ESCAPE FROM BENGHAZI

Escape from Benghazi

Diary of an Impostor

Elia Meghnagi

VALLENTINE MITCHELL
LONDON • CHICAGO

First published in 2022 by Vallentine Mitchell

Catalyst House,
720 Centennial Court,
Centennial Park, Elstree WD6 3SY, UK

814 N. Franklin Street,
Chicago,
IL 60610 USA

www.vmbooks.com

British Library Cataloguing in Publication Data:
An entry can be found on request

ISBN 978 1 80371 020 4 (Paper)
ISBN 978 1 80371 021 1 (Ebook)

Library of Congress Cataloging in Publication Data:
An entry can be found on request

In memory of my parents and of my in-laws

Yaakov and Esther Meghnagi

and

Jack and Renee Freedman

and dedicated to

my wife and family

Contents

PART TWO

England

PART THREE
Extra-curricular

Foreword

Why, you may ask, have I subtitled this book *Diary of an Impostor*? Simply because, wherever I've been in my eventful life, that's what I have felt myself to be—or been told that I am. As a teenager in Libya, where I was born in 1941, I was told by a police officer, 'Go back home to Italy'; arriving in Italy a year later I was welcomed as 'a guest from Libya'; later still, British naturalisation documents described me as 'of unknown nationality'; and to this day, depending on where I attend religious services, I am either 'the Sephardi Jew' or 'the one from the Ashkenazi shul'. It seems to me that I am not who I think I am; therefore, I must be an impostor!

This book aims to (briefly) share the history of the Jewish community in Libya, and to tell the story of my life in, and then my escape from, the city where I was born, bred and almost battered. I then go on to recount how I somehow managed to integrate into a new country and culture, and sidestep efforts to get me back. The qualifications I gained in my new home equipped me for my professional life, which saw me travelling worldwide to fascinating places, far removed from the parochial lifestyle I had known in Benghazi.

Benghazi: how I loved that beautiful, sleepy but cosmopolitan city, a melting pot of people of all nationalities and backgrounds. The Italians, who in 1912 had snatched the region from the Ottoman Turks after nearly four hundred years of Ottoman rule, turned Benghazi and its sister capital Tripoli into showcases of the best of Italian architecture and landscaping. Although Arabs and Berbers made up the vast majority of the population of both cities, there were also black Africans, Italians, Greeks, Maltese and, of course, Jews. Despite an ostensibly happy coexistence between these different groups, nascent Arab nationalism and unrest, together with frustration born of widespread unemployment, were frequently expressed in attacks on the various minorities in Benghazi, especially by the young. The Jews in particular bore the main brunt of this frustration. One of these attacks precipitated my departure from my beloved country.

When I found a group of young Arabs holding down my younger brother, Ever, and raining kicks and blows on him, I leapt to his defence.

My fury lent me strength, and by the end of the fight, I left the principal assailant bleeding. The rest of them had fled. This incident made me a marked boy; although I was just a teen, this traumatic event above all the other threats to my safety was the one that cemented my determination to find a way out. I had to escape from Benghazi, leaving my dear town, family, friends and indeed Libya, or end up in prison…if not in a coffin.

Now, over sixty years since I left Libya, large sections of Benghazi and Tripoli are in ruins due to that most ferocious and senseless type of war that pits brother against brother—civil war. As I write these words in early 2021, I am hearing genuine moves towards peace and with it, hopefully, a rapprochement with expatriate Libyan Jews. *Inshallah.*

PART ONE

Benghazi

1

Tracing an ancient community

Jews have lived in the territory now known as Libya since at least the fourth century BCE, 2,400 years ago. Over the centuries, the various rulers of Libya often treated the Jews as second-class citizens and useful scapegoats for all the country's problems. They faced attacks by Greeks, Romans and Arabs and then, during the Second World War, internment and the threat of death by Italian fascists and Nazis.

Persistent attacks by Arab nationalists against Libyan Jews in the years immediately after the Second World War resulted in many deaths, and consequently, as soon it was made legal, the majority turned to aliyah, immigration to Israel. The years 1948–51 saw a huge immigration to Israel, during which some 30,000 Libyan Jews, over 90 per cent of the community, departed for their new home. Only about 4,000 Jews remained behind, mostly in Tripoli, with a few hundred left in Benghazi. They were a wealthy and influential minority, but had to tread very carefully, living subject to the whims of the Arab population. More fled in subsequent years, until the eventual total expulsion of the last remaining Libyan Jews by Colonel Muammar Gaddafi ended over 2,000 years of the Jewish connection to the land of Libya—a connection that preceded the births of both Christianity and Islam. Today, the descendants of that vital community can be found in Israel, Italy, Great Britain, America and throughout the world—except in the land of their birth.

That's the overview; now to look at the history in slightly more detail.

The beginnings

To begin, as they say, at the beginning: there is evidence of a synagogue in Libya in Solomonic times, but the organised Jewish community set down roots in the third century BCE in Cyrene under the Greeks, specifically Ptolemy I Soter, one of Alexander the Great's generals and companions. Cyrene was the capital of Cyrenaica—one of the three provinces that make up the country known as Libya (the other two being Tripolitania and Fezzan). Soon they achieved positions of importance and even trust. When the Romans displaced the Greeks, the Roman authorities, Augustus and Julius Caesar in particular, were well disposed towards the Jews of Cyrene, even allowing them to send money to Jerusalem. Within a few generations the Jewish community of Cyrene had become numerous and powerful, although not very popular with the native Greek-speaking populace, which resented the way the Romans favoured the Jews.

The Jews of Judea rebelled against the Romans, which led to a series of wars that lasted many years, from 66 until 135 CE. In 115 CE, the Jews of Cyrene, followed by those of Egypt and Cyprus, joined their kinsmen in rebellion. According to the Roman historian Cassius Dio (who was born decades after these events): '...the Jews in the region of Cyrene...were destroying both the Romans and the Greeks. They would cook their flesh, make belts for themselves of their entrails, anoint themselves with their blood, and wear their skins for clothing.... In all, consequently, two hundred and twenty thousand perished.'[1] While the huge number of people reported as killed by the Jews is most likely a gross exaggeration, it must reflect the ferocity of the fighting. However, Dio's monstrous allegations relating to the Jews' barbaric treatment of the corpses, which is completely alien to anything in Jewish culture and practice, may well be the first published anti-Semitic blood libel. General Hadrian (who would become Emperor Hadrian two years later) eventually defeated the Jews, although judging by the final outcome—the total destruction of Cyrene—it was more like nil–nil. After the war, the surviving Jews escaped into the Atlas Mountains, where they were welcomed and given every assistance by the indigenous inhabitants, the Berbers, who have remained good friends of the Jews to this day.

After Cyrene was destroyed, the city of Berenice, about 200 kilometres to the west, became the new capital of Cyrenaica, although under the Vandals and the Byzantines, the city dwindled. With the advent of Islam in the seventh century, and its invasion of North Africa under the Rashidun caliphate, Berenice became Barneeq; at that time, it was only an insignificant village. In the sixteenth century it became known by the name Marsa ibn Ghazi, which then morphed into the name we know today—Benghazi. Today it remains the capital of Cyrenaica, and has become Libya's most populous city after Tripoli.

Over the centuries after the Cyrene community was destroyed, Jewish immigrants started trickling back into Libya from such countries as Spain, Italy, Egypt, Portugal, Morocco and Turkey. The community grew significantly under Ottoman rule, from the sixteenth century onward. Although the Ottomans labelled any non-Muslims living in Muslim countries *dhimmis*, including the Jews, considering them to be second-class citizens, as long as they paid the *jizya* tax they were allowed reasonable freedom and were able to achieve a high standard of living. Thanks to their knowledge of European languages, many of them even became consuls all over Europe. In the sixteenth, the eighteenth and then again in the twentieth century, there were large influxes of Jews from Italy, especially from Livorno (Leghorn), a port city on the west coast, and from the south. The Livorno Jewish community built up a very successful network of commercial contacts around the Mediterranean. They established centres in both Tripoli and Benghazi, and hundreds settled there. These newcomers integrated into the community in due course and took an active part in all communal affairs. They learned to speak the local Judeo-Arabic while at the same time retaining their Italian language, culture and schooling. As a result of this mix of cultures, Libyan Jewry became blessed with a rich, multicultural cuisine combining North African, Spanish, Portuguese, Turkish and Italian dishes. Many of these have now become part of Israel's culinary tradition, and continue to grace Sabbath tables in Italy, Israel, and many other countries.

Shiver me timbers

When I was a child the last thing on my mind was the origin of my name; no one had a problem pronouncing it because Italian is spelled phonetically: what you see is what you say, to coin a phrase. It was only once I arrived in the UK that the fun and games started. If the spelling was difficult, saying it correctly was practically impossible! I have been called Magengi, Macnosy, Macnajy, Mackenzie, Medangi, and various other distortions over the years. Hearing so many Brits mangle my name led me to investigate its origin. For many years I would tell my friends that my name came from the Hebrew word for 'tune', *nigun*, so the Hebrew form Meghinati would mean 'my tunes, my songs'. This theory was especially convincing to me because there are an unusual number of cantors and singers in the family, going back generations.

However, some time ago I was a guest of the secretary of the Spanish and Portuguese Jewish community in London. He had researched much Sephardi history, and he told me an entirely different and astonishing story, revealing to me a dark period in Libyan history in which—he told me—my ancestors had been deeply involved.

Although I grew up in Benghazi, the Meghnagis were actually from Tripoli (my father grew up in Tripoli and then moved to Benghazi). And between the sixteenth and nineteenth centuries, Tripoli was one of the bases of the Barbary pirates, or corsairs, who would patrol the Mediterranean, capturing merchant ships and also plundering European coastal towns and villages. They would take the people they captured to Tripoli (and other ports along the Barbary Coast), and either sell them into slavery, or hold them for ransom.

Because of the local Jews' knowledge of European languages, they were sometimes used as interpreters. Among the captives being held by the pirates there were quite often Italian, German and French Jews, so the community in Tripoli set up a fund to free them. Apparently, according to the secretary, the man who started this fund and became its custodian was an ancestor of mine. He would board captured merchant ships looking for Jewish captives and negotiate their release with the pirates. Some of those thus freed even stayed and became part of the community. In time, people started referring to the treasurer of the ransom fund by his function—the word *magen* in Hebrew means shield, or protector—and this became the basis for my ancestor's last name. It must have gradually morphed in pronunciation and spelling over time—'Mr Magen/Meghnati/Meghnagi' (my custodian, my shield). As for the correct pronunciation? In Italian, gh is pronounced as a hard g, as in spaghetti, while g is pronounced like j.

I was quite surprised to hear this story, but the secretary was adamant that it was correct. Given that he was born in Tunis, whose Jewish community had extensive and close ties with the Libyan Jewish community, he may well have been right.

Evviva Italia

When, in 1911, the Italians captured Libya from the ruling Ottoman Turks, they found a large Italian-speaking community already present, many of whom were Jews. For example, the local committee of the Societa Dante Alighieri, a cultural institution founded in 1889 to preserve and spread Italian language and culture around the world, boasted two Jews on its governing board. Seven of the twelve councillors on the governing board of the Banco di Napoli, an Italian bank in Tripoli, were Jews.[2] Moreover, the percentage of Jews in the general population was high: of Tripoli city's almost 30,000 inhabitants, 8,509 were Jews; in Benghazi, where I was born, there were fewer than 5,000 people, and nearly half of them were Jews.

Many of the Libyan Jews were highly-educated Italian speakers. Accordingly, the Italians hired many of the Jewish elite to help them in their administration of the colony.

The Italians abolished the demeaning *dhimmi* tax, and encouraged the natural unity of Italian-speaking Libyan Jews with the mainland Italian Jewish community under one chief rabbi. Jewish educational and social institutions in Italy and Libya were integrated, creating an ever-greater closeness between the two communities. The Jewish community in Libya rose to a position of great importance.

Much of the Arab population fared less well. There was resentment against the Italian occupation, and rebellions broke out under the leadership of Omar al-Mukhtar and Sayyid Idris. They became national heroes (I grew up on Omar al-Mukhtar Street) and were a thorn in the side of the Italian rulers until al-Mukhtar was captured in 1931. The tale I grew up hearing, told with great admiration, was that the Italians gave al-Mukhtar a choice between capitulation and hanging, and he actually chose execution by hanging rather than give up his fight for freedom (Idris managed to evade capture, and much later became King Idris).

By this time, Italy was under fascist rule—the dictator Benito Mussolini was in power. He realised it was necessary to appease the Arabs of Libya after al-Mukhtar's execution. This, plus his eventual decision to side with Hitler, caused a gradual volte face in his attitude to the Jews, which had previously been quite favourable.

Mussolini had come to power in Italy in 1922. Back then, not fully aware of the true nature of fascism, some of the Jewish youngsters in Libya even enrolled in fascist youth groups. They were mainly seduced by the grandiose building works the Italians had undertaken to transform Libyan cities—new streets with colonnades, modern shopping centres, beach promenades and civic centres—which were rapidly turning Tripoli and Benghazi from sleepy, dusty North African backwaters into advanced, modern European metropolises. The country became a showplace for Italian greatness and culture. Some Jewish youngsters were so naive that they proudly sported the fascist uniform, albeit displaying the Star of David on their caps. Most of the community distanced themselves from the activity of these youngsters, but could not openly show their revulsion. As a teenager, my own mother attended a college of fashion design in Benghazi which carried the name of The Women's Fascist College of Domestic Science. She even received a diploma from this college, a very rare document to be given to a young Jewish girl, which I still have in my possession.

SCUOLA DI ECONOMIA DOMESTICA
DEL FASCIO FEMMINILE DI BENGASI
SEZIONE TAGLIO CONFEZIONE
La Fiduciaria dei Fasci
La Dirigente della Scuola

My mother's diploma from The Women's Fascist College of Domestic Science.

Gradually most schools, colleges and other institutions were appropriated and subjected to fascist doctrine and propaganda, though at the beginning Italian fascist doctrine did not espouse the extreme anti-Semitic views which developed later. When Mussolini arrived in Tripoli in the 1930s, he was presented with a silver menorah by the Jewish community (and with a silver scimitar by the Arabs). As a young representative of the local Maccabi Association, my father was one of those who shook Mussolini's hand. When he told us this story I asked him what he did next, and his answer was, 'I washed my hands, of course'.

On a state visit to Tripoli, Mussolini noticed how quiet everything was. The shops, the banks, the ports...everything seemed to be closed. Baffled, he asked the governor whether it was due to a local holiday, but the response he got was simply, no, it was '*Sabato*' (Italian for Saturday, but also meaning Sabbath or Shabbat). When it was explained to him that most of the shops and businesses were run by Jews, who did not open on Saturdays, he became enraged and instructed Air Marshal Italo Balbo, who was the Governor-General of Libya, to order them to open all businesses. Balbo was in fact an admirer of the Jews, but he wanted them to play a full role in the economy and believed that they should open their businesses on

Shabbat. To 'encourage' Jewish cooperation (and possibly fearing that Mussolini would intervene with more drastic measures), Balbo had a few of the leading Jewish businessmen publicly flogged.

To avoid further flogging while still safeguarding the sanctity of the Sabbath, the rabbis came up with an ingenious solution. They obviously didn't want the community subjected to violence but were worried that if the Jews gave in to Balbo's demands, they would get used to breaking the Sabbath, and this would become the norm even after he was gone and forgotten. Consequently, they advised the shopkeepers to attend early shul services on the Sabbath and then open their shops. However, they were to display specially increased prices, in order to deter customers from buying. People would come to the shops and find the price tag showing an increase of 30 to 40 per cent, and when they queried the increase, they were told to come back on any other day of the week to buy the item at the lower price. The idea was that the shopkeepers would not make many sales, if any, and would not get used to earning money on the Sabbath. It was thought that as soon as Mussolini got involved in bigger problems, he would forget this business and the Jews would again close on Saturdays. That was the theory, and it worked to some extent, but things are never that simple: obviously this ploy could not work for professions like banking.

Balbo later apologised for enforcing the Sabbath opening of the businesses. In fact, at a Blackshirt reunion in Tripoli in 1937 he paid tribute to the 'industriousness, discipline and loyalty' of the Libyan Jewish community.[3]

It's worth mentioning a related incident that could have ended in tragedy for my family. It happened before I was born, when the governor of Benghazi sent an official to my father's luxury home-goods store to buy a complete set of crockery for a big civic dinner in honour of Mussolini's visit. My father persuaded the official to buy a new product he had imported from Italy: drinking glasses made from 'completely unbreakable' glass. He demonstrated how good they were by throwing one on the ground without its breaking. The problem occurred during the dinner, when one of the glasses did suddenly shatter into smithereens. The official was going to take my father to jail, pending an enquiry, but he let him go when he was shown the packaging, which clearly said 'Made in Italy'. It was obviously a completely legitimate product. It was later discovered that this type of very tough glass had one weakness: sometimes tiny air bubbles would be present, which would eventually burst, with a small explosion. Luckily on that occasion Mussolini was in a good mood!

Fascism's true face

In 1938, Mussolini began implementing anti-Semitic racial laws in Italy, which he wanted extended to Libya, too. Italian passports, which had been issued to some Libyan Jews, had to be sent to Rome, and were returned stamped with the words '*Razza Ebraica*' (Jewish race). Most Jews, including my mother's eldest brother, Frigia Dabusc (pronounced Dabush), were so incensed that they tore up their passports, repudiating their Italian nationality, even though it left them stateless and trapped in the country. Jews were removed from municipal councils, public offices, and state schools. The governor general of Libya, Italo Balbo, was not happy about the racial laws, and he tried to prevent them from being implemented across the board in Libya. He wrote to Mussolini trying to dissuade him from enforcing all of them. Reassuring him that Jews had been dismissed from government employ and barred from attending school, he argued that implementing the rules universally would have a negative effect on the economy. In any case, he added, 'Why are you bothering with the Jews [of Libya]? They are already dead; it is not necessary to rage against them.'

Mussolini agreed to Balbo's request, but famously responded, 'The Jews appear to be moribund, but they have a habit of springing back to life.'

He certainly got that right!

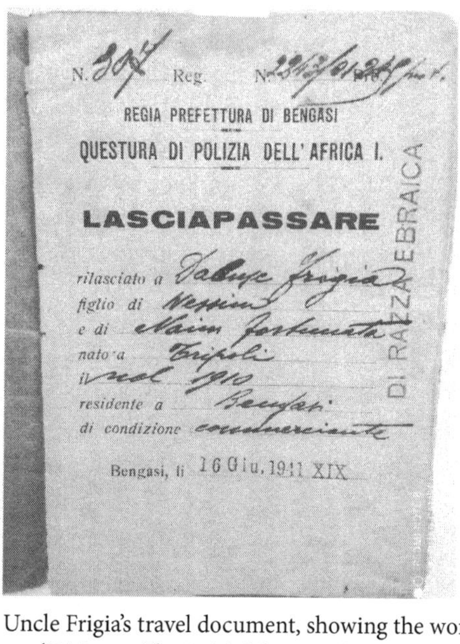

My Uncle Frigia's travel document, showing the words '*Di Razza Ebraica*' (of the Jewish race).

Casa Nostra

Here I'll take a brief break from Libyan Jewish history and tell you something about my family, as this is essentially where I enter the story. Sadly, I don't know many details of those who came before my parents' time. My paternal grandfather was Rachamim Meghnagi, and my paternal grandmother was Diamantina. To my regret, I never met either of them, because while I was born and grew up in Benghazi, they lived in Tripoli, and moved to Israel in 1950. In fact, I met very few of my Meghnagi relatives in Libya. I did discover that one ancestor, first name unknown, was a member of a group who travelled to Jaffa in Israel (then Palestine) in the 1700s and founded a shul. The building is still there, though now disused, and a plaque over the door shows the names of the committee members, including 'Meghnagi, *Parnas*' (treasurer). This may even have been the same person who arranged to ransom pirates' captives, but it's too far back to be sure.

Since most of my mother's family lived in Benghazi, I knew more of them, though I only found out when she was in her sixties that part of her family had lived in Turkey at one time (and that was only when I overheard her telling a friend, who was originally from Turkey. I felt like saying 'Thanks for telling me!'). My maternal grandfather was Nissim Dabusc, and his wife was Fortunata. His father, my great-grandfather, was Rabbi Rafael Dabusc. Descended from a long line of distinguished rabbis, my great-grandfather was a famous kabbalist and the head of the Beth Din (rabbinical court) of Tripoli. The author of a number of books on the Bible, he was frequently consulted by colleagues in Jerusalem on Talmudic questions. He was one of the spiritual leaders of the community, greatly admired for his learning, charity and humility, but mostly he was loved and respected by all for his caring attitude towards Jews and Muslims alike. His father, Frigia, was also a kabbalist and also the head of the Beth Din. Unfortunately I never knew their wives' names.

Moving further back, I found out fairly recently, through a son-in-law's encounter with long-lost relatives in Israel, that the Dabusc family descends directly from the rabbi, kabbalist and poet Shlomo Alkabetz, who was born in Greece in 1500 and moved to the Holy Land later in life. His teachings, and his world-famous hymn to the Sabbath, '*Lecha Dodi*' ('Come, my beloved') have made him one of the luminaries of Jewish learning. (My wife jokes that if I'd known I had this illustrious ancestor, I might not have married a commoner such as her…but I remind her that her late uncle, Rabbi Dr Harry Freedman, was head of the Beth Din of Melbourne for many years, and published many volumes of Torah writings.)

My mother's grandfather, Rabbi Rafael Dabusc.

My mother's father, Nissim Dabusc, looking noticeably more modern than his father.

My father's father, Rachamim Meghnagi. I never had the pleasure of meeting him, as he lived in Tripoli before moving to Israel.

Yaakov Meghnagi, my father, was born in Tripoli in 1912, and Esther Dabusc, my mother, was born in 1922. Her grandparents lived in Tripoli; I am not sure whether she was born in Tripoli and moved with her family to Benghazi when she was little, or whether she was born in Benghazi. As a young child my mother, known affectionately as Esterina, was unable to walk. This mystified all the doctors she was taken to, none of whom could find anything wrong with her. Frequently her maternal grandfather Rabbi Rafael Dabusc, mentioned above, would sit with her to massage her legs and murmur encouragement. He died in a tragic accident in 1926, at the age of ninety-one. He had been officiating at a wedding, and the stage on which the chuppah had been erected collapsed; he died from his injuries about two weeks later. (I've always felt sorry for the young couple; what a way to start married life!)

The whole Jewish community and a large number of Arabs were at his funeral, but of course my mother couldn't go. She was only four, and was unable to get out of bed, so she was left in the care of a babysitter. When the sad and subdued family returned from the cemetery, Esterina's mother, my grandmother Fortunata, went to check on her. She was amazed to see her out of bed and taking a few steps. Totally shocked, she asked, 'How did you manage to get up?'

Esterina replied, 'Nonno came and helped me.'

She was talking about her grandfather, who had just been buried.

The babysitter had seen and heard nothing, but the family were so glad to see Esterina walking that they accepted it as a miracle.

Of course, you could argue that the whole story was the product of a child's imagination, except that there's a sequel: some years later, my uncle, David, who was younger than my mother and only knew what Rabbi Rafael looked like from photographs, arrived at shul early for the evening service and was quite sure he saw his dead grandfather in the seat he had been told was his usual place. He was so terrified that he turned and fled…and that was the last time he voluntarily entered a shul to pray. (A further, equally weird, sequel is that during the last five years of her life my mother was unable to walk, though doctors were mystified as they could find nothing physically wrong. My theory is that she decided that the blessing given to her as a child had 'run out', as it were, and nothing would induce her to try to walk.)

My parents must have met in Tripoli, where my father grew up, possibly when my mother was visiting family there. Though my father was ten years her senior, they clearly fell for each other; he followed her to Benghazi, where they married in 1938. Two years later my older brother Clement was born, followed only eleven months later by yours truly in June 1941. Unlike Clem, who was named for our grandfather Rachamim, I wasn't named after a relative. My mother was fond of telling me the story of my name—she had a vivid dream about the prophet Elijah the night before she gave birth to me. Taking this as an omen (I'm not sure of what) she decided that had to be my name, Elia being the Italian form of the Hebrew Eliahu (Elijah). She would also frequently remind me that I had been born 'wearing a shirt', as the Italians say; that is, still inside the caul. This is quite an unusual occurrence, and is meant to be a sign of good fortune…and I really can't argue with that.

In 1944, my brother Ever was born (a biblical name from which the word 'Hebrew' comes, used mainly by Libyan Jews), and in 1948, my sister Yvette. The traumatic circumstances of her birth are described later in the book. After Yvette, my mother had a set of twins, a boy and a girl, but neither survived. The girl was stillborn, and the boy lived for a month before dying of malnutrition. My mother was so ill that she was unable to feed him; there was no formula available, and no wet nurses. I have a dim memory of seeing a small bundle in the bathroom, and realising later that it was a baby who hadn't survived. It's a pretty grim picture, and the trauma of those losses probably contributed to the frequent tensions that arose between my parents, and my mother's later problems with mental illness.

My older brother and I were born under the shadow of war. Benghazi was a battleground between the Axis and Allied forces, and changed hands several times. In February 1941, just a few months before I was born, Benghazi was captured from the Italians by the British. Unsurprisingly, given the Italian's discriminatory anti-Semitic laws applied to Libyan Jews, Benghazi's Jews welcomed the British enthusiastically. My father even contacted the British and gave them information which helped them locate Italian military food sources to feed their troops.

Unfortunately, Axis powers recaptured Benghazi only two months later, in April. I was born when Benghazi was under Axis control; it was taken back by the British in December 1941, when I was six months old, only to be conquered once more a month later by Axis powers on 29 January 1942. With all the time that has passed since then, and with my father having been gone now for many decades, precise details of what happened are unclear, but we do know that the Axis powers punished the Jews of Libya severely for their "collaboration" with the British, and during one of the periods of Axis control, my father was arrested and charged with treason, because he had helped the British. Two of his friends were arrested on similar charges, and hanged, but thanks to some friends in the Italian military, my father was somehow spared.

Internment

When the Axis forces retook Libya in 1942, the situation for Libya's Jews went from bad to worse. Different policies were put in place depending on whether the Jews had French, British, Italian or Libyan citizenship. In Benghazi, the governor was ordered to arrange the deportation of Jews with Italian or Libyan citizenship to Giado, a former army camp made up of a few barracks about 100 miles south of Tripoli, deep in the desert. The governor of Benghazi sent for my mother's eldest brother, Frigia Dabusc, with whom he enjoyed a close friendship. He had been a frequent visitor to my uncle's home, especially on Friday nights, to enjoy Shabbat food, which he loved, along with a game of cards. Frigia Dabusc was a tall, imposing man. His fair complexion and penetrating blue eyes, together with the dashing style of his hand-stitched Italian suits, made him a compelling figure in our small Jewish community, and he was equally at home in Italian government circles. His friendship and connections with

My uncle, Frigia Dabusc, in his debonair heyday.

many members of the Italian colonial government had often enabled him to intervene on behalf of the Jewish community, especially after he became the only civilian with honorary membership of the Italian Military Officers' Club.

Over the years, the governor had not been the only Italian guest frequently at his home; military top brass had also joined him for dinner and friendly card games, but this had changed slowly as fascism had become more entrenched in Italy. He had felt the change in the atmosphere, especially at the Officers' Club, which had seen a surge in new young members with fascist leanings. In the late 1930s, he had one day approached an officer whom he heard making some anti-Semitic remarks and whispered, 'You do know that walls have ears?'

The startled officer had blustered in reply, 'What's it to do with you?'

'I'm a Jew, that's what it's to do with me, so keep your mouth shut!'

The officer, noting the disapproving looks of some of his colleagues, had backed down, shrugging his shoulders and muttering obscenities. Still, after that incident my uncle's thoughts had turned to the various escape plans he had devised, just in case, with some trusted Italian and Arab friends, although he knew that, in those changing times, nothing would be easy to implement. He started carrying a gun.

I vividly recall, when I was probably three years old, seeing my uncle, followed by cousins and others, rushing up our stairs waving a gun and screaming '*Tedesco*!' (German). I do not remember if a German was found, but I do remember the tense atmosphere, and the high state of alert and fear that was engulfing us all.

That tense atmosphere already held sway on the day that my uncle was asked to call on the governor. Full of foreboding, he made his way to the town hall. This was one of the many splendid buildings that had sprung up in Benghazi during Italian rule, testimony to Italy's colonial pride. In better times, Frigia had looked forward to his visits there. This time, however, the building was cold and ominous, with its fascist flag flapping from the cupola and Mussolini's Blackshirts guarding the entrance.

After the preliminary pleasantries, the governor explained the order he had received from Mussolini to deport the Jews. He was very reluctant to carry out the order, he explained, but really he had no choice. He then asked Frigia to help organise the deportation of the Jews to the camp in the desert, assuring him that if he could accomplish the task within twelve months he and his family would be spared.

Frigia was furious that his friend thought him capable of betraying his community. He flatly refused to co-operate and stalked out of the office, ignoring the governor's reassurance that he would still ensure his family's safety. That Friday evening he went straight to the packed shul and warned the congregation about the impending deportation. A feeling of helplessness and foreboding descended upon the community, as there seemed little possibility of escape.

After Shabbat, a member of the community (name withheld to protect his totally innocent family) presented himself at the governor's office and offered to organise the deportation in three months rather than twelve, in return for safety for himself and his family. Thanks to him, every Friday evening, when the shul was full, a new list of five families would appear on the notice board, along with an announcement informing them that they were to report the following week, to be loaded onto trucks and taken to a reception camp, presumably 'for their own protection'. Some clothing and a few personal belongings would be allowed. Those listed were given very

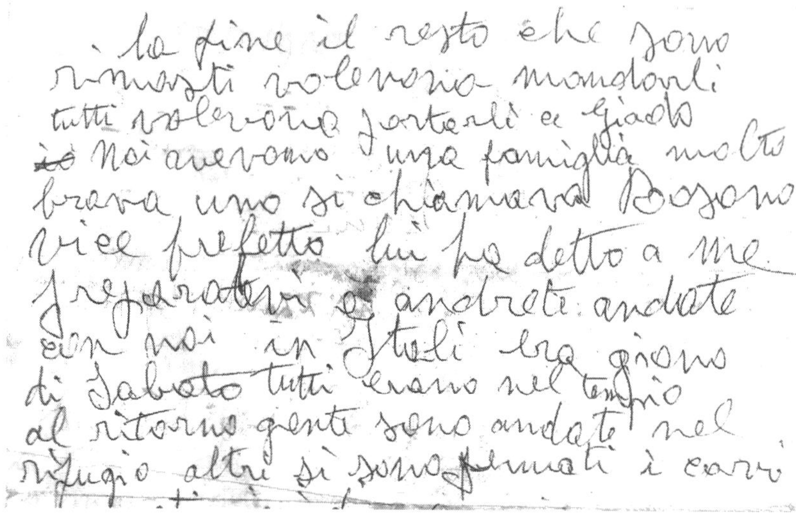

. la fine il resto che sono
rimasti volevano mandarli
tutti volevano portarli a Giado
~~io~~ Noi avevamo una famiglia molto
brava uno si chiamava Bosono
vice prefetto lui ho detto a me
preparatevi e andrete: andate
con noi in Itali era giorno
di Sabato tutti erano nel tempio
al ritorno gente sono andate nel
rifugio altri si sono fermati i carri

An extract from my mother's diary. She writes, in Italian: '...in the end, the remainder [Jews who were not being sent elsewhere] were being assigned to the Giado concentration camp. As for our family, we were close friends of a lovely family whose head was Mr. Bosono, the vice prefect [assistant governor] who told me in person to get ready, for "You are all coming with me to Italy" [as Italian expatriates returning to Italy].' The text continues (not pictured here): 'One Saturday everyone was in the synagogue. After the service some went to the shelter, others stopped in the big square to chat. Suddenly two tanks full of soldiers appeared and stopped. A bomb exploded, killing Italians, Jews and others.'

little time to collect their things before fascist thugs in military uniforms pushed them unceremoniously into waiting army trucks.

One Friday evening during this chaotic and terrifying period our family's name appeared on the list of deportees. My mother rushed to the home of the governor to remind him of his promise. He assured her that the truck drivers rounding up the deportees had been told not to go to her house.

Of course I was too young at the time to know what was going on. Accounts of what happened have been passed down over the years, but now that I am writing about those times, there is sadly no one left who can fill in details for me. I may have got events in the wrong order, but I do know that people, including those Jews still in Benghazi, had to rush to bomb shelters during the frequent and heavy bombardment of the city. On one such occasion, somehow in all the rush and confusion, little one-year-old Elia was left behind. When my mother realised I was missing, her shrieks sent her 18-year-old brother, David, diving out of the shelter to rush back through explosions and falling debris to rescue me. (A few years ago, I gave a *hesped* (eulogy) at his funeral here in London and recounted this story, reminding family and friends what a selfless hero my Uncle David was.)

As the situation deteriorated, the danger to Jews increased because young fascists began reviling them in the shelters, often forcibly ejecting them. This may be what impelled my parents to seek refuge in the desert, where they were sheltered for a while by kindly Bedouins.

The remaining Jewish families in Benghazi lived in constant fear of seeing their names on the dreaded list which appeared every week. Having seen those selected being roughly manhandled into trucks, allowed to take only a few belongings, they had a good idea of what kind of camp they were being taken to. Those selected faced a terrifying journey to the Giado camp, over six hundred miles away, which took many hours and had to be endured under typical desert conditions—freezing cold at night and unbearably hot by day. The camp compound itself was enclosed by a fence topped with barbed wire. Italian fascists guarded the inside area, while the outside was patrolled by Arabs on horseback, wielding whips and swords. Living conditions were terrible: survivors later recounted that there was no sanitation or running water; each family was allocated just one square metre of space, and had to sleep on the floor. Blankets were thrown over ropes to provide a modicum of privacy. Food rations consisted of a few grams per day of rice, oil, sugar, and coffee substitute, with an intermittent and meagre supply of drinking water. Men and boys over eighteen were taken outside every day for forced labour, their dwindling strength used to build roads for the Italian military effort.

There were some strange inconsistencies in the treatment of the Jews in Giado. On the one hand, the Italian and Arab supervisors of the camp enjoyed mistreating and harassing the prisoners. On the other hand, when the Jews totally refused to work on Saturdays, determined to keep Shabbat, the camp commandant acquiesced, and even agreed to allocate a hut to be used as a shul. He also allowed the Benghazi Jews to receive regular food parcels from the Jewish community in Tripoli, which had not been deported. This supplemented their starvation rations and allowed more people to survive, though a few parcels of food didn't go far in a camp full of people!

Of the 2,700 men, women and children deported to Giado, 550, including Benghazi's Rabbi Hammus Fellah, died of starvation, beatings and disease. Rabbi Fellah was made to sweep the whole camp daily, which hastened his death. The dead were buried by inmates on a hill outside the camp, the site of an ancient Jewish cemetery. (The few hundred Libyan Jews who did end up in European concentration camps were those who had British or other passports, or who were already in Italy studying, on business, or visiting family.)

A friend of mine, Meir El Saiegh, was actually born in the camp. His father was a pharmacist, and had taken medicine with him to the camp when his family was deported. Using some of it to bribe guards, he was able to sneak out to a nearby village and buy milk and other necessities for his wife, thereby saving her and their baby. Doubtless, without that, Meir would never have survived to grow up. His father told him many tales of their time in Giado, and he shared them with me. The following liberal translation of one of the stories he shared with me is my own:

> One morning, the fascist guards, screaming like frenzied madmen, pushed us out of the barracks, aided by the *ascari*, as the Arab collaborators were called. It was about eight in the morning. They had picked only men and boys, shoving us out without giving us time to get dressed. I looked around; some were naked, some had simply collapsed on the ground as we were all herded towards the central square.
>
> One of the officers was screaming like a lunatic. 'We will kill the lot of you! We have received our orders!'
>
> We waited for these orders, shaking with terror and with our hearts in our mouths. Many of us covered our eyes with our right hands while reciting the *Shema*, believing that the end had come.
>
> It was obvious from their behaviour that things were not going well for the Italians; news of the defeat at Tripoli must have started trickling in. Whilst lining us up, some of the officers were screaming expletives and threatening to exterminate us all. They kept us standing there all day and well into the night, watching as men collapsed. Many died right there from heat stroke, thirst and exhaustion.
>
> Then something miraculous happened; we could hardly believe our eyes. Suddenly the Italian guards and all their collaborators started jumping into military vehicles and barrelling out of the camp as fast as they could. Soon after that, a number of British army trucks entered the camp, and the soldiers started freeing us.
>
> Later, when we had time to reflect, we realised that there must have been a struggle raging between the Italians guarding the camp. When news of the fall of Tripoli had reached them, the diehard fascists had wanted to finish the job by rounding up the prisoners

and having them shot. Others, knowing it was all over for Italy, didn't want such a crime hanging over them, and argued against it. The struggle had saved us; the British arrived in time. We were overjoyed to find that with them were Jewish volunteers from Palestine, who helped us recover from our experiences.

Notes

1. Cassius Dio, *Dio's Rome*, Volume V., Book 68, paragraph 32, translated by Herbert Baldwin Foster, Project Gutenberg E-book: https://www.gutenberg.org/files/10890/10890-h/10890-h.htm.
2. Piera Rossetto (2021) 'We Were all Italian!': The construction of a 'sense of Italianness' among Jews from Libya (1920s–1960s), History and Anthropology, DOI: 10.1080/02757206.2020.1848821
3. Claudio G. Segre, *Italo Balbo: A Fascist Life* (University of California Press, 1990), p.348.

2

Rebuilding

After the liberation of Giado by the British, they immediately improved the hygiene in the camp, stamping out the typhus that had already killed so many inmates. They moved inmates to better housing nearby, and made sure they had medical treatment, and were fed. Over the spring and summer of 1943, they gradually transferred families back to Benghazi, using British military trucks. The American Jewish Joint Distribution Committee helped fund the return of the Benghazi Jews to their homes—many of which they found looted or destroyed. Once home, they were later joined by those who had survived being sent to Bergen Belsen. They had been helped to return by Allied and Jewish organisations, and the Red Cross.

In the meantime, my family had settled back in Benghazi after their sojourn with the Bedouins. Although under the British my parents at last felt safe to stay in Benghazi, times were hard for them, as for the vast majority of Benghazi's returned Jews. The community was a shadow of what it had been.

At our *asilo* (kindergarten) run by nuns. I am in the third row back, sixth from the right and looking worried. Clem is in the row behind, with a finger up his nose!

My father's store had been ransacked and reduced to rubble. Not one to give up, he determined to start a new business. Due to the disruptions of war there was a severe food shortage in the city, and he took a gamble that he could help solve it. He borrowed money from a bank and, via his family in Tripoli, ordered four lorry-loads of all kinds of food, including fresh.

The convoy should have reached Benghazi within twenty-four hours, but it failed to arrive. It transpired that the lorries had become stuck in the desert sand and the food had been carried off by a gang of marauders. The lorries were too badly damaged to be brought back, and the whole thing became a nightmare. He despaired of finding the money to repay the loan, and the bank was already threatening to sue. Then the Axis forces were driven out of Libya once and for all, and the Italian lira practically collapsed. Thanks to this he was able to buy the number of liras he needed very cheaply, and went to the bank to repay the loan. However, they refused the liras and insisted on being paid in sterling or dollars equal to the pre-war value. He waited till he was summoned to court. He walked up to the judge, laid a bag full of liras in front of him, and said words to the effect, 'Here is the money that I owe, but the bank is refusing it.'

He won the case, but he was penniless.

This was when the British army came to my father's rescue. They were still in need of a local food expert, and in recognition of the assistance he had given them earlier in the war they appointed him manager of local food supplies to the NAAFI (Navy, Army and Air Force Institute) division of Cyrenaica, a job he kept until 1952, when Libya gained its independence and the British returned to the UK.

The job was a good one. However, the NAAFI centre was outside Benghazi, and it was dangerous to travel out of town, especially for Jews. This was because of the fact that although Libya was under British administration, it essentially had no government. There were few jobs available, and the Jews were a convenient target for the local Arabs to vent their frustration. Furthermore, local leaders took advantage of the frequent news of fighting between Arabs and Jews in Palestine to stoke up hatred of all Jews, everywhere. This is why an army jeep used to arrive every morning to take my father to work at the NAAFI inside the British Army HQ, and would also bring him back at night. Unfortunately his hours were not regular, and often he would not get back till 10 p.m. or later. Nevertheless, we were very proud of our dad. At a time when the town was in chaos, security was practically non-existent and food supplies were erratic and often inedible, there we were, enjoying the best that the British army could get.

As adults, my siblings and I reminisce about those mornings when we would keep a lookout for the army jeep. How proud we were when our father shook hands with the military driver and accompanying soldier, then turned to wave goodbye to us. My own sweetest memory is of his return with trays of fruit pies and all kinds of goodies. At a very young age these treats triggered in me a strong desire to see—and perhaps live in—this country called England. Even now, decades later, I cannot resist a jam tart or a Mars bar!

Attack and counterattack

Sadly, the joy everyone felt following the end of the war was soon dampened. The local Arab population, inspired by the 2 November anniversary of the Balfour Declaration of 1917, which had promised the Jews a homeland in Palestine, and spurred on by similar attacks in Syria and Egypt, vented their hate on the Jews. There were some incidents in Benghazi, but far worse occurred in Tripoli, where gangs of Arabs went on a killing spree, and burned synagogues and shops. From 5 November to 7 November 1945, over 140 Jews were murdered, and five synagogues were destroyed completely. This attack was followed by more, and the situation could have become even worse but for the somewhat tardy intervention of the British military police.

Jews from Palestine had volunteered to join the British army to fight the Nazis; there was a Jewish Brigade within the British army during the Second World War. Some of those soldiers were now in Libya with the British, along with Jewish soldiers from Britain and other Allied countries. After these attacks on the Jews of Libya in 1945, some of those soldiers secretly taught Tripoli's Jewish youngsters self-defence, and smuggled some pistols to them. One of my older cousins told me that, at some point afterward—I don't know exactly when, but the attacks on Libyan Jews continued sporadically from then on, in both Tripoli and Benghazi—it was decided to mount an offensive against the fanatics. The offensive would not be directed against the general Arab population, who were believed to be unhappy with the murderous behaviour of some of their own. An 'army' of able-bodied Jewish men and boys was organised into squads of eighty, placed strategically to lure the attackers into chasing some of them. Other squads lay in wait to close in on the attackers from behind.

Women and older men were ready on the rooftops with copious supplies of hot water, stones, and anything else available to shower on the attackers, who ultimately sustained many injuries. This put an end, for a while, to the large-scale attacks, although isolated incidents continued. It must be said that at that time Libya was not yet independent, and it was the governing British who were responsible for maintaining law and order. For many, complex reasons, they were often slow in their efforts to keep the peace and guard the safety of the Jewish community. In fact, some kind of peace and co-existence was achieved after a delegation of senior Arab clerics met with the leaders of the Jewish community to plan intercommunal policing and co-operation. This did work to some extent, proving that dialogue and good sense were achievable between Jews and Arabs.

Istituto De La Salle

After the war, the Jews of Benghazi had to reorganise the devastated community, and most important was schooling. Many children continued attending the Jewish school, which soldiered on for a time despite the emigration of many teachers and pupils. However, there was a need for a school on a firmer footing, and there my parents were able to help. During the war, they had agreed to store valuable furniture belonging to the Italian Officers' Club when the Italians had to withdraw. This meant that one room in our apartment was out of bounds and unusable for years. After the war my parents contacted the Italian consul, who represented the now non-fascist Italian government. He could not believe their honesty in hanging on to the furniture all that time, instead of selling it. A friendly relationship developed, and we were allowed access to the extensive library at the Italian consulate, which became my favourite haunt on Friday afternoons. More to the point, the consul used his influence to reopen Italian schools that had been in operation before the war. As Italian speakers, we had gone to a kindergarten run by Italian nuns, but now we needed proper schooling. The Istituto De La Salle reopened in the late 1940s, run from the Vatican by the De La Salle Brothers (also known as the Christian Brothers). It had a sizeable number of Jewish students, including myself and my older brother.

A warm relationship of mutual respect developed between pupils and staff; the teachers, called 'brothers', became family friends. They came to our bar mitzvah ceremonies; we attended celebrations in church when there was a special event like a visiting archbishop from Rome. I look back on those days with affection, and consider them the epitome of successful, positive inter-religious coexistence. We were Italians, Jews, Arabs, Maltese

Class of 1956 (eight of us Jewish) with myself second from right in the front row, Clem behind me, third from right, and Fratello Roberto next to Clem.

and Greeks; Christians, Muslims and Jews; and one big family. The Catholic Brothers did do their best to convert us, but their efforts were gentle and good-natured (and futile).

The brothers were dedicated to teaching, and I found learning exciting, lapping up whatever was on offer. I also enjoyed sport, and was good at rope-climbing, running and wrestling. Football was less successful because I kept missing the ball—until I realised that I needed glasses. Then I began to enjoy it.

One feature of the school day that did nearly cause conflict was that every morning started with a prayer. Out of consideration for the large number of Jewish boys, the headmaster composed a 'universal' prayer, but nevertheless an awkward situation developed when we Jewish boys still showed reluctance to participate. This was because there was a large crucifix hanging on the wall in front of us, before which we would not pray—and we did not want to offend the brothers by articulating the issue.

The dilemma was solved when our rabbi suggested a compromise. That morning we all said the prayer together. Peace and friendship reigned once more. So what if our faces were turned towards the window? We were discreet, and the brothers didn't notice—or more likely, they pretended not to.

Despite some objections from Rome, the principal also made our lives easier by turning a blind eye to the Jewish boys' non-attendance on Saturdays (the school timetable was full days from Monday to Thursday, and mornings only on Fridays and Saturdays). When increasing pressure from Rome threatened this happy arrangement, the principal came up with a compromise solution: we would attend early shul services on Shabbat morning, and then walk to school to do sports for a couple of hours, with no need to carry school books or do any writing. Then we were able to get home in time for Shabbat lunch. (This system worked very well until 1959, when a firm instruction came from Rome requiring all Jewish pupils to attend regular Saturday classes, or leave. Most of them left. By that time I was in England, and I'll never forget the letter my brother Clement sent me. In it he explained what had happened, and told me how upset he was at missing his final year exams, as that was likely to affect his chances of getting a job. However, he ended with the memorable words, 'I am not worried, because God sees the smallest black ant in the blackest night'. Now that is pure faith, typical of Clem.)

Ordeal in the desert

Having settled our secular Italian education through the Istituto De La Salle, my parents had to consider our Jewish education. At this time the main provider for this was the Talmud Torah, which was in the old ghetto of Benghazi, where the boys spoke Judeo-Arabic. We attended three or four times a week, but I recall little else about it because, as it turned out, we didn't stay there for long. Because my brother and I were Italian speakers from the European part of town we were regarded as oddities, and came in for considerable teasing. This was harmless until one hot day when Clem was about eight. He dozed off leaning against a window, and one of the boys put a carob seed in his right ear.

It was meant as a joke, but when Clem woke up the seed was firmly lodged, and he couldn't get it out. At first he thought it was just an irritation, and said nothing about it to my parents, but by night time he was in excruciating pain. The next morning my mother called in our doctor, an Egyptian. After a careful examination, he advised my parents to take Clem straight to hospital. My parents had grave misgivings about this, as it was common knowledge that there were German doctors working there, who might well have been Nazis. Many of the Italian doctors who had once worked in Benghazi's hospital had returned to Italy, and defeated Nazis fleeing prosecution had found safe haven in post-war Libya due to the total chaos created by the Italians' hasty withdrawal. However, there was little choice—it was the only hospital in Benghazi.

Hoping that the Italian nurses would keep an eye on Clem, my mother took him to the hospital, where her worst fears were soon realised. She soon heard horrendous screams coming from the direction of the operating theatres. She was frantically trying to find Clem when an Italian nun, a nurse, came rushing towards her. '*Signora, signora*', she implored, 'quick, take your son out of here! It's a German surgeon and I'm sure he's a Nazi. Take your boy quickly or he won't survive long.'

With the help of the nun and sympathetic Arab male nurses Clem was wheeled out and taken home, unconscious. His face looked like something out of a horror film, but at least he was out of Nazi hands. Our own Egyptian doctor did what he could to make him comfortable, but strongly urged my parents to take him to another hospital. This, however, posed an enormous problem. The nearest hospital with modern facilities that was still staffed by Italian doctors was in Tripoli, some 650 miles away. It could be reached only via a poorly maintained desert road that was riddled with pot holes. Old coaches and trucks converted into people-carriers were the only means of transport, and the journey could take up to two days. Furthermore, aside from probable stoppages due to engine problems, there was the added danger of attacks by armed gangs. But Clem's condition was worsening. He simply had to be taken to Tripoli. To complicate the issue further, the only person who could take him was our mother, and she was eight months pregnant. It was vital for my father to keep his job; there was no way of knowing how long Clem would need to be in Tripoli, and he could not risk being replaced if he was away for long. He agonised over letting his pregnant wife make the journey. To make things a bit easier for my mother, and alleviate his worry, the wife of the shul president volunteered to go with her. My maternal grandmother and aunts would look after me and my toddler brother during the day when my father was at work.

Everyone understood the potential dangers. Clem might not survive the journey; my mother could go into labour in the desert. Before leaving, she went to our rabbi and made a vow before him: if the Almighty granted that she and Clem, and her unborn child, got through the journey safely and successfully, she would fast during the daylight hours of Rosh Hashanah for the rest of her life.

Two Jewish women and a sick child set out on the perilous trek to Tripoli, in the company of a dozen Arab men. Their travel companions behaved impeccably, giving my mother and her friend the best available seats in the truck, and soothing Clem's tears of pain with sweets. The truck driver stopped frequently so that the passengers could buy dates and goats' milk from passing Bedouin, but even so they were all hot, hungry and uncomfortable, and some of them suffered from travel sickness. At one point, the truck was indeed targeted by a band of robbers; they took the men's wallets, but left the women alone. Further on, my mother felt so unwell that the driver made an unscheduled stop at a Bedouin encampment so that they could spend the night in relative comfort before continuing the journey.

After some thirty-six harrowing hours, during which my mother and her friend were constantly reciting psalms, they arrived at the hospital in Tripoli, where they were greeted by relatives who had been alerted to their imminent arrival by my father. Clem was whisked off in one direction, to be given life-saving treatment (though he was left with permanently impaired hearing); my mother was wheeled to the delivery room, where she very shortly gave birth to my sister, Yvette. In Hebrew, she was named Chava, meaning 'life'.

It was about a month before my mother returned, as she and Clem both needed to recuperate after their ordeal, and travelling through the desert with a newborn would have been unwise. She stayed with family until they had recovered, and travelled back in a respectable coach. I have only hazy memories of that time, but I do remember being worried and feeling rather lonely, while at the same time looking forward to welcoming a little sister. It was quite pleasant to be pampered a bit, but there was little to do as it was holiday time, and I missed my mother and Clem. I think I did my best to entertain Ever, but the three-year gap between us meant we had different interests. We were overjoyed to see them when they finally got back, and probably made nuisances of ourselves mauling the baby.

My mother did indeed fast during the two days of Rosh Hashanah, until the end of her life. As children we had not been told of her vow, and we were mystified as to why our father would take her coffee and cake before daybreak, and why she would not eat with us during the day, and only after dark. We assumed this fasting was an obligation on all Jewish women and it was many years before we realised it was peculiar to our family, and learned the dramatic story behind it.

When, eventually, the family came to England, we tried to persuade our mother that it was time to nullify her vow, especially after our father died suddenly on Rosh Hashanah 1976, aged only sixty-four, but she was adamant she would always keep it. So, depending on where she was spending the festival, either Clem or I took on the task of taking up her very early breakfast to her on Rosh Hashanah mornings.

One year, when my mother was staying with us in our home in Edgware, we met the eminent rabbi, Dayan Michael Fisher, on our way back from shul. Seizing my chance, I appealed to him to tell my mother that fasting on Rosh Hashanah was forbidden. Much to my chagrin, and her smug satisfaction, he replied that on the contrary, it's a *mitzvah* to fast on Rosh Hashanah! I should have realised: mothers always know best.

3

The aliyah years

The continued state of insecurity regarding the future of Jews in Libya, as well as their love of Zion and the declaration of the State of Israel in 1948, resulted in the immigration of about 90 per cent of the Jewish community to Israel between 1949 and 1951, leaving behind some 4,000 Jews in Tripoli and only a few hundred in Benghazi, all of whom were heavily involved in commerce and the local economy.

My parents were uncertain whether going or staying would be best. On the one hand it was very tempting to join those heading for the newly independent Jewish homeland; on the other, life there would be uncertain, whereas my father's NAAFI job was secure. For many months, nearly all our household goods remained packed in wooden boxes whilst my parents vacillated, until eventually we could no longer live with all the basic necessities of life packed away waiting for shipping. The decision was made to stay put, keep the job and take our chances.

My brothers and I were deeply disappointed. As a nine-year-old I had been very excited at the prospect of travel, and had been looking forward to seeing the family and friends who had already left. We had been used to spending time with grandparents, uncles, aunts, cousins and friends, and now we felt we would become lonely and isolated. One of the saddest memories of my childhood, which haunts me to this day, was waving goodbye to these dear people as the ships carrying them away receded into the distance. Unfortunately, I never saw many of them again. We kept in touch for a while, but then when Libya attained independence, and the British left, telephone communication was cut off by the Libyan government. Any contact with the State of Israel was forbidden, and they were lost to us completely—at least while we remained in Libya.

The shul of my youth

The shul of my formative years, known as the Grand Synagogue (Tzelat Alkebira in Judeo-Arabic), stood in the European section of town, catering to the slightly larger congregation of mostly Italian-speaking Jews still hoping to make a life in Benghazi. It was of more recent construction and modern design, with a very high ceiling, rows of comfortable benches with backrests facing inwards towards the central *bimah*, a ladies' gallery, a social hall, and a Talmud Torah classroom.

Like all shuls, ours had its characters. Over half a century later, I can still feel and hear the heavy footsteps of the *shamash* who used to summon us for *Selichot* services, which Sephardim maintain for forty days from Rosh Chodesh Elul. He would walk the streets at the crack of dawn, giving two knocks with his walking stick on the gates of Jewish houses. It was uncanny how we could tell when he was getting closer and then moving away from our home. Years later I learned about the Doppler effect, whereby you can tell when a sound is moving towards you, and then away, by the changes in pitch. I still feel a slight shiver when I recall my father (and often my older brother and I) jumping up to get ready for *davening*.

There was Mr Mushi, who used to walk up and down the aisles of the shul to ensure complete decorum during *davening*. Just a look from him was enough to freeze you on the spot and stop any idle chatter. Then you had Vittorio, who watched us like a hawk, and would run from one end of the shul to the other to warn someone whose *tallit* was sweeping the floor. (In a Sephardi shul, this is extra important; Sephardim tie their *tzitzit* according to a special *minhag* (custom) that hints at Hashem's Name: the four groups of coils on the strings number ten, five, six, and five windings, reflecting the numerical value (*gematria)* of the Hebrew letters *yud-hei-vav-hei*. Sephardim are therefore particularly scrupulous about not letting *tzitzit* drag on the floor.)

The most fascinating and mysterious of all the congregants was Mr Meyohas, a multi-millionaire who usually came to shul only for festivals. At the auctioning of the *aliyot* on Yom Kippur, he would bid as high as necessary to obtain *petichah* (the ceremonial opening of the Ark). His contribution for that *mitzvah* alone would keep the shul going for the whole upcoming year.

Oh, yes, the auctioning of the *aliyot*: this was a very jolly and noisy time, providing a needed break from the solemnity of prayer. Lots of people used to bid for a particular *aliyah*, only to then offer it to a friend, visitor, or *ba'al simcha*.

From this I learned two valuable lessons: the value of an *aliyah*, and the importance of not judging your fellow man. According to our 'religiousness' scale, Mr Meyohas was not truly observant, but he kept the community economically afloat, and was always ready to help those in need.

Then we had Rabbi Madar, a pint-sized man who spoke Judeo-Arabic rather than Italian. He had wanted to make aliyah as soon as it became possible, but eventually decided to stay on in Benghazi to look after those of his flock who also remained behind. A product of the previous generation, he resisted changing over to European clothing as everyone else had, instead wearing white trousers, a long jacket, and a fez. Then one day, when I was about twelve, he turned up in shul with a hat, suit, and tie, to the amazement and spontaneous applause of the congregation. He spent much of his time in his office, concentrating deeply on learning Gemara. He had a good relationship with the local Arab clergy; several times they asked him to organise a prayer for rain during a lengthy drought. He was an excellent peacemaker, arbitrating domestic disputes and following them doggedly till they were resolved. He was probably the only one who was happy when Gaddafi expelled the last remaining Jews of Libya in 1970, for he ended his days in his beloved Eretz Yisrael.

The real beauty of my shul in Benghazi was its magnetic atmosphere, the people's warmth, and their readiness to embrace each other with genuine affection. But what I miss most is the respect people had for each other, and especially for the elderly. When an older person entered the shul, we youngsters would stand up or bow as he passed by. When a father or grandfather was given an *aliyah*, their children and grandchildren would stand, and remain standing from his first blessing, through the *leining*, to the final blessing. Then they would go up to the *bimah* to kiss his hand.

The Nazi butcher

The following events happened towards the end of the long summer break in late September, when I was about nine. It must have been 1950. Our grandparents, uncles, aunts and cousins had not yet left for Israel, so there were plenty of people to visit and play with. Clem and I spent time in our Uncle Frigia's store, admiring the marble he imported from Italy. Whenever we were there, he would send us to his mother's house in the afternoon to fetch him a clean handkerchief, and give us a few coins on our return. Then, once a week, he would give us the empty tins from his cigarettes, which we then took to sell to sailors as containers for their tobacco. That was quite an adventure.

It was an exciting time, as we youngsters were eagerly looking forward to our favourite festival, *Sukkot*. We would be spending a week eating all our meals—and maybe even sleeping—in a specially constructed hut (a

The young Meghnagi siblings. Left to right: little Yvette, Clem, myself, and Ever. This must have been taken in about 1950.

sukkah) with no proper roof, just a covering of leaves, to commemorate the way the Israelites lived in the desert after the exodus from Egypt. As in previous years, the local farmers had brought in their carts full of wares—palm branches to serve as the roofs for our huts, along with large bunches of fresh dates and other seasonal fruit for us to enjoy on the forthcoming festival. Lots of children had rushed out to greet them, climbing on their donkeys, picking the dates and just generally enjoying themselves. The whole place was agog with excitement and impatient anticipation.

Even from the back of our building, where we were 'helping' our father build our *sukkah*, we could hear Arab boys playing just below our balcony that fronted the street. They were pushing bicycle wheels and kicking old footballs, much to the annoyance of the hairdresser and other shopkeepers trying to rest in the afternoon siesta. We were probably being just as noisy, banging in nails, making posters, and tying pieces of wood into the shape of an enormous Star of David, which would end up as a large oil lamp chandelier. It was when our father was called away that the mischief started.

My brothers and I, even little Ever, who was only six, were running around, sawing and nailing wood to make a frame for flowers and fruit, when one of them tossed a piece of wood in my direction.

My brother had meant for me to catch it, but instead it hit my leg, with a heavy blow. I left the *sukkah* in pain. Not wanting to make too much fuss, I went to my grandmother's house next door, where I fell asleep in the spare room. She must have put a blanket over me, because during the night I felt its oppressive weight on my leg. The pain was excruciating, and I was shivering and crying, though I tried not to make a fuss.

The next morning, my mother took one look at my now-swollen leg and took me straight to the local hospital by taxi (which, in Benghazi, was a horse-drawn carriage). She was still very uneasy about this hospital, but it was the only one we had access to, and this was an emergency. An Italian nurse examined my leg. She said there was a large splinter lodged deep inside, and immediate surgery was required to remove it. I was taken to an operating room, where a German-speaking doctor appeared with two male assistants.

The two men held my leg while the German 'doctor' grabbed a knife and got to work on me. Unbeknownst to me, this duty doctor was a Nazi, maybe the same one who had hurt Clem.

My memories are hazy, but I do remember that there was no anaesthetic, and hygiene was not very high on the list of priorities as the surgeon's knife bit deeper and deeper into my leg, breaking the splinter into many pieces. My screams must have been heard outside the room, but of course my mother was not allowed anywhere near me. But for the kindness of an Arab nurse I would surely have lost my leg, if not my life. He somehow grabbed me from the operating table, rushed out of the room and thrust me at my mother, telling her to get me home. She escaped from the hospital and managed to take me to our own physician. He examined the leg, which was by this point dangerously infected. While cleaning and bandaging the wound as damage limitation, he warned my distraught parents that my leg would become gangrenous unless it was treated properly. I needed a hospital.

The problem, again, was which hospital? We already knew that the only safe one was in Tripoli, and that was simply too far away to deal with something so urgent. However, I had better luck than my brother Clem had had. When my father's boss at NAAFI heard what had happened, he arranged for an army ambulance to pick me up from our house and take me straight to the British military hospital near Benghazi, ordinarily out of bounds for regular Libyans. The British doctor who examined my leg looked horrified, and I understood enough English to be scared stiff. He wanted to inform the Red Cross about the doctor who had done this to me. Still, they managed to calm me and give me a general anaesthetic to prep me for surgery. All these years later I can still smell the ether and hear the sweet nun singing me a lullaby *'Amore mio…dormi, dormi'* ('my love… sleep, sleep') while I drifted off.

When I came round, my whole leg was throbbing and swathed in bandages. Thereafter I had to go to our own doctor nearly every day to have the wound checked and cleaned, and it took a long time before I was given the all clear to go back to school. The leg was still painful and not completely healed—that would take many more months, using miles of bandage and tons of cotton wool—but I was still excited to see my friends and teachers. After an absence of over a month and still heavily bandaged, I limped into the classroom, whereupon my teacher, Fratello Amedeo, simply looked up and remarked, 'You're an hour late!'

4

The gathering storm

My father thoroughly enjoyed his job at the NAAFI, so much so that his luxury home-goods store, which had been a regular supplier to the governing bodies before its destruction, became a distant memory. However, in 1951, Libya attained its independence and the British forces departed forever. This meant that my father's NAAFI job came to an end and, with it, some of his self-confidence. He struggled to find a new job. At one stage he opened a small drapery shop, but could not pay the rent and had to close it. I remember the occasion very clearly. I happened to be awake that Thursday night and heard him telling my mother the disastrous news. I lay there, worried sick, wondering where we would find the money for Shabbat food that week. To my amazement, the next morning I watched as my mother pulled a box from under her bed and produced a handful of liras. This 'magic box' disgorged money every week for what seemed to me ages, until my father found a job as a teacher for the community's Hebrew classes.

My parents never knew that I understood the precarious state of our family finances. My mother was able to help make ends meet by making soutanes for the local friars, and sewing dresses for friends. Once I turned thirteen, I helped too; from 1954 to 1957 I spent each three-month summer holiday working at different jobs—I worked variously for a barber, a gas fitter, in a hardware store, and at an import-export office. There was a one-off job in 1956, when I was entrusted with the task of organising a complete census of Benghazi's Jewish community. 'Complete' meant just that; it had to include property, bank accounts, jewellery, businesses, cars, and even the number of children per family. I had to fill out a form for each household and get the head of household to sign a declaration that he was aware of the consequences of any misinformation or omissions.

I can't pretend I didn't sometimes miss joining my friends on their holiday jaunts, but I was glad to hand over my earnings to my mother. There was no welfare state, and I knew my father would not accept charity from the community. My jobs helped me develop a work ethic, and a determination to become self-sufficient.

One of the features of our life in Benghazi was the way attitudes to us Jews tended to fluctuate. Often there was a difference in attitude between the younger and older Arabs. I recall well one particular example of the cordial interactions we often enjoyed. I was about twelve. My mother sent me to buy six lots of *sfenz* (a type of pancake made with yeast). These were either sugar coated or filled with an egg, and we wanted the latter. I didn't understand why the Arab stall-holder asked me to break the eggs before he used them, until later my father explained that this was very decent of him: if an egg contains blood it is not kosher, and has to be thrown away. Knowing this, the vendor was prepared to lose money if we found blood spots. I also vividly remember how we and other families used to take the food which had been prepared for Shabbat to be kept hot in the Arab baker's huge oven.

There were also, unfortunately, negative interactions. Benghazi, being on the Mediterranean coast, is usually blessed with the most beautiful weather, but occasionally a sandstorm would sweep up from the Sahara, bringing with it fine sand that was actually thick, red powder. A red haze would fall over everything and, try as we might, it was impossible to stop it penetrating indoors. It was a menace; the powder would lie on the staircase up to our apartment so thickly that the stairs became more like a slide, and every nook and cranny inside was covered. During these sandstorms most people stayed indoors for their own safety, but that meant we could be stuck at home for several days. It was a Friday afternoon in springtime, 1956, just after we had been released from one such confinement, and I was on my way home from the lending library at the Italian consulate. I was very happy to have found a whole new consignment of books there, as I had read virtually everything they already had. I was hurrying through nearly empty streets, laden with an armful of books and looking forward to immersing myself in a good read, when I turned a corner and saw what looked like an ugly situation developing further down the road.

Three young Arabs had surrounded a teenager who was dressed for Shabbat. They were gesticulating, apparently angry. I was pretty sure he was in trouble. I knew I should help anyone who was being threatened, Jewish or not, but to my shame I hesitated, wondering if it was worth two of us getting beaten up instead of one. Then my less cowardly nature took over. I marched towards them, as boldly as I could, and once I got closer I realised that the boy being threatened was actually a good friend of mine named Maurice. But then I was stopped in my tracks. One of the Arabs threatening him spotted me and, in a friendly voice, greeted me by name! My astonishment turned to relief as I recognised him; he had recently done some work in our apartment, and we had made sure to give him something to eat and drink while he was with us. Within a few minutes we were all the best of friends. He insisted on escorting us safely to my home, where Maurice and I chatted about everything except what had just happened, and how close we had come to a nasty confrontation.

A few months later, I saw Maurice again, under rather different circumstances. Having worked hard at my holiday job throughout the summer, I thought I'd earned a day off and so I rode my bike to one of the best beaches in Benghazi, where most of my friends had beach huts and would spend whole days relaxing and swimming. My friend Meir El Saiegh welcomed me to his hut so I could change into my swimming trunks, and off I set for a swim. No big deal, you might think, but I had to be very careful because of my absolute lack of buoyancy. I now know that this is typical for my body type, but back then I just knew I didn't want to make a fool of myself.

I struck out, and started swimming parallel to the beach. At first I was doing fine, but then suddenly I felt myself being caught in an undertow and swept well beyond my comfort zone. The harder I struggled to get back to the beach, the further out I was carried, until I panicked and thought my time had come. I don't know how many times I went under before a strong pair of hands grabbed me, first by the hair and then by the shoulders, and dragged me coughing and spluttering back to the safety of the beach.

Those heroic hands belonged to the friend I had 'saved' from being beaten up by those youths. When I had recovered we had a good laugh, which we continue to do over sixty years later. I, thank God, lived to become an engineer, while he went on to become the highly respected historian, with many books to his credit, Professor Maurice Roumani, now living in Jerusalem.

Death to the Jews

The worst negative interaction with our Arab neighbours that I experienced—one that nearly ended in utter disaster—came in late 1956. Although it was early November, there was not a single cloud in the sky. I was fifteen, Clem sixteen, Ever twelve and Yvette eight. We boys were busy at the Istituto De La Salle, while Yvette was at a girls' school run by nuns. Nearly all our relatives and friends had moved to Israel, and Libya's hostility to the Jewish state meant that aliyah was no longer possible for the remaining Jews. It was the year of the Hungarian revolution and, much more scary for us, the escalating Suez crisis. The news of Israel's invasion of Sinai, in response to Egypt nationalising the Suez Canal and blocking it to all Israeli vessels, had given some Arabs in Benghazi an excuse to organise attacks on the Jewish community. Egyptian president Gamal Abdel Nasser's inflammatory diatribes on the radio were continuing to trigger attacks on Jews in most Arab countries.

It was a Friday, and normally I would have been going to class at the Istituto De La Salle. I always looked forward to school, especially on Fridays when there was a more relaxed atmosphere. Another good reason for relishing Friday mornings was that much of the time was devoted to my favourite lesson, Italian literature. I especially enjoyed the writing of Giovanni Pascoli, whose poetry held a touch of sadness. When he was only eight years old, his father had been murdered on his way home, shot by an assassin while riding in his carriage, and young Giovanni never got over seeing his father's body borne home by the mare pulling the carriage. That vision haunted me, maybe because of our own precarious existence, which seemed to echo his.

Benghazi being predominantly Muslim, on that day schools and shops closed after lunch. Consequently, the Jewish children who went to the Italian school not only enjoyed a free Sunday, but also a school-free Friday afternoon. We would arrive home soon after midday, then bathe and put on our Shabbat clothes before making our way to the Italian consulate lending library to spend a few relaxed hours reading and chatting with the consul and a few friends. Later, we would meet the rest of the community at the shul for evening prayers, before the whole family eventually walked home together for the Friday night meal.

On this particular Friday, however, we had been kept at home, and it was apparent from our parents' hushed voices and the fear on their faces that something was seriously wrong. It was the fifth day of fierce fighting between Israeli and Egyptian forces. Looking out of the window, we could see an ugly crowd growing around the mosque beyond the end of our street. The street itself was deserted; the shops below weren't just closed, but had their metal shutters down. The silence did not reflect the typical relaxed Friday calm. It was frightening. In the past, threatening situations such as these had usually amounted to nothing but noise that soon fizzled out. On these occasions we would seek refuge with our upstairs neighbours, Mr and Mrs Amin, a lovely Egyptian couple (we called him Amin Effendi, a term of respect). He was a senior diplomat, and his wife and my mother had become very close friends. This time, however, they were in Egypt. They couldn't help.

Soon we saw the mob moving inexorably towards our neighbourhood, which was still mainly Jewish. The crowd was really angry, with ringleaders screaming to urge everyone on. We began to make out shouts of 'Death to the Jews!'

Arabs of courage

Our father started implementing defensive measures. He rushed to bolt the main doors of the building, before securing all the doors and windows in our apartment. My younger brother and sister clung to us and we huddled together, trying to put on a brave face, but fearing for our lives. Peering through a small gap in the heavy curtains I could see the terrifying mob advancing towards us, swelling in number as more joined in. On they came, wielding knives, sticks and stones, and yelling threats and curses: '*Filastin arduna walyahud kilabuna*' (Palestine is our country and the Jews our dogs).

If the mob managed to break into our home, we would be sitting targets. The only possible means of escape was via the laundry-cum-*sukkah* area, an open-roofed space at the rear of our apartment, but that would involve a four-metre drop to the narrow alley that ran behind the building, on the other side of which were one-storey houses belonging to Arab Libyans. Our only means of egress would be through one of those houses; we could only hope that the residents might take pity on us and offer us shelter.

We ran to drag our mattresses to the rear of the apartment, ready to drop them down to soften our landing, then we children took up our positions by the window again. My father was whispering prayers which, of course, only filled us youngsters with more terror.

We watched the approaching mob helplessly. I, at least, was wondering why we hadn't followed our wider family to the relative safety of Israel back in the early 1950s. But then, all at once, we were stunned as we witnessed an unbelievable spectacle unfolding before our eyes...a true miracle. Some dozen Arab men broke away from their fellows and formed a human chain, blocking the entrance to our street. Facing down the mob, one of them managed to grab a megaphone from one of the agitators and yelled repeatedly, 'Leave the Jews alone, leave the Jews alone! They've done no harm, they are our friends!'

What we witnessed that day was an incredible act of courage. Those few men unquestionably put their own lives in danger as they stood firm against the mob to protect their Jewish compatriots. They could easily have been trampled to death. Thankfully, their brave actions were successful and probably averted a massacre. After the initial pushing, swearing and screaming at the men holding them back, the mob gradually dispersed and drifted away.

The threat was gone for the time being, but that was the moment when I, at fifteen years old, resolved to find a way of leaving. There was no future for us in Libya. Leaving aside such terrifying outbreaks of violence as we had just experienced, Libyan Jews were, at best, moderately liked by the older population and the business classes and tolerated by the youth. Certain Jewish practices were respected, especially regarding dietary laws; our status as the People of the Book meant that there was a certain affinity between Judaism and Islam, and a reasonable tolerance and respect for our attendance at shul and the celebration of our festivals. Nevertheless, we could never relax our vigilance; we always had to be on our guard against individual attacks, and deal with the periodic flare ups of animosity against the community. Much of the animosity stemmed from the Jews' natural closeness to the State of Israel, and the Arabs' hatred of that state. We could not show any support of Israel at all. Only a few weeks earlier we had narrowly averted trouble when an onlooker had mistaken our celebration of a religious festival for a celebration of Israel's Independence Day. During the festival of *Hoshana Rabba*, our custom was for the whole family to don their best clothes and make their way to the shul at about 6 a.m. for the morning service. A young Arab had seen us all dressed up and, assuming we were surreptitiously on our way to celebrate Israel's Independence Day, threatened to call others to attack us. He took some convincing that our service was primarily a prayer for rain, but eventually calmed down and let us continue without further trouble.

Leaving Libya was not simple, for Jews. We were not normally granted Libyan nationality, and therefore had no passports. Permission to travel abroad with a stateless travel document was given only in exceptional circumstances, such as for special educational or urgent medical reasons, but only if the rest of the family remained in the country as 'guarantors'. A few Jews who had managed to obtain foreign nationality such as British, French, Italian, etc. were in a better position, but there was always the risk of losing the right to return. As I mulled my options during the aftermath of this latest flare up of rage against the Jews, I was inspired by the story of two Jewish teenagers who had recently swum to an Italian ship that was anchored off the port of Tripoli; they had stowed away to Italy, and from there made their way to Israel. However, I knew there was no way I would or could follow their example, for two important reasons. First, I would not abandon my family, knowing that if I did it was highly likely that the authorities would make them suffer for my illegal escape. Second, and more immediately relevant, I have the buoyancy of a brick, and the only direction in which I can swim any distance is down. Any escape plan involving swimming would not be a good option for me.

5

Kidnapped

Notwithstanding my intention to leave Libya somehow, the even tenor of our lives went on mostly undisturbed. However, when I was about sixteen, a twelve-year-old Jewish girl unaccountably disappeared from home. Hers was one of the most respected families in town, one which unusually and courageously lived in the heart of the Arab district rather than in the safer European/Jewish section of the town. When it became clear that family and friends had not seen her for quite some time, the chilling realisation that she might have been kidnapped left everyone in deep shock. Our small community felt exposed and insecure.

As soon as my brothers and I arrived at the shul for prayers we realised something very serious had happened, but we had no idea what. The usual quiet and decorum had been replaced by agitated whispering from small groups of men dotted around the main prayer hall, distracting those trying to concentrate on their prayers. In vain the warden tried to keep some semblance of order. Usually one look from him was enough to quell any idle chatter, but this time he had no chance.

Gradually the whispering stopped as all eyes were drawn to the elder of the shul, who had been quietly chanting the twenty-third psalm but was now lifting his head and standing up. He started sobbing quietly. To us children growing up in an intermittently hostile environment the sight of a grown man weeping was scary and unnerving. The fact that he was the pillar of our close-knit community made it even worse.

The adults had no time for explanations, so we children went outside to the courtyard, where everything seemed quite normal. Soon the men filed out of the shul in tight-lipped silence. My father took firm hold of us and briskly led us straight home. As soon as we arrived he bolted the front door, gathered us in the lounge and forbade us to go out for the immediate future. After a quick meal we were sent to bed with none of our questions answered. Our parents did not understand that keeping us in the dark, in both senses of the word, only intensified our fear. Eventually we fell asleep.

The next morning, during a tense breakfast, our mother finally explained the mystery. The shul elder had been so distraught because it was his daughter, Sara, who had disappeared. Her bed had not been slept in. We were all thunderstruck.

Community in shock

Nothing like this had happened in living memory. We had heard stories of Jewish girls being abducted in earlier decades, but those were only rumours of events from long ago. Leaving aside the danger to Jews posed by nationalistic Arab firebrands, this was a society that treasured children—even Jewish ones—and would rarely attack, let alone abduct them. This new development was alarming not only for us, but also for other minorities in Libya like the Greeks, Maltese and Italians, although they at least had their embassies to run to. We had no one. This worrying turn of events further undermined our already precarious sense of security.

The elder whose daughter was missing was a successful businessman with an unusually close and friendly relationship with his Arab neighbours. Everyone was speculating on the whereabouts of his youngest daughter. Had she been abducted by Arab nationalists? Was this their new way of attacking Jews?

The police were informed, but by the next day, there was still no news of any kind. The air of helplessness and gloom in the community intensified. We children were kept indoors again whilst the rabbi and the president of the community appealed to Arab friends for help.

Early that afternoon, an elderly Arab, a friend of the community, turned up at the rabbi's house with a message from the abductor, saying the following: 'Sara has left her home of her own accord. She is staying at her friend's house. He loves her deeply and intends to marry her. This will be carried out in accordance with Muslim tradition. In the meantime, she cannot be visited until things settle down, and even then only in the presence of her host's family.'

The rabbi was stunned and shaking with anger. How a young girl had been lured out of her house in the middle of the night and into this Arab man's home was a mystery, and a very frightening one. What made it more sinister was the pretence that this twelve-year-old child was in love with this man. No unmarried girl was now safe.

At a hastily organised meeting of the shul elders a rather subdued rabbi explained the facts and promised to contact Muslim clergy and other influential Arabs. He cautioned against unnecessary gossip and advised everyone to go home early, lock the doors and only go out if absolutely necessary. He reminded them that the Arabs' respect for women meant they would not harm Sara, and that she would not be touched until after a wedding ceremony. Thus, they had time to calm down and form a plan of action.

What was needed was some miracle, and a modern-day saviour.

Esther to the rescue

Later that evening my mother, Esther, went to visit Rabbi Madar, a friend and mentor who had a tremendously calming influence on the whole community. He had occasionally mediated in my parents' sometimes stormy relationship, so knew them personally. She told him baldly that she intended to go to the abductor's house and stay there until they released Sara. Aghast at this idea, Rabbi Madar did his best to dissuade her, citing his hero the great Rabbi Rafael Dabusc, her grandfather, who he claimed would have definitely disapproved of her plan.

She countered by saying that, as a woman who spoke the local Arab dialect well, she stood a good chance of being allowed in and treated well. Also, she would be well placed to appeal directly to the man's mother, as well as to him.

From past experience the rabbi knew how intrepid, not to say stubborn, my mother was. This was a woman who had crossed the desert at eight months pregnant, to save her son! Reluctantly he conceded that she might be right, and gave her his blessing. He knew that something had to be done, and urgently. Esther had as much chance of success as anyone, if not better.

That same afternoon, my mother baked some cakes to take with her, then, as darkness fell, she draped a scarf over her head so that it resembled a hijab, and proceeded on foot through the Arab quarter. Arriving at the abductor's house she was greeted politely, but just as politely told to go home. Ignoring all this, she pushed her way inside and staged a sit-in.

We found out later that the whole night was spent in argument and counter argument. It became clear that Sara had been drugged. My mother finally won them over by saying the child was in no fit state to agree to convert to Islam, which would be necessary for a wedding to take place. She insisted on taking Sara back home to give her a chance to recover and reflect. There was plenty of time for the families to meet and discuss things, she said. At last the mother of the enamoured young man relented and persuaded her husband and her son to let Sara go, at least for the time being. She acted with the decency of a mother feeling sympathy for another mother.

As dawn broke, early-morning Arab traders were surprised to see a European-looking woman with a dazed-looking girl leaving an Arab home. My mother was so tired and emotional she forgot to arrange her head covering as before, and her light brown hair was escaping from under her usual head scarf.

Quickly Sara was returned to her grateful family, and my mother went home to rest. It transpired that the Arab youth had become obsessed with the beautiful Sara. He had stalked her for weeks and beguiled her with gifts until he managed to lure her to his house (she was only twelve, after all). The tremendous relief everyone felt at her homecoming was tempered by the fear that copycats might use this incident to attack Jews.

On the pretext of improving her education Sara was quickly sent to Italy, and from there I think to South America. She never returned to Benghazi, and I believe she is now living happily in Israel with her Jewish husband and children. As for my mother, we all knew she had made herself a target for revenge, because the abductor's family obviously believed Sara would be returned to them. There followed a period of stress and fear for my mother, as she anticipated attacks. However, everything went quiet; it seemed that the abductor's family had realised there was no point in further action since the girl was gone. Still, after these events our family was left feeling very uneasy. By this time I was not the only one in the family to feel the need to leave Libya. The rest of the family were reluctantly coming round to the idea, but it would be some time before anything definite was done. Our dream was to go to Israel, Italy, or America.

6

Life changes

By 1957, I had completed my studies at the Istituto De La Salle. There was no Italian higher education available in Benghazi, so my mother and I travelled to Tripoli, where there were many Italian schools that offered courses leading to university entrance. I was hoping to find a course which included maths and other subjects which would lead towards engineering.

After a short stay my mother went home, and I remained with my aunt, Communa Pagani, whose son, Herbert, would go on to become a famous Italian artist and musician. I remember standing on Aunt Communa's balcony and watching a few minutes of the British film *Ice Cold in Alex* being shot. Although the street and large piazza below were cordoned off, they could not stop people looking on from their own balconies. I remember seeing John Mills and Sylvia Syms having a final embrace. Every time I watch the film I am taken back to the sights and sounds of Tripoli.

At the college interview I was told that one of the basic entry requirements was Latin. This meant that I had to return to Benghazi to cram three years' study of Latin into one. When I had started at the Istituto there had only been one path of study, with an emphasis on maths, science and business, and no classics. Later, they began a course that included the arts and classics, but I had already been committed.

Back home, I was allowed to sit in on all classes except Latin, since I was a beginner and they weren't, but I had private tuition in Latin. In order to pay for the tuition I gave maths lessons to two brothers in the year below me, and their father paid my Latin tutor directly. This went on for seven months, at the end of which I took a test at school and found I had progressed enough to join the Latin class, then in its third year of study.

Our neighbour's tragedy

It was during my year of intense study that our lovely upstairs neighbour, Mr Amin, knocked on our door one day and tearfully broke the news that his beautiful wife had died suddenly while in Cairo. She had divided her time between Benghazi and Cairo, where their younger children were staying with family and attending school. He told us he was going to Egypt to organise the funeral, and would not be returning as he had to look after the children.

He told us his apartment would now be occupied by his eldest daughter and her dentist husband, who would set up a practice locally.

For my mother this death was a terrible shock. She and Mrs Amin had been like sisters, spending hours together swapping stories and recipes. The charming couple had always been there for us with help and advice. Now the poor widower tried to make my mother feel better by asking her to look after his daughter when she arrived...and indeed the young bride turned out to be just as friendly as her parents.

While we were still taking in this tragedy, events occurred which were not only very upsetting, but completely changed my life and that of my family.

A fateful decision

It all started when the community decided to mark a special anniversary of the passing of one of Benghazi's great rabbis. A full programme of individual and group study was organised in the ancient and imposing shul, Tzelat Bramli, in the ghetto district. The ghetto had housed the Arabic-speaking Jews of Benghazi, most of whom had made aliyah by then; the congregation, once in the hundreds, now numbered only around twenty families. Tzelat Bramli was a very old, imposing edifice built in the grand style, with wood, marble, colonnades, a semi-circular ladies' gallery, a *bimah* big enough for a children's choir, and a large Ark.

People were encouraged to spend as much time there as possible. Various rabbis were to give lectures throughout the day, ending with the evening prayer and a big communal meal. One unusual feature was that the day was declared a *Ta'anit Dibbur*, literally a 'fast from talking' day, during which idle chatter was discouraged; it was to be a day of quiet prayer, psalm reading and personal reflection.

For the children, the day started as usual by going to school. The Istituto De La Salle was about two miles from home. The main roads of central Benghazi were laid out in a number of concentric arcs; our home was at one end of the outer one, and the school was at the other. Usually we walked round that arc, taking what we called the sea route, rather than cutting across the diameter, which went through an Arab area where youngsters at a loose end might start trouble. Occasionally, if we were late, or my father was in a really good mood, we would ride in horse-drawn carriages. To get to the shul we had to pass our apartment and continue on for some way, and on that particular day we wanted to get there as soon as possible. The Jewish boys from school, about ten of us in all, decided to risk taking the quick route. We ranged in age from eight to seventeen, so we walked in single file, with the older boys at the front and back to sandwich the younger ones. As the eldest, Clem and I brought up the rear. We told everyone to keep on walking and not to retaliate if anyone started throwing stones. On the Arabs' home ground that would be disastrous. If it came to it, our boys should just use their satchels as shields, but not run.

So off we went, encouraged to see the distant lights of shops where we might be able to seek refuge if necessary (shopkeepers of all nationalities and religions were usually sympathetic). We had not gone very far when we were confronted by a sight which would haunt my dreams for years to come. There on our left appeared a large open area, a bombed site which had been left untouched since the war, where some thirty young Arabs were kicking a football about. As we drew level with them the name-calling started; then, as I had feared, they started pelting us with stones.

We stuck to our plan, merely warding off the stones and increasing our pace without running, and as we got past the danger zone I thought we had got away with it, and sighed with relief. Suddenly, though, I heard a blood-curdling scream from behind me. Don't ask me how our younger brother, Ever, had managed to fall behind without our noticing, but there he was on the ground, being kicked and pummelled by one of the stone-throwers, while another held him down.

Immediately Clem and I raced back, yelling. Launching myself at the main culprit, I used my aluminium lunchbox to lash out at heads and arms...whatever I could reach. I was in quite a frenzy, and seeing this Clem dashed up and pulled me off before I could do too much damage. The youth scrambled up, and he and his friend darted towards the bombed-out buildings nearby. In the glimpse I caught before he ran, he did not look as bad as I'd feared, since my punches had landed mainly on his clothes and not his face, yet there was a lot of blood from somewhere. I realised it was from Ever.

Clem and I started chasing the fleeing youths, screaming at them, fuelled by adrenaline and the impetuosity of youth. What happened next still strikes me as incredible: As we charged after the assailants, the whole gang who had been throwing stones, some thirty of them, turned tail and fled. There were only two of us, but it was as if they saw an army coming after them. Most likely they feared the possible outcome of their attack. Maybe their reaction shocked us back to our senses, maybe not, but we realised the rashness of what we were doing; at any minute the tables might be turned, and they would be the ones giving chase again. Clem skidded to a halt, catching my sleeve to stop me, and we gradually backed away, still screaming taunts at the offenders.

Thankfully they decided they had had enough and just scattered, so we were able to return to Ever, who was still lying on the ground. He looked like an extra from a horror film; his nose had been flattened, and his face was covered in blood. We helped him up and supported him as he hobbled home. The rest of the group with whom we had set off from school were long gone, but we couldn't blame them for that. There was no help offered by any of the people we passed on our long walk home, though at least they looked sympathetic.

At last, we staggered into our apartment. My mother took one look at Ever and had a screaming fit. Our father was still at work, so she had to deal with the situation herself. Calming down as she sponged his gory face, she decided to take the patient to our doctor, the Egyptian who lived across town, which meant taking a horse-drawn cab. My mother was always a lioness in defence of her young; she asked the driver to follow the route we had taken earlier, in case Ever was able to spot his attacker. Amazingly, he actually did so. With the culprit pointed out, our mother stopped the cab, got down, and looked around for someone in uniform. She found a policeman, and although he explained he was from another town and had no jurisdiction, and despite constant heckling from onlookers, she persuaded him to hold the youth until a local policeman arrived to take him for questioning.

The next day we got a call from the police station telling me to come and make a statement. My father went with me, so I was rather surprised when they asked just for me, and told him to wait at reception. Once inside, alone, the senior officer's demeanour completely changed; his civil air disappeared and he became angry and aggressive. He began accusing me of attacking the Arab. Noticing I had difficulty answering in Arabic, he shouted at me, 'Go home, go home, back to Italy!!'

I protested, 'This *is* my home', at which he shook me violently and almost punched me. Only the arrival of another officer stopped him. Then he told me to get out, but he warned me I would be hearing from them.

As I made my way home with my father, I was too shocked to explain to him what had happened, but once we were in our apartment I had to explain that I was in serious trouble. I had now become a target.

My mother was beside herself when she realised she had inadvertently given the police the name and address of the youth (me!) they considered to be the guilty party. It was clear that they had no interest in punishing anyone for breaking Ever's nose; rather, I was to be punished for daring to defend him. Obviously, they preferred to believe the Arab youth's version of events.

A few days later, once news of what had happened had spread, the president of our community warned my parents that sooner or later I was bound to suffer a revenge attack, and that I should leave the country as soon as possible. Easier said than done! Permission to travel abroad was very seldom given. Those who had the right contacts and, of course, the money, might be allowed to leave for educational purposes that would ultimately benefit the country, but even that was dependent upon them guaranteeing their return. Needless to say, we had neither contacts nor money, and I knew that if I left, I would not return. Generally speaking, it was not worth the risk of drawing attention to yourself by expressing any kind of desire to leave, but my situation was becoming desperate. In the past, our friend and neighbour, Mr Amin, would have been only too happy to help, but we couldn't turn to him any more since he had left for Egypt to be with his younger children.

Then a gift landed in my lap.

PART TWO

England

7

Cambridge, here I come

The Pye Radio Company of England offered scholarships to international students to study at its Cambridge-based college for nine months. These were to be for young people who seemed suited to study electronics, and my name had been put forward, together with that of my very good friend, Shlomo Gean, affectionately known to family and friends as Mumu.

My mother's reaction was an instinctive, 'Oh no, absolutely not!' She feared I'd never come back; that she'd never see me again. For my part, I was determined to go. I was thrilled! Although I knew that I would miss my parents, brothers, cute little sister and friends of all nationalities, including Arabs, my main thought was that I would no longer have to stay alert, constantly anticipating and dreading being attacked.

I was invited to see the president of the community, who had connections in government circles and overseas communal contacts. Having congratulated me, he stressed that I *had* to go, for the honour of the community but also, more to the point, for my own safety. Not only were the police probably after me, but it was likely that the family and friends of the boy I had beaten would be looking for revenge. The threat of a stab in the back was very real, and I could not lose this opportunity to get away. He said he would try to assuage my mother's understandable fears. My father was more pragmatic, but my mother had visions of her seventeen-year-old son adrift, without his family, in a strange country, with a strange language and culture, never to be seen again.

The president was as good as his word and, with help from the rabbi, prevailed upon my mother to accept (grudgingly) that I had to go. We had about a month to get everything organised. Permission to go was obtained fairly easily, since the invitation came from a well-known international company. Getting a passport was a different matter, as my family was not considered Libyan, despite having lived there for generations. In the end, the president of the community managed to arrange a stateless travel document for me. Weeks before Mumu and I were due to leave, the president again called me to his office and gave me some money and a one-way air ticket, both gifts from the community. He urged me to stay in

England, or go to Italy or Israel, but to on no account return to Libya. He asked me to keep his advice confidential, to which I agreed, thanking him for all his help and assuring him I would do my best to follow his advice. Our departure was set for Sunday 24 August 1958. Everything seemed in order during the week leading up to my big send off, but then, as bad luck would have it, on Shabbat I developed an excruciating toothache and headache which threatened to call the whole thing off. While sympathising with my agony, my mother was clearly half pleased that I might have to stay. It was Clem who saved the day by reminding us about our upstairs neighbour. We all trooped upstairs, where the dentist good-naturedly agreed to examine my mouth. To my huge relief, he announced that the problem was just an erupting wisdom tooth, and that rinsing with salt water should take care of it.

'Don't worry, madam!' he beamed at my poor mother. 'Your son will be fine for his flight tomorrow!'

My memory of my actual departure is hazy. I know I flung a few things in a case before my mother could stop me, and there were tearful farewells at home. Who knew when we would see each other again? In my heart I knew I was unlikely to return to Benghazi. I think Mumu came with his family to pick me up and go to the airport. My family stayed at home, so as not to draw undue attention to ourselves at the airport; after all, I was the one in possible trouble with the police. I certainly remember feeling the excitement of embarking on a great adventure, tempered with apprehension at the prospect of being thousands of feet up in the air.

Still, deep down I feared I would not be able to leave; I was worried that I would be stopped at passport control, where the fact that I was travelling on a stateless travel document could easily identify me and raise suspicions. In fact, only recently did I realise what must have happened: the travel document showed my Hebrew/Italian name, Elia, whereas all previous documents used its diminutive, which was Lillo. Family and friends still call me by that name. I now assume anyone looking for me at that time would have been checking for Lillo, not Elia, and by the time they realised that Elia and Lillo were one and the same person, I was already in Cambridge (which is where they caught up with me).

On a wing and a prayer

Mumu and I had chosen to stop over in Rome because we had spent so long studying its history and achievements. I particularly wanted to see its famous monuments and statues, especially Michelangelo's sculpture of

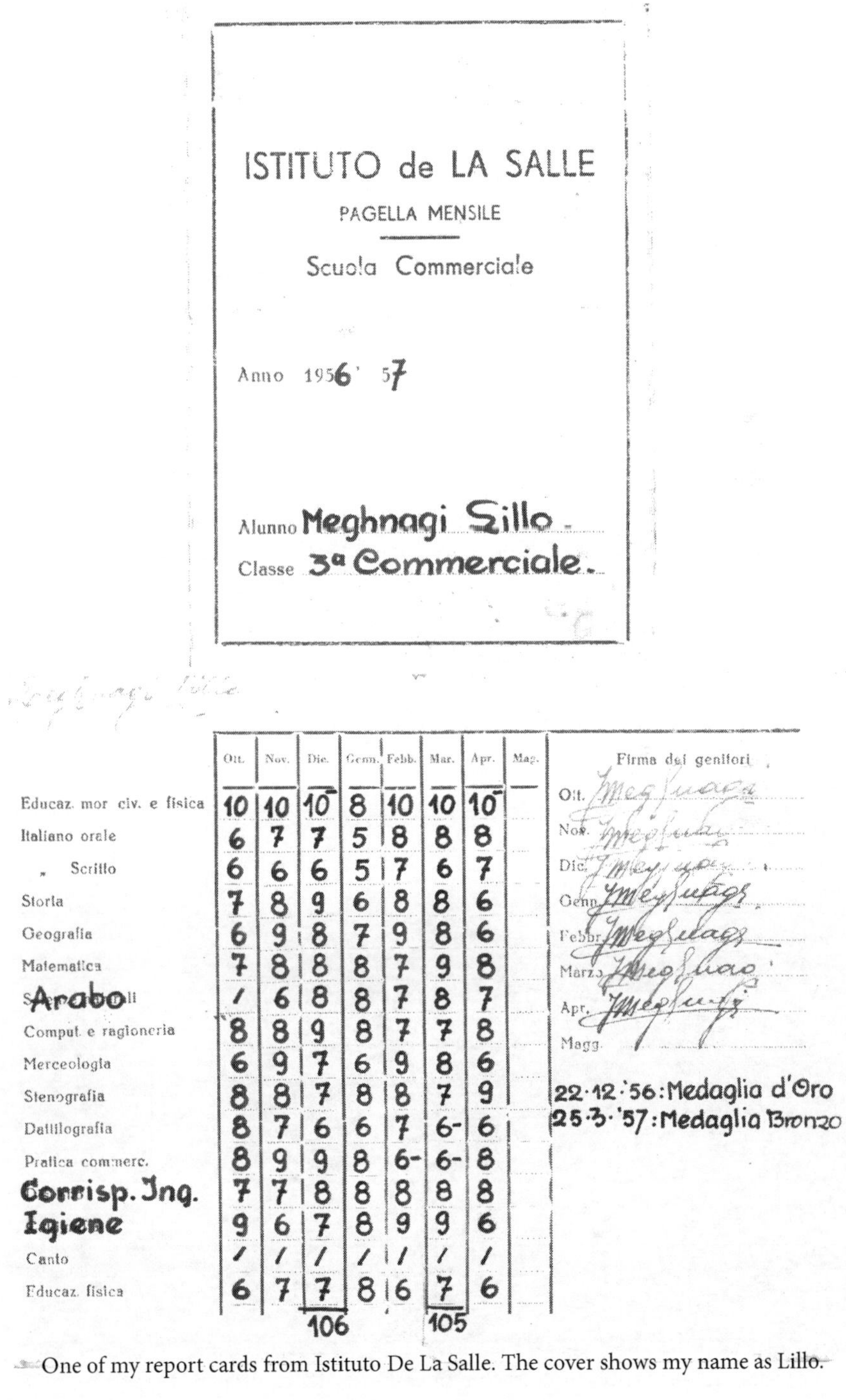
ISTITUTO de LA SALLE

PAGELLA MENSILE

Scuola Commerciale

Anno 1956' 57

Alunno Meghnagi Lillo

Classe 3ª Commerciale

	Ott.	Nov.	Dic.	Genn.	Febb.	Mar.	Apr.	Mag.
Educaz. mor civ. e fisica	10	10	10	8	10	10	10	
Italiano orale	6	7	7	5	8	8	8	
" Scritto	6	6	6	5	7	6	7	
Storia	7	8	9	6	8	8	6	
Geografia	6	9	8	7	9	8	6	
Matematica	7	8	8	8	7	9	8	
Arabo	/	6	8	8	7	8	7	
Comput. e ragioneria	8	8	9	8	7	7	8	
Merceologia	6	9	7	6	9	8	6	
Stenografia	8	8	7	8	8	7	9	
Dattilografia	8	7	6	6	7	6-	6	
Pratica commerc.	8	9	9	8	6-	6-	8	
Corrisp. Ing.	7	7	8	8	8	8	8	
Igiene	9	6	7	8	9	9	6	
Canto	/	/	/	/	/	/	/	
Educaz. fisica	6	7	7	8	6	7	6	
			106			105		

Firma dei genitori

Ott.

Nov.

Dic.

Genn.

Febbr.

Marzo

Apr.

Magg.

22·12·'56: Medaglia d'Oro

25·3·'57: Medaglia Bronzo

One of my report cards from Istituto De La Salle. The cover shows my name as Lillo.

Moses, but the monument which ultimately made the deepest impression on me was the Arch of Titus. Erected to celebrate Rome's final triumph over Judea, it depicts the glories of the Temple in Jerusalem being borne away by triumphant conquering Romans while Jews are led into slavery. When I got close enough, however, I found Hebrew words scratched into the arch that read '*Am Yisrael chai*' (the Jewish people are alive). This alone made our short stay in Rome worthwhile; it moved me deeply. I concluded that Rome may have been visited by millions because of its great past, but Jerusalem would be visited by millions because of its great future.

We stayed at a pensione run by a childhood friend of my mother. Besides running the pensione, this fascinating lady set herself up as *Il Mago d'Africa* (the Magician of Africa) and received a steady stream of clients who would come to her to ask advice and to take part in séances.

When I asked her what she knew about magic, she explained that many years before she had befriended an African man who called himself the Magician of Africa. He had made a very good living dressing as a tribal chief and 'prophesying' for many clients, mainly from the entertainment world. Eventually, having made plenty of money, he decided to go back to

Arriving at Rome airport with Mumu, after the first leg of our journey to the UK.

Africa, and offered her the chance to take over. To her laughing reply that she was no magician, he explained that he knew nothing about magic: he just told people what they wanted to hear; praise, mixed with some criticism, plus a lot of blessings. 'Works like magic!' he had told her.

Thus encouraged, she had sat in on a couple of sessions before taking on his mantle, and had never looked back. She had a thriving business 'consulting' with men and women from the media and from Cinecittà film studios, who really just wanted to air their personal problems, fears and frustrations.

If only my mother knew what her childhood friend was up to!

'Why don't you stay, and I'll teach you?' she suggested.

I caught Mumu's eye and said, 'Thanks, but no thanks.'

It was just as well that I had Mumu, and my ticket to London, as it was quite a tempting offer, especially as I suspect she had her eye on me for her very attractive daughter! But I resisted the temptation, and before long we were on our way to Ciampino Airport, bound for London en route to Cambridge.

Where are your horns?

As we came in to land at Heathrow I looked out of the window and my heart sank. What I had heard about London was true: all I could see was a blanket of cloud. Once through the clouds, however, we could see the breathtaking London skyline. As someone brought up in a small town I felt as though I were watching a technicolour, cinemascope film. After a smooth landing we were guided to passport control, where, in our hesitant English, we had to field a barrage of questions about why we had no proper passports and where we were going.

Showing the letter from Pye finally did the trick, and we were allowed out to be greeted by a tall, smiling gentleman from the company. Mr Hovell drove us to 35 Friars Close, Cherry Hinton, a village about four miles from the centre of Cambridge. This was to be our home for the next nine months, lodging with a charming young couple, the Campbells, and their year-old son. Mr Hovell made the introductions and left, reminding us as he went that college would not start for another fortnight, so we would have plenty of time to find our way around.

Once we had taken our cases to our room and freshened up, we rejoined our hosts. They were very welcoming. Giving us our own door keys, they suggested we go for a walk to stretch our legs, but be back by six for supper. Unsure how much information they had been given about us, we hesitantly pointed out that we kept to a vegetarian diet. They assumed that this was for medical reasons, so we had to tell them we were Jewish. On hearing this, Mrs Campbell literally recoiled. 'You're Jewish?' she exclaimed. 'But where are your horns?'

Mumu and I looked at each other, flabbergasted. We had heard about this imbecilic stereotype, but never thought we'd hear it here in Cambridge, supposedly one of the most cultured cities in the world. Recovering myself, I replied matter of factly, 'Sorry, I don't wear them during the day. I keep them under my mattress.'

There followed a few seconds of embarrassed silence, then we all laughed, and Mr Campbell suggested a game of cards till supper was ready.

A few weeks later his wife took me aside and sheepishly explained that as a child she had been to a church Sunday school, where she was taught that Jews have horns. We were the first Jews she had met, and she was most apologetic about her faux pas.

After that initial awkwardness we all got on very well. There was no television, so we would often spend evenings playing card games. One evening Mr Campbell taught me how to play chess, and to my embarrassment thereafter he was never able to beat me at it. We laughed it off and I just kept saying what a good teacher he was.

Student life

Soon after arriving in Cambridge, Mumu and I did what every self-respecting student there does: bought ourselves bikes. In our case, however, we promptly rode the wrong way down a one-way street. Luckily, we did not come to harm! Once having sorted out which side of the road we should be on, we spent many evenings cycling around the beautiful Cambridgeshire countryside and beyond. One day we visited the American War Cemetery and noted the names of Jewish soldiers whose graves were marked by a Star of David. We stood in the non-denominational chapel and said a short prayer, concluding it by listing their names. It was a very sobering experience, but we were impressed by how well maintained it all was.

Once we started our course, we were allowed to join the Cambridge University Students' Union and the Cambridge University Jewish Society, even though we were not at the university itself. We took an active part in the shul services in Thompson Lane, and at last we were able to have kosher lunches, which were provided there. Much as we appreciated these, it took time to accustom ourselves to the rather bland cuisine. Back home we had enjoyed plenty of dates, nuts and pomegranates, with our daily fare often featuring spiced beans, meat and fresh vegetables, shakshuka and sometimes fish, while Shabbat and festivals had their own special menus: on Shabbat, chicken (less often available there than England, because we had to take the chicken to be slaughtered), and couscous and mafrum, a labour-intensive dish of sliced potatoes stuffed with herbed mincemeat, fried in flour and egg, then simmered in a tomato sauce; each festival had its particular dish, with names which sound exotic to British ears: basin, chreime, cherchi, mokides/nokides, ghizata, bastil, boulo, mergaz…the list goes on, and if I describe them all this will become a cookery book. Today the recipes can be found online.

The only meal we continued to eat with the Campbells was breakfast—not a full English, of course, just cereal, maybe boiled eggs, and tea. This was different from my Benghazi breakfasts, when we sometimes had

Hard at work at Pye College, Cambridge, 1959.

Working alongside Mumu at college.

zabaglione, or bread and jam and occasionally milk with a dash of coffee, before rushing off to school (in Benghazi milk was not plentiful, as we usually had to collect it from a farm, which was not always possible, and we had no fridge). For supper we got by on fruit, vegetables, maybe nuts, and any cheap snacks we knew were vegetarian.

The next few months were like living in a dream. I was coping well with the course in radio and telecom engineering at Pye College, and I also joined a class at one of the local colleges to further polish my English. I participated fully in the Jewish Society and others, and made many new friends. We were free to do whatever we liked: we could go anywhere, read any newspapers, join any societies and political parties. It was a breath of fresh air: our first experience of democracy.

Mr Nichols, a fascinating, pint-sized man in his fifties, was one person with whom I became friendly through the shul. He had a cute little jewellery shop right in the middle of a bridge over the River Cam, and he ran his business with great enthusiasm and a disarming smile. I came to realise that he was something of a pariah in the local Jewish community, as he lived with his non-Jewish housekeeper, Gladys. They clearly loved each other, and she kept a strictly kosher home, but they had not married, as changing religion was a step too far for her. Though he regularly attended shul services, he never took part in communal activities. That was hardly surprising, since nine out of ten of those who attended were students, and the older residents who attended regarded him with disapproval. Despite this, he made it his mission in life to welcome and help lonely Jewish students, especially those from overseas. When he saw me and Mumu in shul, he took us under his wing and became our friend and adviser. Mumu and I became very active in all aspects of shul life, often helping with the running of the services as well as doing cleaning and helping to prepare the Sabbath meals. However, one contribution made us really famous...or notorious. We had seen that whoever was honoured with taking out the Torah scroll had great difficulty pulling back the curtain covering the Ark because the rail was so rusty. This rail ran from one side of the eastern wall to the other, and had clearly not been oiled for years, so one Friday morning we decided to do a good deed, and clean and oil it. I suppose we should have told someone, because next morning, the young man called upon to open the Ark braced himself, gave an almighty heave, and shot across the whole length of the wall, taking the curtain with him. Amidst somewhat unseemly laughter we apologised profusely, and the service continued. At lunch the young man was very gracious, and we were congratulated on a job well done.

Every Friday afternoon before Shabbat, Mumu and I cycled to shul for the service, followed by dinner, then walked back the four miles to our lodgings. Then we walked back for the service on Shabbat morning, had lunch, and stayed for the rest of the day, cycling back after dark. The Shabbat services and meals in the company of undergraduates, graduates, teaching staff and other local residents made for an exciting, intellectually stimulating and often inspiring day. During our long walks to the shul and back home Mumu and I got to know each other even more deeply, and to really appreciate one another. It was during these walks that I learnt how precarious Mumu's father's life had been during the war. Taken to the Giado camp with so many other Benghazi Jews, one day his father and a dozen other young men had been rounded up and made to stand all day under the hot desert sun. After hours of baking heat, hunger, and thirst, they had started collapsing, one by one, only to be whipped as they lay prostrate on the ground. According to Mumu, this may have been a punishment for their refusal to work on Saturdays.

We shared family stories, we talked about our lives back in Libya, and we talked about our life in England. In fact, the only time we disagreed was when we discussed what we would do when we finished our course with Pye: Mumu was set on making aliyah and settling in Israel, whereas I was determined to stay in Britain to finish my education and to find a way of bringing my family out of the dangerous place that the lovely town of my birth had become. Besides, going to Israel would have resulted in a complete break in communication with my family.

Family ties

After a couple of months of this carefree life, I decided I should try to contact my grandparents, uncles, aunts and cousins, who had left Libya years earlier to make their new home in Israel. Libyans were forbidden to correspond with anyone in Israel, so it was over six years since we had been in touch. I didn't have any addresses or telephone numbers, but I had a vague idea that my mother's parents had settled in a small town called Pardes Channa. I wrote a letter saying that I was in England and would love to hear from them, and I addressed it, simply, to Nissim Dabusc, Pardes Channa, Israel, and hoped for the best.

About a month later I got a letter back from my Uncle David. The family had been surprised and delighted to receive my letter, but he had to tell me the sad news that my grandfather, Rabbi Nissim Dabusc, had in fact just died. He enclosed a photograph of him as a young man in his Ottoman army uniform, holding a rifle almost as tall as himself (in our several homes, we have always had this photograph on display). To me, he looks uncannily like King George V. Uncle David himself was looking after his brother Frigia's family, because Uncle Frigia himself was unfortunately in a mental institution. After the war, Frigia had built up a successful business, married and started a family, but mentally he had deteriorated. Possibly fear of attacks on his children made him over-suspicious; he became paranoid about anyone he imagined to be a threat, especially Italians and Arabs. My mother was the only one who dared try to calm him during his rages. Over the years, Frigia was detained in hospital for increasingly longer periods because of frequent epileptic attacks, and what today would be called post-traumatic stress disorder. Yes Frigia, that larger-than-life, imposing, fearless man, had become a shadow of his former self. When he and his family had left Benghazi for Israel, it had been a case of 'out of the frying pan, into the fire'. Israel was still busy coping with the huge influx of refugees from Europe and North Africa while defending itself against attacks on its territory, and had no time for his problems. Sadly the authorities, who were of European extraction, regarded immigrants from North Africa as uneducated and barely literate, and gave them only menial jobs (when I learned about this, I understood why my parents had decided to stay in Benghazi). Frigia was hidden away in an asylum, where he languished for many years until, as I have been told, an Israeli newspaper published the story of his heroism during the war years. This brought his plight into the public eye, and was probably a factor in his release. (By the time I was able to visit family in Israel, years later on a trip with Clem, they had managed to attain a good quality of life, and they didn't tell me the stories of their traumatic absorption into the country. I just remember being greeted at the airport by a smiling, waving crowd who virtually fought over whose home we should visit first. More than once we had to eat two lunches and two suppers, so as not to upset anyone. We joked that our best day there was the fast of the Ninth of Av, when we could legitimately refuse food.)

Despite the depressing news from Israel, I continued to enjoy my studies. To improve my English I vowed to avoid any Italian speakers except Mumu, and to increase my sophistication I even took classes in—wait for it—ballroom dancing. Well, that didn't last long. The instructor was a buxom lady, about twice my height and width (I am a fairly slim 5' 3"). As she dragged me round clutched to her ample bosom, I must have looked more like a ventriloquist's dummy than a dancing partner. I gave up when I decided I needed to breathe!

Mumu and I had become friendly with young people we met in shul, and at the university's Jewish Society once term started in late September, but because we were following the course with Pye and shared a timetable, it was generally just the two of us. One warm Sunday afternoon we were enjoying a bike ride in the green countryside when we noticed a large group of white-clad men playing some kind of ball game in a well-kept park. Dismounting, we strolled over and sat on the grass to watch.

Most of the men were standing or walking about, and occasionally one would run, trying to catch a ball that had been hit ferociously by another man with a bat. We watched and watched, trying hard to work out what this game was. One thing we did understand: this was not football. There was no hustle, it was polite, relaxed and good humoured. Eventually we were told that what we were watching was cricket, supposedly the 'gentleman's game'. To us it seemed a little too gentle! It is said that on average, in an hour's game, a player stands for forty minutes, walks for fifteen and runs for five. No wonder matches can go on for days! I can't say that the sport ever became a favourite, but since England has been good to me, it would not be polite to criticise the national sport. Now that wouldn't be cricket!

I learned to love everything English, especially since I kept being reminded of the days when my father worked for the NAAFI. I still love my cuppa. As for fish and chips, well, they have almost overtaken spaghetti.

Hilton Hotel calling

After I had been in England for about six months, with just a few letters to and from home, I received a phone call from a guest at the London Hilton; an Arab gentleman who said he was a friend of my father's and had a message for me. Would I visit him at the Hilton the next day?

One Sunday afternoon on the River Cam, helping the punt along.

Relaxing with a grinning friend on the River Cam, while Mumu does the hard work.

I was quite excited to visit London, so I decided to make a day of it. I arrived early at Victoria Coach Station, and from there I walked and walked and walked: Victoria Station to Oxford Street, Piccadilly Circus, Trafalgar Square, Regent Street, Leicester Square, and many other famous landmarks, in no particular order. I was just happy to take in the sights I had read so much about and even 'visited' when playing Monopoly.

In the afternoon I walked from Marble Arch down Park Lane, spent an entertaining half hour or so enjoying the very English peculiarity of Speakers' Corner, and at exactly 3 p.m. arrived at the Hilton Hotel. Mr Al-Mazri was waiting for me in the lobby.

After exchanging pleasantries he assured me that all my family were fine, and that they missed me very much, but there was a problem; my father had been called to the municipality and told he must sign a document guaranteeing my return to Benghazi. He had told them that was impossible, since I was in the UK studying, and he could not force me to return. In response, they had told him that the government's permission for him to send me money was withdrawn. Mr Al-Mazri then handed me an envelope containing some money that my father had sent with him. The ultimatum my father had received from the Benghazi municipality meant that there could be no more contact, and this was the last money I could expect. I should not go back. I was on my own.

I was very upset, as much for my parents' sake as my own. Seeing my emotional state, Mr Al-Mazri put his arm round my shoulder and reassured me that my family had faith in me and were sure I would manage. I thanked him over coffee, and scribbled a note to my family for him to take back with him, telling them that somehow I hoped to bring them to Britain to join me one day.

I left the hotel feeling downcast and lonely. On the coach back to Cambridge I mulled over my situation; I was seventeen years old, in a new country, I wouldn't be getting any more money, and there was to be no more communication with my family. I was all alone.

Well, not quite alone. After all, I had my dear friend Mumu. We shared a room, we cycled for miles together, we went everywhere together. And we never exchanged a cross word, or disagreed on anything. He was very sympathetic when I shared my predicament with him. He was not in the same situation; he was not wanted by the Libyan police, and would be happy to leave the UK at the end of our course.

I had to continue to do well on the Pye course; I had to work out how to survive with hardly any income, and I knew that I was going to have to 'lose myself' in the UK somehow, in order to avoid the possibility of being sent back to Libya. Now that they had withdrawn my permission to study abroad, they might try to extradite me.

A few days after my life-changing visit to the Hilton, I went to see Mr Nichols. I confided to him my fear of being extradited, though I didn't mention that I would shortly run out of funds. His reaction was immediate and typical: 'Don't worry, you're only seventeen. If necessary, I'll adopt you.'

I was too young to even understand the implications of what he'd said, and I couldn't imagine how Gladys would react to such a decision, but just having his support gave me hope. I began to think of him as Uncle Jack.

We had another three months of studying to do, so I concentrated on that. Then shortly after this, Uncle Jack told me and Mumu that he had arranged for Mrs Rabinowitz, the widow of the previous rabbi of Cambridge, to provide us with evening meals from Sunday to Thursday, at a very reasonable price. Gratefully we agreed to give it a try, but I was really worried about the cost.

After a few weeks of enjoying delicious meals, we told Mrs Rabinowitz we couldn't carry on coming until we were given the bill, as we had to be sure we could afford to pay. Nobody had mentioned a price, but we couldn't assume that she was doing it out of the kindness of her heart. That was when we found out the truth. Begging us not to let on that we knew, she confessed that Mr Nichols was already paying her for our meals; there would be no bill. How typical of him to combine two good deeds, paying for our meals while helping her.

By the middle of 1959, Mumu and I had almost completed our course in radio with Pye. One of the Pye directors came to get our feedback on the course, and I dared to pipe up. The course had been very useful, I said, and we were grateful, but I was surprised that it had not included television, as that was clearly the coming thing. He looked rather taken aback, and agreed that I had made a good point.

The next day we were told that the course was being extended to cover television, and would last a further four months. This was brilliant for me, as it meant Pye would continue to pay for my board, and it gave me time to think about other arrangements for afterwards.

At the end of the new course Mumu left for Milan, to do another engineering course with the ORT Institute, a college set up for Jewish refugees. He had to return to Libya at one point to sort out a problem with his travel document (with some help from Tunisia, the country of his mother's birth), but was able to return to Milan to finish his course. Once qualified, he went to settle in Israel, fulfilling his life-long dream, and spent his working life as a television engineer.

Our friendship has survived time and distance. Whenever we speak, or see each other, we just pick up where we left off.

The German beauty

After Mumu left I carried on in a rather depressed state, missing my best friend's company and his always helpful advice. We had come to a new country and encountered a new culture together, and shared a room for months. Being without my kindred spirit took some getting used to.

On top of that, lack of money was now a big worry. Uncle Jack invited me to have evening meals with him, as Gladys didn't mind cooking for just one extra, but during the day I subsisted on a diet of carrots, packets of dates, bags of nuts, and sometimes windfall apples. Being by myself, and no longer funded by Pye, meant I had to find cheaper lodgings. I was so hard up I had even borrowed £1 from Mumu before he left, which I'm ashamed to say I never repaid, though I did offer to do so the last time we met up in Israel (he said he'd settle for a signed copy of this book). I managed to find cheap, room-only accommodation, and said goodbye to the Campbells. I hoped to make some money to support myself by doing odd jobs.

One thing which did cheer me up was the arrival in Cambridge of a group of youngsters from the Sinai youth movement. They were from North West London, and were on holiday for two weeks. As one of the few students still around in Cambridge during vacation I befriended them. I spent some mornings showing them round, and took them punting (they paid). Their afternoons were spent on Jewish learning, and I was impressed by their enthusiasm and the intense way they studied the Torah and Talmud. Back in Benghazi I had been to Hebrew classes for years, and was certainly familiar with the laws of Shabbat and the festivals, but I had never done any in-depth studying of that kind. It was thanks to the eye-opener they gave me that I became interested in such study myself.

I really valued the time I spent with them, both for their friendship and for the insight they gave me into the beauty of learning. (Many years later, when I moved to their area of London, I met several of them. They invariably greeted me as 'Mr Cambridge'.)

A few weeks after Mumu's departure I was drawn to a newcomer in shul, a quiet young woman who kept mostly to herself and seemed to concentrate intently on her prayers. One Shabbat during lunch I invited her for a coffee the next day. To my pleased surprise she agreed, and we met at a popular café.

During our conversation I asked her where she was from, and was taken aback when she replied 'Germany'. I was quite naive in those days, and remarked, 'I didn't know there were still Jews in Germany.'

'I'm not Jewish,' she replied.

I was very confused, and asked her, if that was the case, why she was coming to shul.

'After what my people have done to your people', she explained, 'the least I can do is get to know you and do anything I can to help.'

I was very moved. I thought about how hard it must be for decent Germans of the post-war generation to grapple with what their country, possibly even their parents, had done. I could see how conscience-stricken this young woman was.

Much as I admired her and enjoyed her company, I made up my mind not to pursue the relationship. I couldn't risk our falling for each other. My future partner and home had to be Jewish and strictly Orthodox. Even if this pleasant and attractive young woman might be interested in converting, aside from the fact that my needs in a partner would probably be too onerous for her, I was due to leave Cambridge in a few months. I was glad I could tell her that, truthfully. I wished her every success. I do hope she found the answers to her questions, and peace of mind. I wouldn't be surprised if she did convert and marry one of the many Jewish Cambridge students, in which case I sincerely hope they are happy.

Despite my financial worries, thanks to Uncle Jack I soon started really enjoying the next few months in Cambridge. I did all kinds of odd jobs in his shop, and for friends, to earn enough money for food and my lodgings. On Thursdays and Sundays, Uncle Jack and Gladys would take me for rides in his luxury car all over the beautiful Cambridgeshire countryside. Then we would indulge in the very English affair of afternoon tea.

Jack disliked crowds, and at this point he began sending me to represent him at a number of weddings and bar mitzvahs in London, all expenses paid. In this way, I met people who were able to help me sort out my future. This was insecure at that time, since I was no longer considered a student, and might be required to return to Libya…the one thing my father had warned me against.

One of the people I met was Rabbi Dr Norman Solomon, an eminent musician who had studied in Cambridge. After we started chatting at a wedding, he told me that he wanted to help me stay in the UK, and invited me to his home in London to discuss my future. When I expressed my wish to study Judaism in greater depth before going to university, he contacted Rabbi Alexander Dominitz on my behalf. This most amazing man, a 'mensch' with a permanent smile on his face, spent his time helping young people with food, money, temporary accommodation and jobs. His house was always open to anyone in need. People would just come in, go to the kitchen and help themselves to food. His wife remained in the background, but clearly supported him in this charitable work.

He made all the arrangements for me to study for a few months at Gateshead Yeshiva, a world-famous Talmudical college. Whilst most students spend a year or two there before going to university or taking a job, many spend up to eight years there, learning to qualify as rabbis. Rabbi Dominitz paid my fare, gave me some money and sandwiches, and directed me to Victoria to catch the coach for Gateshead, in the northeast of England. I arrived there in October 1959, intending to stay a few months; I ended up staying over two years.

8

What are you still doing here?

Gateshead Talmudical College (Gateshead Yeshiva)

I arrived at the coach station in Gateshead, and set out for Bewick Road to find the yeshiva. Not knowing the full address (don't ask me why, it's ages ago) I was looking for a large, modern building. Most of the houses in the clearly residential street were rather small and unimpressive, but then halfway up the road I came to a more impressive looking house, and spotted a mezuzah on the doorpost. This must be it, I thought, and rang the bell. Shortly, several teenage girls appeared at the door, looking rather bemused to see me.

'I don't suppose this is the yeshiva,' I faltered.

'No', they laughed. 'This is the women's seminary! The yeshiva is the building at the end of the road.'

Well, that was a great start! A few minutes later I arrived at a set of large buildings, comprising one of the most prestigious Talmudic colleges in the world, where some three hundred boys and young men ranging in age from sixteen to their early twenties study Talmud, Bible, Jewish law, and ethics, from early morning to late at night.

It was Thursday evening and I had been travelling all day. A young man let me in with a beaming smile and gave me a *kippah* to wear; until then I had not been used to wearing one except in shul (in Libya wearing a head covering all the time was seen as a Muslim practice). This friendly chap introduced himself as Abe David, whom I soon got to know as an outstandingly brilliant student. (He is now known as Dayan David, a leading figure in the Sephardi community, famed for his lectures and writings.)

After showing me to my room in a nearby house, where I deposited my bag, he took me on a tour of the yeshiva, which was made up of a central building that housed the main study hall, a number of classrooms, a prayer hall, a dining hall, a library and all the other facilities needed to cater for the students. This central building was surrounded by a number of houses which served as sleeping accommodation.

After the tour we went to the prayer hall for *ma'ariv*, the evening prayer, and then to the dining hall, where we helped ourselves to the DIY supper which I learned was the norm for Thursday evenings. The cook took this opportunity to give her sense of humour free range, as one of the foodstuffs she provided was great piles of eggs, with no indication of which were raw and which hard boiled. We had to work that out for ourselves, so there was much spinning of eggs (since raw eggs spin slowly as the liquid inside sloshes about). Having been used to just one meal a day at Uncle Jack's, supplemented by a few carrots or dates when I could afford them, the prospect of three meals every day was very comforting. I tucked in happily, and so to bed.

There were three beds in the room, but I had been told I would have just one roommate, a Londoner called Joshua. Exhausted, I fell asleep before he came in and didn't meet him until the following morning. He turned out be a charming, strapping fellow whose appearance belied what I later realised was a shy personality. We would become good friends. After morning prayers and a much appreciated breakfast I had some time to myself, not yet having been assigned a study partner, and wandered around to see what was going on.

I had to be honest with myself; at first, I felt slightly let down. The place was somewhat ramshackle and run down. Most of the buildings needed a coat of paint. Still, when I entered the study hall I stopped in my tracks, confronted by the amazing sight of hundreds of students, '*bochrim*' (literally, unmarried young men), learning together in pairs. I had expected to find a quiet, intense atmosphere, but as I surveyed the packed hall, while I did indeed see some pairs sharing focused, quiet study, others were engaged in vigorous debate, disagreeing with each other, their voices raised; some were even standing up, shouting and waving their arms as they made their points. After such heated exchanges the student, or students, would resume their seats, smile at each other, and carry on studying. To me, this was amazing and exciting, and my disappointment at the poor state of the buildings slowly melted away.

Since it was Friday, after a quick lunch the study hall slowly emptied. The yeshiva became like a very busy airport, with *bochrim* rushing around preparing themselves and their rooms for Shabbat. I followed suit and went to my room to wash and change. About two hours later I returned to the main building to find it completely transformed. The place was now immaculate, with books tidied away, and all the tables and desks straightened. In the dining hall the tables were covered with clean white tablecloths. However, the difference was more than visual; it was tangibly spiritual. My mistake earlier on had been to see my new home as just a group of disparate buildings. Now I saw the yeshiva for what it really was: a centre focused on love of learning and the enhancement of spiritual values, epitomised by the excited anticipation of Shabbat.

That Shabbat, with its communal prayer, inspiring talks and shared meals, set the mood for the rest of the week, and I soon settled into the routine. I came to love the lived-in appearance of the yeshiva, every cranny or loose nail acquiring a special beauty and significance to me. (When, months later, a new modern building was built to replace the old one, we had mixed feelings.)

Soon after my arrival, I was called in to see the student counsellor, a sincere, modest and charming man, Rabbi Moshe Schwab, affectionately known as Rav Moshe. You couldn't meet a more warm, friendly person. After discussing my background and my level of knowledge he introduced me to a personal study guide from among the senior students, and allocated a fellow student to act as my *chavruta* (study partner), with whom I would be sharing not only my learning but also any personal problems.

Even after a few weeks there, I could still hardly believe my good fortune at being at Gateshead Yeshiva, one of the greatest Jewish institutions in the world. Eagerly I plunged into the many hours of shared learning that took up most of the day and sometimes continued well into the night, always punctuated by times for prayer and meals. We were literally bent over pages and pages of the Talmud, in Hebrew and Aramaic, extracting its laws and arguing over possible interpretations. Our discussions did sometimes become heated, and if we couldn't resolve a point we referred it to a more senior student, or if necessary to one of the rabbis. This was a much deeper level of learning than I had experienced back home, and all in the name of getting at the truth. I found it all stimulating and exhilarating, and thoroughly enjoyed it.

Naturally I had to cope with homesickness, especially at the meal on Shabbat afternoons, when the communal singing was so different from our tunes at home that I just sat at the back by myself, feeling miserable. I also faced the demands of another new language, since most of the lectures were in Yiddish! But at the same time I began to make new friends who came from all over the world, from Israel, France, America, Morocco and, of course, the UK.

The midnight strangler

I had settled in well with my new roommate Joshua, even if I still missed Mumu. We didn't see much of each other outside of our room, as we weren't

The main study hall at Gateshead Yeshiva. I am in the middle block, two rows back, second from the right.

in the same classes, but in the evenings we would chat easily. One evening soon after I arrived, we were both getting ready for bed when he came over to me looking very serious and a little embarrassed. He said he had something important to tell me. 'It's nothing to worry about', he stammered, 'it's just that I'm prone to sleep-walk'. That didn't seem so terrible, but what he said next was pretty unsettling. I can still hear his exact words: 'If you see me walk to the window and try to jump out, don't worry; I've never actually done it. Just gently turn me round and guide me back to bed.' And there was even better to come: 'And just sometimes, I might put my hands around your neck, just gently mind you, nothing to worry about. Just take my hands away, take me back to my bed and I'll settle down without even opening my eyes.'

Nothing to worry about? He was a big lad, and it was quite a drop to the ground from our room. As for being strangled... *That's all very well for you to say, Joshua,* I thought, *but I'm not going to stay in this room with just the two of us!* Out loud I said, 'I'm sure you're harmless, but if you don't mind, I'll be happier if we get another person to join us. In any case, there is a third bed.'

The next morning I went to Rav Moshe and told him about my roommate's potentially suicidal and homicidal tendencies. He wasn't too worried, but seeing my concern undertook to find me an additional roommate by that evening. Sure enough, at lunchtime a congenial fellow named Abe Kramer strolled over and introduced himself as our new roommate. He had arrived from South Africa a few months earlier, and was happy to share our room. We went on to enjoy peaceful companionship, with no nocturnal wanderings from Joshua (as far as I knew), and many games of chess. I even forgave Abe for always beating me!

Much to my satisfaction and surprise, despite my initial struggles with Yiddish I progressed quite well. After a few months Rav Moshe suggested I move to a higher class, run by Rabbi Kahane, who not only taught, but was responsible for the smooth running of the yeshiva. At the same time, having realised that I had no source of income, Rav Moshe gave me an envelope containing enough money to buy a suit for the coming Passover. In addition, he told me that from then on I was to receive a weekly allowance, for which I was extremely grateful. As it happened, I had few outgoings, being a determined non-smoker (unlike most of the other *bochrim*), so I resolved to save whatever I was given for when I would truly need it.

As well as enjoying my studies, I also had the pleasure of being a guest at a number of fellow students' homes during Jewish festivals, when the yeshiva emptied. One of these hosts was a friendly fellow called Icky Sufrin, affectionately known as the yeshiva's 'postman' because he distributed letters as they arrived. The festival of Sukkot took place not long after my arrival, and I had been prepared to be almost on my own, with just a few other students who, like me, had no homes to go to. Then, one by one, friends remembered them and phoned to invite them to their homes. I was becoming resigned to being truly on my own when I also got a phone call, from Icky Sufrin, inviting me to spend the festival with his family in Manchester. Knowing how tight my finances were, he had even asked Rav Moshe to give me money for the train fare. I have never forgotten how the Sufrins treated me as an honoured guest, as if I were doing them a favour by being there.

I was similarly touched the following April when another fellow student, Simcha Fordsham, insisted on my spending the whole Passover break with him and his family in London. The warmth of the hospitality shown both to me and other lone students demonstrated that such people practised true *hachnasat orchim*—welcoming guests. With my wife's help, I have tried to live up to their example.

A worrying letter

Out of the blue, after a few months at Gateshead I received a letter from the Home Office, which controls immigration, requesting my presence in London to explain why I had not returned home to Libya. I still don't know how they knew my address, as I certainly hadn't told them. My nightmares of being dragged to the airport and back home returned with full force. I went to Rav Moshe for advice, and he introduced me to a fellow student whose father, Julius Jung, was closely involved with the Jewish Refugees' Committee in London. He also had connections in the Home Office and was deeply involved in helping hundreds of Jewish refugees from Europe to settle in the UK. I got in touch with Mr Jung directly, and he invited me to visit him when I was in London to work out a reasonable strategy. I soon made that journey, and was reassured when he said he would mention my case to his contacts. Obviously he couldn't guarantee success, but was prepared to explore every avenue for me. In the meantime, we agreed that I should write to the Home Office asking for more time, explaining that I was now studying at a rabbinical college.

With Rav Moshe's approval, I sent a letter saying that I needed at least another two years to complete my studies, and that I was waiting for my travel document to be renewed (a white lie which I thought justified).

Whilst in London I went to visit my old friend, Rabbi Dominitz, who was very pleased to see me. When he heard the reason for my visit he suggested that I stay in the city for a few days so that we could plan my next move. He telephoned Rav Moshe to explain that I needed to stay to sort out my problems. After evening prayers we had dinner together at his house, and then he took me to the home of an elderly lady who kindly gave free accommodation to needy yeshiva *bochrim*. But I couldn't sleep. All the worries I had pushed to the back of my mind came back to haunt me: Would I be sent back to Libya? Would I have to go into hiding to prevent that outcome? If I couldn't stay in England, and had to emigrate to Israel, what would happen to my family? My mother's fears of never seeing me again would be realised.

As it turned out, I need not have worried about having to leave the UK. Mr Jung was as good as his word, and I heard nothing further from the Home Office. However, I was still deeply concerned about my family in Benghazi. My parents had had very hard lives in an unpredictable and often hostile country. When they had been in their twenties, the fascists had taken over Italy and, by extension, Libya. They had suffered first under Italian fascists, then the Nazis, and now Arab ultra-nationalists. Their community was a fraction the size it had once been, and they were cut off from their relatives, who had moved to Israel. It was increasingly hard for them to make any kind of living. However irrational it was, I felt I was letting them down.

The next morning I expressed my fears to a very understanding Rabbi Dominitz, and explained to him the plans I had worked out during a sleepless night, asking him if he thought they were possible. I wanted to get official permission from the Home Office to continue at Gateshead, and I would visit London regularly to work on implementing my plans, which were:

1. Get my brothers accepted at a yeshiva in London, where I hoped the whole family would eventually settle. Gateshead would not have suited them, and in any case it had limited places and was very selective. I needed to get them out of Libya, and a very unstable political situation, to a place where they could make a new life without the constant danger of attacks. Ever was young to go to yeshiva, but I hoped they would make an exception for a refugee;
2. Find a job for my father in London, and possibly a part-time one for my mother. I felt that with his years of work at the NAAFI, he shouldn't have any difficulty obtaining a work permit for the UK, once he had a job offer;
3. Find an apartment for my parents and Yvette;
4. After settling my parents and completing my time in Gateshead, finish my studies in electronics at a London college.

Rabbi Dominitz agreed that getting my brothers accepted into a yeshiva in the UK was the easiest part of the plan. Although yeshivas normally needed some payment, this could be waived in special circumstances, and my brothers' situation certainly qualified. He managed to enrol them at the North West London Talmudical College in Golders Green, better known as Yeshivas Chayei Olam. It took a few months of cutting through red tape, and letters from Rabbi Dominitz, Rabbi Warhaftig of Golders Green, and Rabbi Madar of Benghazi, to convince the Libyan authorities to grudgingly issue the stateless travel documents that would allow my brothers to travel. Libya was clearly still displaying the equivocal attitude of not really wanting Libyan Jews to remain, but not wanting them to leave, either.

Reunited

Eventually, it was time to check that my brothers' room at the yeshiva they would be attending was ready; they were due to fly to London, and they would be pretty tired after the twelve-hour journey. The 24th of May 1960 saw me travelling to Heathrow Airport, ecstatic to welcome my brothers after two years apart. I will never forget the date, because it had been an extraordinary week: the Mossad, the Israeli Secret Service, had captured the monster who had organised the Final Solution, Adolf Eichmann. They had found him in Argentina and snatched him away. This was world news on the very day my brothers were arriving in London. The date is indelibly imprinted on my memory because the London Underground was full of passengers reading newspapers bearing the dramatic headline: *BEAST IN CAGE*.

Having enjoyed a joyous reunion with my brothers and seen them settled in, I spent a few days with them at their yeshiva. After so long apart we were allowed this time together, and gladly toured the sights of London while becoming reacquainted. Clem looked no different, being less than a year older than me, but the more grown up Ever took some getting used to.

Whilst in London I also visited the Jewish Refugees' Committee, in case they might be able to help sort out the rest of the family. There I met the wonderful Mrs Epstein, who was dedicated to helping Jews who had escaped from tyranny and anti-Semitism to settle in their chosen new home. I returned to Gateshead full of joy, and tremendously relieved that my brothers were finally safe. The first stage of my plan had succeeded, but I still had to worry about bringing my parents and Yvette.

Happy in the knowledge that my brothers were safely settled in London, I returned to Gateshead ready to concentrate on my learning. This took up most of my time, but there was one area in which I was happy to be able to contribute my expertise to others; thanks to the skills I had learned at Pye in Cambridge, I was able to help when rabbis, teachers and other locals encountered minor electrical problems. Although I was happy to do this without payment, some insisted on paying me something, which of course helped my always precarious finances. On one occasion, I was called to Rabbi Kahane's home to sort out his time switch. It was Friday, 5 May 1961; I remember the date clearly because it was the day the first American went into space. As I approached his house I could hear the radio blaring, and Rabbi Kahane himself let me in, looking very excited. This was an unusual sight, and rather amusing, as he was usually a very serious man. He was waving his arms at the ceiling and repeating, 'They are up, they are up!'

Thinking he meant someone was upstairs in his house, I asked, 'In the bedroom? Who, who is up?'

As excited as a child, he screamed happily, 'It's the Americans! The Americans are up in space!'

I had known nothing about it. We didn't read the newspapers in yeshiva, nor were we normally allowed to listen to the radio, as it was considered a waste of precious time. As a special concession I was allowed to keep a crystal radio set that I had managed to put together myself, in order to keep up with the news, but this particular item had passed me by.

I fixed the time switch and after a chat about my family and my progress I returned to the yeshiva happy. I was tremendously impressed that this amazing man, who spent a good ten to twelve hours studying nearly every day, still found the time to keep in touch with the outside world. This was a man I had seen a few weeks before, standing at a lectern for hours, struggling to unlock a seeming contradiction between the pronouncements of two eminent rabbis from the past. He had still been standing at the lectern when the last student left the study hall, at about 2 a.m., and he was still standing there when the first students came in the next morning. Then, halfway through the morning, he triumphantly exclaimed, 'I got it, I got it, I got it!' and finally went home to sleep.

Sometime in 1961 I got a call from an excited Rabbi Dominitz, who asked me to come to London as soon as I could: he had had a good idea for my parents. I didn't ask why he couldn't tell me about it on the phone; if Rabbi Dominitz wanted to see me, I would do as he asked!

As usual Rav Moshe offered to pay for my ticket, but he asked me to delay my departure until after the first lecture he was giving in a new *mussar* series (*mussar* translates roughly to ethics, or ethical living). I have always remembered Rav Moshe's introduction to the lecture series. Imagine a lion, he told us, that's been starved for a few days, and then someone puts a joint of meat in front of it. What does it do? It pounces on it and devours it voraciously. That's its nature; that's what it does. Now imagine a yeshiva *bochur* at the end of Yom Kippur. He's been fasting and praying for twenty-five hours, with only a few hours of sleep. After the fast ends, along with his fellow students, he hears *havdalah* (the blessing just after the end of Sabbaths and festivals) and then, still before eating or drinking, recites the evening prayers. Repairing to the dining room, he goes to wash his hands, then to the table laden with food. He sits down, says the blessing over bread, and only *then* does he start to eat. That, concluded Rav Moshe, is the difference between man and beast.

(Incidentally, years later I met him on one of his regular visits to London. The personal interest he took in his students, even years after they had left the yeshiva, was evident when the conversation turned to education. He was not very impressed with the local Jewish school our eldest was attending, and suggested a more Orthodox one some distance away. I doubted that they would have room for her, and in any case it would have been a problem to get her there, since my wife did not yet drive. Even so, he undertook to arrange for her to be enrolled next time he was in London. Before that could happen, he passed away. I was deeply upset at the passing of this charismatic man, who did so much to make me feel at home and give me hope. I treasure the memory of Rav Moshe Schwab's care and concern.)

Extraordinary people

Having obeyed Rabbi Dominitz's summons, I was rather puzzled when he took me to look over a three-storey building on Seven Sisters Road, right opposite Finsbury Park in North London. He told me that this huge house was going to be a boarding school for up to sixty boys aged ten to fifteen. They were either orphans, or their families lived in areas where there was no Jewish education available. I didn't understand why Rabbi Dominitz was showing me his next project until he turned to me and explained that the school would need house parents, and asked if I thought the job would suit my parents.

Would it suit them? It was ideal! My father had been a Hebrew teacher and *chazan* (cantor), and the skills he'd used when managing the Benghazi food department of the NAAFI would no doubt also come in very useful. My mother was used to looking after children, and was a good cook and seamstress. I could have kissed him (in fact I think I did). This was the perfect position for my parents, and I was overcome with gratitude. Rabbi Dominitz went on to assure me that there would be a full time cook who would just need some help, and the flat on the top floor of the building would be large enough for my family. We discussed logistics and timing; my parents would need to receive an official invitation so that they could get a work permit for the UK and an exit visa from Libya. If all went as it should, then I would return to London in a few months to redecorate the flat for my parents, and to sort out the electrics, plumbing and anything else that needed fixing. After agreeing on a possible timetable for my parents' arrival, and visiting my brothers, I returned to Gateshead aware that my time there might have to end sooner than planned. If my parents were going to start a new life in London, I would need to be close by, to help them settle in the UK. Gateshead was simply too far away.

At Her Majesty's pleasure

In the following weeks and months I had to travel to London frequently to make sure that the arrangements for my parents, both legal and financial, ran smoothly. I decorated and rewired the flat they would be occupying (nearly electrocuting myself in the process, because the way the original wiring had been done was actually illegal). I also managed to furnish it with kind people's unwanted furniture, with the help of Rabbi Dominitz and his friends.

More often than not I made the journey to London as a hitchhiker, and one trip in particular stands out in my memory. As bad luck would have it, the weather was terrible, with strong winds and torrential rain. Several drivers took pity on me standing there drenched on the side of the road, so I had no problem getting lifts, but the conditions made driving slow, and when I finally arrived in London it was much later than I'd expected. I had arranged to stay the night in the home of the elderly lady whose hospitality I had enjoyed before, who hosted yeshiva students for free, but by the time I rang her bell it was after midnight. She looked out of an upstairs window at my bedraggled and disreputable looking self, and told me in no uncertain terms to go away and come back in the morning.

I had spotted a police station nearby and went to seek help. Maybe they could persuade her to let me in. But no, she would not be moved, especially as it was now after one in the morning, so the helpful policeman who had accompanied me took me back to the station to 'see what we can do'. This proved to be a very welcome cup of tea, and an overnight stay in an empty cell. He apologised for the spartan conditions, but as far as I was concerned it was luxurious; I had running water, a toilet, and a hot radiator over which to drape my sopping wet clothes. I was more than grateful.

I slept well on the hard bunk, and woke up ready to face the day. However, when I tried the door, it was locked, and when I knocked on it to be let out, no one answered. I could hear dim voices outside, and I made out a puzzled conversation:

'Can you hear knocking?'

'Don't think so. Nobody was booked in last night.'

This was becoming material for a comedy sketch. I had to hammer on the door for what seemed like forever before the officers who had come on duty finally conceded that they weren't hallucinating, and there really might be someone in the cell. When they finally approached close enough to hear my explanation, they let me out, understandably amused. Their colleague, who had locked me in for my own safety, had not recorded my presence at the station as I was not under any suspicion, which is why they had not known to let me out. This did mean that, for a while, I felt some sympathy for convicts.

Having been fortified by the ever-comforting cup of tea, I was sent on my way full of appreciation for the good old British bobby.

Reunion at last

Finally all the pieces of the puzzle fell into place, and the date for our reunion was set. Looking back now, I don't remember the exact date, but it must have been early 1962. At last, we were all going to be together again. My father, mother and sister landed safely at Heathrow, where my brothers and I fell upon them before taking them straight to their freshly painted and furnished apartment.

It was wonderful to have the family together again and actually hear their voices for the first time in so many years…though it was impossible to have a proper conversation at first as everyone was talking at once. My parents had changed little, but Yvette was quite the young lady. I was amazed when my father told me they had left the dining table set ready for a meal, to give the impression to anyone who might come calling that they would be returning shortly. They had certainly obtained permission to leave the country, but it was always possible that some mischief-maker might want to make trouble and stop them. When I think about it now, I realise they would not have wanted to give the game away by emptying the little that was in their bank account, so they came to the UK with virtually nothing.

Just before my parents left Benghazi to fly to London, my mother visited the archive where her grandfather's writings were kept. It was in its own room, lined with copies of his books and manuscripts, and attended by an Arab who had taken it upon himself to guard it...such was the reverence in which he had been held. In fact, this fine man took his task so seriously that he refused to let her touch anything until she finally convinced him that she was a Dabusc, and then he allowed her to take a couple of manuscripts as a keepsake.

It was nearly four years since I had left Benghazi aged seventeen, not much more than an innocent child. What a difference those few years had made. Now I found myself taking on responsibility for sorting out any problems my parents faced in their new country, whether legal, financial, or simply helping them adjust to a new language and culture. When I let myself think about it, I felt quite overwhelmed.

There were a few hiccups at the beginning, though my father adjusted well. He was happy helping the boys with their Hebrew reading, prayers and other educational needs. He also found himself an honorary position as a chazan at the local Sephardi shul; he had always loved being a chazan, and this new shul was a venue where he made friends and developed a flourishing new social life. Having worked for the NAAFI in Libya, he was already used to English language and culture, and found that side of the move easy.

My mother, on the other hand, found the move harder. She was happy on the pastoral side of their job, comforting boys who were homesick, and making sure they were all properly clothed, but she found English challenging despite going to evening classes, and she didn't make new friends. She was quite lonely.

Ever had not settled well at the yeshiva, and had not stayed long. Instead, he was now a pupil at JFS, a Jewish secondary school which was conveniently nearby. Yvette, who was fourteen, was enrolled at a local girls' school. Although she actually hated the school (I now know), she nevertheless quickly gained confidence. I don't know why she didn't go to JFS with Ever.

I had been staying in the flat with my family, but once everything seemed to be going well, I felt justified in going back to Gateshead, intending to spend another year learning in the yeshiva while looking for an engineering course in London.

9

Goodbye, Gateshead, I must leave you

I was really happy to see everyone settling down. However, after a few months I had to return to London unexpectedly. My poor mother suddenly started suffering from bouts of mental illness. All the tension and stress she had endured for so long, combined with the loneliness of her experience in a new country and missing her home and friends, had a drastic effect on her wellbeing. She was seen by many doctors in our efforts to diagnose what was going on. Ultimately, they could not decide whether her condition was clinical depression or schizophrenia, but whatever it was, the effects were devastating. While there were many symptoms she experienced, the most distressing was that she would hear voices threatening her loved ones.

I had no choice but to move down to London and try to help my family. I said my sad goodbyes to all the rabbis and my friends in Gateshead, and returned to London for good, moving in with my family in Finsbury Park. Rav Moshe tried very hard to persuade me to stay and study for *smicha* (rabbinical ordination) but I knew deep down that it wasn't for me. I did like the idea of teaching and lecturing, but I also felt a strong pull towards engineering.

I still feel greatly indebted to all my rabbis for their care and understanding. Rabbi Moshe Schwab saw over the years that I was not able to give as much time as necessary to my Talmudic studies, but nevertheless he was still ready to help me with advice and financial help. He was a truly great man, as were Rabbis Eliezer Kahan and Zev Cohen, and of course Rabbi Dominitz, who were all there when I needed them. These were people whose time was precious, yet they always managed to find time for us students.

In the autumn of 1962, I enrolled at the Northern Polytechnic in Holloway (which later became the London Metropolitan University) to take a three-year course in electronic engineering, leading to a chartered engineering qualification. Since my existing qualifications were Italian, I couldn't start the course immediately; I had to do a preliminary year of concentrated study in maths and science at the college to bring me up to A-level standard.

Once the academic year started, I took an after-school job at the New Synagogue Hebrew classes in Stamford Hill, teaching three evenings a week, plus Sunday mornings. With my pay from this, a small grant from the Jewish Refugees' Committee, and very careful money management, I somehow covered the cost of the course.

The deep freeze

For a while things went on fairly smoothly. My father continued enjoying his position at the boarding school and leading prayers on Shabbat at his new shul. He had renewed his acquaintance with some Italian- and Hebrew-speaking friends who were living locally. My mother was on medication and we thought she was coping reasonably well, but she was not thriving. When we called a doctor, we were shocked to be told she was suffering from malnutrition. That just shows how easy it is to take someone for granted.

This was horrifying, but then matters got even worse. Something happened that threatened to upend our existence entirely. England was hit by one of the most severe winters of the century. It started to snow on 26 December 1963, and snow lay uninterruptedly on the ground until March 1964. The deep freeze was total, and affected countless homes and businesses. At the boarding school, some of us had to climb up to the loft armed with hammers and chisels to break off lumps of ice, which we then melted in order to get water for drinking, washing and cooking. The pupils were all put up in various homes whilst the cold weather persisted, but our family had to put up with those horrible conditions.

Early in March the long-awaited thaw arrived, but it caused greater damage and more chaos than anyone had expected. Pipes all over the building burst and water came cascading down from the loft and flooded the school. Given all the work and money it would take to repair, the charity which had been funding the school decided to close it permanently and sell the building (which was eventually rebuilt as a modern hotel). All the pupils were found permanent homes within the community and attended various schools. My family was now homeless, and my parents without a job. All the months and months of planning to find a home and a job had ended with this catastrophe.

Rabbi Dominitz agreed to take me to see the heads of the charity. We pointed out that they had a responsibility and a duty to find my family alternative accommodation, and they reluctantly offered my parents a small apartment on a short-term basis. My brothers were already working. Ever had finished secondary school and had managed to get a job at, of all places, a branch of the NAAFI. He was already making very good progress. Maybe someone there recognised our surname and put in a good word: some small compensation for having had his nose broken by those hooligans back in Benghazi. Clem had become a salesman for Osem, the Israeli food company, which had offices in London (later Ever also joined Osem). My father found a job at Frohweins, the kosher butcher. I carried on with my education while we all shared the cramped flat.

Unfortunately, one of the directors of the charity was rather cold, and after only a few weeks, began sending letters demanding our family vacate the apartment. I told my father to ignore them because they were not from the charity itself, but from this individual (I'll call him Mr C) allegedly on behalf of the charity. His co-director was not in agreement with him, and had even come personally to meet my parents and welcome them. Then, to make my father even more uncomfortable and humiliated, Mr C took him to the rabbinical court for a hearing on the matter.

I felt terrible, as though I had betrayed the family. The least I could do was go to court with my father to help him put his case forward. When the case began, Mr C opened by insisting that he had given us plenty of warning that he needed the place for another family. 'You have to get out,' he snapped.

Then it was my turn to speak. I started by telling the court a story that all Benghazi Jews of my generation had grown up knowing. After the war, some eight hundred Jewish refugees trying to reach Palestine had been abandoned by their ship's captain on the shore at the port in Benghazi. He promised that another ship would arrive the next day to pick them up.

It was an empty promise. A Jewish boy riding his bike near the port saw these hundreds of emaciated men and women looking lost and confused, and realised that they were Jewish. Immediately he turned round and rode to the rabbi, who arranged for every Jewish family in the city to host two or three people. These guests stayed with the families for months, until representatives from Palestine arranged for them to continue their journey. In that time they were made very welcome, and there were even some romances between hosts and guests that led to marriage. In fact, the rabbi's daughter married one of the men. Surely this was a lesson for Mr C.

Next, I outlined briefly the physical and mental hardships my family had gone through to reach London, explaining how important it was for them to have a secure home now. I concluded by saying, forcefully, that I was disgusted by Mr C's attitude.

After a short discussion, the senior rabbi of the court, who normally spoke only in Yiddish and Hebrew, pointed at Mr C and uttered in English the memorable words: 'Listen to me carefully. You are not to write to Mr

Meghnagi again. You are not to call him, you are not to bother him, you are not to evict him. He and his family will remain in the apartment until he finds other suitable accommodation. Now *shalom* and goodbye!'

The Northern Polytechnic

The first year of college, when I was bringing my education standard up to A level, was as easy as it was enjoyable. I became friendly with people from all over the world who were in the same position, and developed a close friendship with a Greek student, George, from Athens. After full days at college, three times a week I used to cycle from college to *cheder* (Hebrew classes), where I was teaching for ninety minutes, then on to George's apartment for a three-hour revision of the day's work. George often had something for me to drink with the sandwiches I had left over from lunch. I regularly got home about ten in the evening. Life at college was great, but I had very little time for relaxation.

One of my fellow students, though on a different course, was my close friend David Stiffelman. We knew each other from attending the Jewish youth group Ezra, and spent most Saturdays together. Now that we saw each other at college, I realised he was a heavy smoker. This surprised me, because he had seemed very health conscious: he avoided any form of sugar because his father had died from complications of diabetes. His blasé attitude to smoking really worried me, and one day while we were queueing for a hot drink in the canteen, I pleaded with him to give up the disgusting and dangerous habit.

In retaliation, he turned round and challenged me to give up putting sugar in my drinks: 'See how long you last!'

This gave me an idea. 'Let's make a pact,' I said. 'For six months you try to stop smoking, and I'll stop taking sugar in my tea and coffee. Let's see who lasts the course.'

'I'm happy to accept the challenge,' he said defiantly.

The result was that I found I enjoyed my drinks unsweetened, and never went back to taking sugar. And David? He switched from smoking cigarettes to a pipe, claiming it was less unhealthy.

He has been living in Israel for many years, and we see each other or speak on the phone only occasionally, but whenever we do, the years between just disappear.

One morning as I arrived at college I was approached by a polite, pleasant Chinese student, who asked me if I had read the Bible. I was rather taken aback; having spent my schooldays resisting the persistent if friendly efforts of the Catholic Brothers to convert me, here I was in London on the receiving end again. I have great respect for Christianity and, indeed, Islam, but I believe the Almighty intended this colourful, beautiful world to be a kaleidoscope of faiths with Judaism as the mother and model, with standards which Christianity and Islam, being daughter religions, should look up to. This does not mean that we Jews consider ourselves superior. It does mean that we have an important, often misunderstood role as guardians and flag bearers of monotheism. I have always believed that our role is to be like a fire that heats up the world with theological and ethical ideas. Unfortunately, fire is self-consuming and must be kept stoked, or it will burn itself out. We are told in Isaiah 49:6 that we are to be 'a light unto the nations'. While this 'light' has sometimes been dimmed by unethical behaviour on the part of my fellow Jews, far more often it has been utterly extinguished during anti-Semitic outbursts by nations who misunderstood our role. Like it or not, we will continue to experience this.

All this was in the back of my mind when I answered my fellow student. However well-meaning he was, he had upset me. I answered, politely, that in fact I did read the Bible—in its original language—and that I'd be happy to teach him Hebrew any time (I know this makes me sound very arrogant; I had not yet learned to be diplomatic).

J'Accuse

After this encounter, I resolved that I must form a Jewish Society to give other Jewish students an anchor: a place where they could deal with the pressures that come with being a minority on campus. I put up a message on the college notice board inviting students to assist in the formation of a Jewish Society, and very soon a dozen young men and women had agreed to join. However, to our shock, the students' union wrote to us refusing permission to go ahead because the college rules did not permit the formation of exclusive societies.

Immediately we responded that we were no more exclusive than the Christian Union, and anyone wishing to join our society would be more than welcome. We challenged the president of the students' union to a public debate, but instead of accepting our challenge he informed us that we could carry on with an unofficial formation of our Jewish Society while the college organised a change in its constitution. They said this actually required an Act of Parliament!

Within a few weeks, there was an explosion of new societies on campus. We were allocated a space on the college's notice board, and after a short meeting I was elected chairman of the new Jewish Society. Dayan Isidor Grunfeld, an illustrious senior judge in rabbinical court, as well as the author and translator of many important religious books, agreed to be our patron. I knew him from Finsbury Park Synagogue, and had tremendous respect for him and his equally renowned educator wife, Judith. Having Dayan Grunfeld as a patron was a great coup because it gave the society a religious dimension, making it more than just a forum for social gatherings. We were able to organise many lectures and social events that resulted in many students finding or returning to their roots.

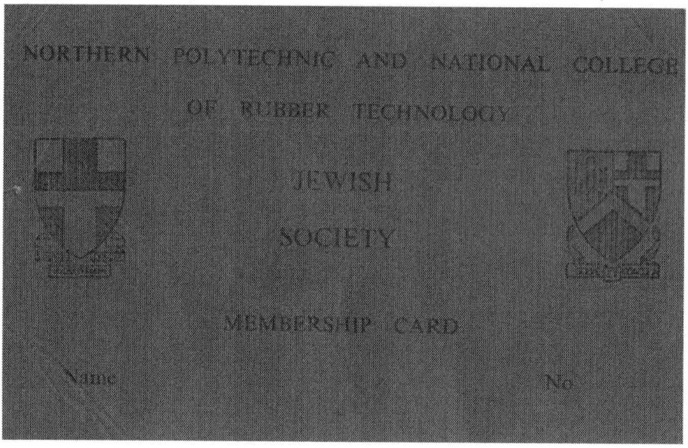
NORTHERN POLYTECHNIC AND NATIONAL COLLEGE OF RUBBER TECHNOLOGY

JEWISH SOCIETY

MEMBERSHIP CARD

Name No.

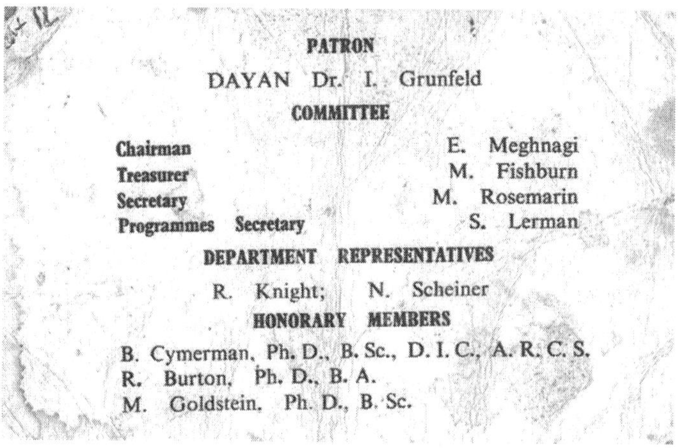
PATRON

DAYAN Dr. I. Grunfeld

COMMITTEE

Chairman E. Meghnagi
Treasurer M. Fishburn
Secretary M. Rosemarin
Programmes Secretary S. Lerman

DEPARTMENT REPRESENTATIVES

R. Knight; N. Scheiner

HONORARY MEMBERS

B. Cymerman, Ph. D., B. Sc., D. I. C., A. R. C. S.
R. Burton, Ph. D., B. A.
M. Goldstein, Ph. D., B. Sc.

The front and back of the Jewish Society membership card.

Although we had sorted our differences with regard to the college's rules on exclusivity, soon after we established the society I had to deal with another minor disagreement with the president of the student union. A few weeks after our founding we decided to have a film show, and we rented the film *J'Accuse*, about the Dreyfus affair. We intended to charge a small entrance fee, but when the president of the union saw this on the notice board he called me to his office to say that the college rules did not permit charging for activities.

When I pointed out that it would only be a small amount, and we had no other way to recoup our costs, his reply was a simple, 'Sorry, no can help.'

Just to be sure, I asked him, 'You're sure we're not allowed to charge *entrance* fees?'

He nodded, and insisted that although he sympathised, he couldn't help us. On leaving his office I duly changed the wording on the notice board.

Later that week we showed the film, as arranged. Halfway through, while the reels were being changed, I switched on the lights and announced: 'Ladies and gentlemen, please note that as we are not allowed to charge an entrance fee, we are charging an exit fee. Thank you.'

Everyone laughed, and everyone paid, and from then on the president of the union left us alone. In fact he even visited us on occasion, and became quite friendly.

Shortly after we screened *J'Acccuse*, I was given space in the college's monthly magazine, *Talking Point*, to report on events in the Jewish Society. Encouraged by this, I somewhat cheekily asked if I could also be the magazine's film critic, and my request was granted. This exalted position gained me free entry to local cinemas, accompanied by a friend, where the manager would usher us to our seats and generally treat us like VIPs. This was definitely a bonus!

Another event that made life more interesting was my appointment as the London correspondent of the Italian Jewish weekly, *Israel*, which was based in Rome. I had contacted them to offer my services, and was pleasantly surprised when they agreed. The press card they sent me opened many doors and I was able to interview all kinds of public and media personalities, including the famous pop singer Helen Shapiro. For that interview I took with me a fellow student who was a keen member of the college Photographic Society. When we arrived at her agent's office, we were asked to wait. We felt like amateurs, but did our best to look and act the part. About an hour later, Helen walked in. The first thing she did was to go straight to the charts to see the position of her latest song, which I think was 'Woe Is Me'. She looked a bit disappointed, but when she turned to us,

My press card for the now-defunct Italian Jewish magazine, *Israel*.

she was very positive and friendly. She answered questions about being Jewish and her recent trip to Israel, and was happy to have her photo taken. We ended up with a full-page spread about her and her future plans.

I must confess that my new 'qualification' as a journalist emboldened me to try all kinds of things. When I read in *Stage* magazine that the casting director, Ron Greenwood, was looking for a Spanish-looking actor for his next film, I examined myself in the mirror and thought I would fit the bill. Using my best 'Spanish' accent I somehow managed to book an audition with the great man.

A few days later I laboured up the seemingly endless flight of steps to his office. Pausing only to regain my breath, I knocked and entered a room cluttered with books, papers and magazines. A small man was sitting at a desk: Mr Greenwood himself. As he looked up, his monocle dropped out, and I had to bite back a laugh, but the laugh was on me. When I explained

I had come for the Spanish part he looked me up and down and shook his head. 'Sorry, won't do', he said. 'This is someone who beats a really big guy in a fight scene. You're just too short.'

I suggested a David and Goliath scenario; I reminded him that Alan Ladd, a successful leading man, was short. He didn't buy it. Still, for a busy man, he spent quite some time with me and tried to be helpful. In answer to his questions, I declared that acting was in my blood (well, my father had done amateur dramatics in his youth), and I was hoping he could find something for me. He was very sympathetic, and to my amazement asked me to keep in touch and call him every other Monday morning. But it was not to be. I never did call back, and my name never did go up in lights. College work took up most of my time.

10

Dark clouds

In the summer of 1961, while still at Gateshead, I had accepted Rabbi Dominitz's invitation to join a team of students to help him run a month-long boys' camp on the south coast. After my first year of college, during which I got used to a routine of long days of studying, three evenings and Sunday mornings teaching, reviewing lessons with friends, and spending time with my family on Shabbat, I looked forward to something different. I went to help at Rabbi Dominitz's summer camp again.

These camps were an enjoyable, if challenging, experience. The participants came from schools where discipline was strongly enforced, and they did not all know how to cope with the relative freedom of a holiday. Days were punctuated by the usual prayers, but the main emphasis was on fun. We would take them to the beach in the mornings, play games in the afternoons, and enjoy singalongs in the evenings led by Rabbi Dominitz, who played the accordion beautifully. Many of the boys were noisy and rowdy at first, and supervising games and excursions for them could be quite a headache. We youth leaders did form a rapport with them and each other, but it was tiring, to say the least.

Inventing games for them tested our ingenuity. One which I devised proved very popular. We leaders would first set up the game by inflating balloons and plastic bags, filling some with water and some with little gifts, and hanging them above head height from a rope tied between two trees. The boys would take turns to be blindfolded and led near the rope, where they were given a golf club to swipe with as they tried to find, then burst, one of the hanging objects. The twist, of course, was that they were taking their chances of being showered with water, or winning a gift.

This was fine in principle, but I nearly came to grief with my very first volunteer, a strapping teenager. As I put the golf club in his hand I warned him to count to ten before making his attempt, but he was over-enthusiastic, and struck out before I could move out of range. The club landed with an almighty thwack, an inch from my left eye, and nearly knocked me out. I was rushed to the nearest hospital, where the doctors confirmed that I was lucky the blow had not been closer. Thankfully I still have the eye—and the scar! We all learned a lesson, and made very sure the game was played safely after that.

Bombshell

I arrived home from that action-packed month to be hit by an absolute bombshell: I found two letters from the Libyan Embassy. One had been delivered by regular post, the second by special delivery. I was overcome by a mixture of shock and fear. I had kept out of their way; I had moved about, from a village near Cambridge to Gateshead, then to North London. I had tried, throughout, to keep my address secret. Now, four years after leaving Benghazi, these two letters seemed ominous. I looked up at the sky. Yes, it was rather cloudy. *God,* I thought, *are You making fun of me? How did they find my address?* Then it hit me: my name was on the college's notice board as chairman of the Jewish Society.

My surname was very well known in Libya; Rabbi Babani Meghnagi had been the last rabbi and dayan (judge) of Tripoli, serving on official Libyan courts with both Muslims and Jews, with his office in the town hall. He had been the last Jew in Libya to be honoured with a state funeral, starting from the town hall. That was the kind of relationship that once existed between Arabs and Jews of the older generation, before Nasser and others poisoned many of the younger generation with dreams of glory, and anti-Semitic diatribes.

I opened the first letter. 'Dear Mr Meghnagi,' it read, 'we have been requested to inform you that you are to return to Benghazi by 24th August. Please come to the embassy to collect a travel document.' The second letter, sent two weeks later, read, 'Dear Mr Elia Meghnagi, We have not received a reply to our letter requesting you to come to the embassy to collect a travel document so you can travel to Benghazi, where your presence is urgently required. If we do not hear from you within two weeks, we will be asking the Home Office to extradite you.'

I couldn't read any more. I was shaking and, frankly, for the first time in my life, really frightened. Were they still after me for beating up that Arab boy? I had visions of languishing in prison and being beaten up mercilessly. I had brought my whole family to England, and now I might be sent back to Benghazi. One thing I was sure of: I couldn't say a word about this to my parents.

I walked over to Rabbi Dominitz to ask his advice. He read the letters, and immediately set up an urgent appointment for me to see the member of parliament for Hackney North and Stoke Newington, Mr David

Weitzman. While I waited for the day of the appointment, I sought the advice of many people, including the principal of the college and advisers on the Jewish Refugees' Committee. They all concurred that the MP would be my best bet.

When Mr Weitzman heard my predicament, he advised me to write to the Home Office explaining that I was a second-year student of engineering, paying for my upkeep by teaching part time. I should also explain that I had not done anything illegal in Libya, except possibly to defend myself in a silly fight over five years earlier, when I was still a teenager. He went on to say that if the Home Office reply was not sympathetic, I should call him immediately and he would raise the matter in Parliament.

There followed two weeks of cautious optimism, but just in case my application to the Home Office was refused I essentially stayed in hiding. The one thing I knew was that I would not go back to Libya, even if that meant staying in Britain illegally.

During the third week, I received one of the most important letters in my life. The Home Office stated that they understood my situation and had no intention of interfering with my education. I was to ignore the threats from the Libyan embassy. The Home Office had no intention of extraditing me.

This was the most exciting news I had had for a long time. Essentially, it meant that I had been officially recognised as a refugee, and I could now relax and concentrate on my studies. When the new year started, I plunged myself back into my college work with renewed fervour, while carrying on with my teaching.

Trouble on the home front

Everything went fairly well till my mother's attacks flared up again, which must have been some time in 1965, when I was in my final year of college. She started having arguments and screaming bouts with my father, accusing him of all sorts of outlandish things. Sometimes the fights would go on into the early hours of the morning. My father bore the brunt of it, but the effect on me was pretty bad, though it sounds selfish of me to say it. As a very light sleeper I would be kept up too, and I often found myself cycling to college tired out. (Unfortunately, over the years my mother's symptoms only became worse, resulting in frequent hospitalisation, and her suffering was exacerbated by the physical side effects of various medications.)

The worst day in my college life came at the end of the year. The screaming had been so bad during the exam period that I had had to keep leaving the house at five in the morning, cycling around till seven, when the college doors opened. Needless to say, I failed the exams. I was going to have to repeat the year, which is something that had never happened in my life. Apart from the fact that this undermined my confidence, I was desperately worried because only by gaining qualifications and, with them, a good job, could I truly be a help to my parents. Plunged into gloom, I allowed myself a day or so of self-pity. Then I saw an advert in the *Jewish Chronicle* looking for responsible young Jewish men and women to act as camp leaders and supervisors for a children's summer camp. That sounded as if it might cheer me up during the long vacation, and also bring in some money. A month spent in the beautiful Hampshire countryside with like-minded people would suit me perfectly. I went for an interview and was offered a position as youth leader.

Jolly Holidays

The camp, called Jolly Holidays, was run by Sydney Palace, a tall, imposing man who looked and still acted the part of the sergeant major he had been in the British army. As an observant Jew himself, he assured me that the camp would be run on strictly Orthodox, kosher principles, though the children would come from a mix of religious and non-religious homes. Mr Palace was a fascinating man. He was proud of having fought alongside his fellow British comrades, Jewish and non-Jewish. He told me with great pride and emotion of the time when his unit was taken prisoner by the Nazis and the men were asked to stand in line. When the German officer ordered all Jews to step forward, all the British soldiers moved forward together, without hesitation.

My time at camp that summer turned out to be an enjoyable and educational experience. There were two sessions; about two hundred youngsters each spent two weeks attending. There was a full programme of activities and outings for the campers, aged nine to fifteen, who were led, controlled and generally looked after by some dozen leaders, plus Mr and Mrs Palace. Perhaps naturally, with his background, Mr Palace ran the camp with strict military discipline.

One of my duties during the very first week of camp was to organise a concert for the Sunday when parents came to visit. I was very impressed by the amount of talent available: singers, gymnasts, comedians and dancers volunteered to perform. One ten-year-old girl had some training in ballet, and was clearly going to be the star of the show. The trouble was that it became clear she was something of a prima donna. When the big day dawned, one of the other staff members told me that this girl was refusing to attend the final rehearsal because, she said, she had fallen and hurt her leg. We were sure this was just attention seeking, so I asked my colleague to bring the girl to see me.

When she hobbled up, I reminded her that we were depending on her, and she really could not let us down. I asked her to walk to a nearby tree, and she obliged, limping pathetically.

'Okay', I said, 'now show me how you walked before the accident.'

Immediately she strode out happily to the tree and back, looking puzzled by the onlookers' laughter.

That afternoon she performed brilliantly, to the delight of her parents and everyone else. The show was a big hit, and after dinner we staff had time to congratulate each other on a successful show. Looking around, I noticed one camp leader I hadn't spoken to up to then. He was keeping to himself, and didn't look particularly happy. I made a point of saying hello to him, and learned that his name was Ralph. Over the remaining weeks of camp, I had the pleasure of getting to know him better, together with his cousin Barry, who was also a leader. The three of us kept up our friendship once we were back home, meeting up periodically for coffee and a chat. Barry lived quite near me, and Ralph would drive from his home in Loughton, outside London.

11

The love of my life

It was at Ralph's birthday party in November 1966 that I met his cousin, Beryl, who was then in her final year at Birmingham University doing an English degree. Her father had driven her to Loughton, and she had arranged to stay the night…as had I. It was all very proper: when all the other guests had left, and his twin sisters had gone to bed (their parents were away), Ralph, Beryl and I sat up talking virtually all night. I remember it was absolutely freezing, and I can still hear Ralph's voice when he announced at about 5:30 a.m., 'I don't know about you two; I'm going to bed!' I also remember Barry's teasing 'Oh, yes?' when I called him the next day to ask for Beryl's telephone number. We quickly became an 'item', but being based in different cities meant that what was then called a courtship was conducted mainly by letter, with infrequent meetings.

One of the things which drew us together was our ability to discuss anything and confide in each other. I admired her intelligence and humility, and delighted in the fact that we could make each other laugh. I was also attracted to her because she shared my love of language, and was (and is) equally fascinated by all things linguistic. She told me early on that she wanted to learn more about Judaism: her parents were proud to be Jewish, and kept a kosher home, but that was all. Her father had such unhappy memories of his own very strict Orthodox upbringing that he refused to send his three daughters to *cheder*, saying that they could decide for themselves how they felt about religion when they were older. This meant that Beryl, who had always been very successful academically, felt there was a huge gap in her knowledge of what was really important. I suggested she should go to the shul in Birmingham on Shabbat and get to know people there. As a fairly shy person it took some courage for her to do this, but she did it nonetheless, and was rewarded by being invited to families for meals. She was able to mix with and learn from Orthodox Jewish people who were not judgemental, and were happy to guide her in increasing her knowledge and observance.

Knowing that my relationship with Beryl was serious spurred me on in my efforts to do well in the final year of my engineering degree. Luckily for me, near the start of this repeated year, a good friend had invited me to share his ground-floor flat for a very reasonable share of the rent. It was very near Manor House station, and within easy cycling distance of campus and my family. I had my own spacious room, and we shared the bathroom and kitchen. This made a fantastic difference to my life. I became independent. I could study in peace when I needed to, but was still able to invite family and friends to visit me. Nonetheless, moving out of my parents' house did not put an end to my responsibility for their wellbeing. Whether I liked it or not, I had to cycle to see them daily in order to keep my mother reasonably calm. My siblings were there, and ready to help, but I had been the first one to come to the UK, and she obviously thought I knew the ropes, and was the one to be relied upon.

Independence

Having moved to my new shared accommodation, I had to be extra frugal. I sought holiday jobs and private teaching, and somehow I got by. I made sure there was always money for my rent and running expenses, and made *very* sure my parents didn't realise how stretched I was.

One of my college friends, a mature student from Scotland who used to come and revise maths and physics with me, understood my financial worries and suggested I apply for a grant from Hackney Council. It had never occurred to me to ask for help. I owed the UK so much for the kindness and understanding I had been shown; I certainly didn't expect to get anything back. He told me that I was entitled to claim as my father paid taxes, and in any case I would be much more useful to the UK with a degree than without.

Well, I thought, what could I lose? So I applied, and I was thrilled when the council offered me a grant of £550 for the year. That was a significant sum in those days, and meant that I would be able to afford small luxuries, like a new pair of shoes. In due course the cheque from Hackney Council arrived, so I immediately wrote to the Central British Fund, the financial arm of the Jewish Refugees' Committee which had been giving me help. I told them the good news about my grant, thanked them for their help and support in the previous years, and explained that I no longer needed money from them. To my great surprise and delight they replied that as I had been honest, and as the money had already been allocated, they were sending it to me anyway. The cheque came with the message: 'For a change have some extra money in your pocket. Good luck.'

Enter British Rail

One event that took place at college that year proved to be very significant. Early in 1967, a senior engineer from the British Railways Board came to give a talk to students about prospective careers in railway engineering. The talk was an eye-opener for me. In my ignorance I had imagined jobs in the railway system were limited to selling tickets and driving trains, while here was this engineer describing an amazing world of advanced electronics and communications; an industry that was at the cutting edge of computer technology. He left a pile of application forms, and I was one of about a dozen students to collect one. I didn't take it too seriously, but I've always believed in the principle 'Nothing ventured, nothing gained'. Along with the usual requirements of name, address and personal details, I had to write a few thoughts on the railways and why I was keen to have a career in the industry. I completed the form, sent it off, and more or less forgot about it.

To my surprise, sometime later about six students, including myself, were invited for interviews at BRB's Marylebone headquarters. In due course I attended, and had a friendly and quite personal chat with the interviewer. Two weeks later I received a letter asking me to attend a second interview with Mr A. Cardani, the chief engineer of British Rail's Signalling and Telecom Department, Western Region. After a pleasant but searching interview, he offered me a paid two-year postgraduate training stint in his department, which was based in Reading, half-an-hour's train journey from Paddington. This would in due course then lead to a full-time position. Since my flat was a short walk from an Underground station, I would be able to carry on living there for the time being.

Noticing that I was wearing a hat, he asked me if I was an Orthodox Jew and, if so, would I need to leave early on Fridays. I confirmed that I was indeed Jewish, but hastened to add that early Fridays would only apply in the winter, and I would make up the time during the week. I was hugely relieved when he said he had allowed this with another employee, and it had worked out very well.

A week later a letter arrived confirming my appointment, to start in October of that year, 1967.

To say I was elated is putting it mildly! Here I was, having brought my family to the safety of the UK and found them jobs and housing. I had a share in a comfortable ground-floor flat, and had been elected to the committee of Ezra, the youth group I was still involved with. I had nearly finished my studies, and could now look forward to a good job with British Rail. But the icing on this magnificent cake, the best thing that had happened so far in my eventful life, was that Beryl agreed to marry me as soon as we reached financial independence.

Israel imperilled

Our personal outlook was positive, but our joy was somewhat overshadowed by the worrying news concerning Israel that spring. Apart from the fact that what happened to Israel was, and always would be, extremely important to me, I had many relatives and close friends living there, many of whom would be called up to the army. For the first time in two thousand years there was a Jewish state, and now it was facing annihilation. The megalomaniacal Egyptian president, Abdul Gamal Nasser, was bent on keeping his promise to seize the Holy Land and throw the Jewish people 'into the sea'. Unfortunately, like all demagogues, he had started believing in his own oratory and invincibility. Instead of using his undeniably enormous popularity to help rebuild Egypt's tattered economy and to confront social inequality within Egypt and the Arab world, his attention was focused on his hatred of Israel and the Jews. He was a gifted orator with tremendous charisma, which he could have used to unite the Arab world and bring it out of the doldrums of post-colonial stagnation and into the twentieth century. He had won the grudging admiration and respect of even those countries like Britain and France from which, a decade earlier, he had been able to snatch victory from the jaws of defeat. Unfortunately for the Arab world, for Israel and especially for Egypt, he missed (or rather messed up) his chance to become the Arabs' greatest leader for centuries because of his blind and obsessive hatred of the Jews and Israel. Having become effectively the leader and the darling of the so-called Non-Aligned Nations, he started exhorting other Arab nations to join him in the 'holy' war to wipe the 'Zionist Jews' from the face of the Earth, promising a swift victory.

Though most countries in the world sided with Israel, few were prepared to do anything about this newest threat to its existence. However, Jews from all over the world volunteered to assist the war effort by flying to Israel or by raising funds. I will never forget a man who ran a clothes shop in London putting his entire business up for sale, and telling the local paper that he was giving the proceeds to Israel. When he was asked what he was going to live on, his reply was: 'I came here from the concentration camps with nothing; I can start again with nothing.'

Like other young Jews from all over the world, many members of our youth group, Ezra, decided to volunteer in Israel, arranging to fly there as soon as possible. They were fortunate not to have to worry about leaving their studies, as the hostilities happened to coincide with the end of the academic year. Most students, including myself, had already taken their end of year exams or, as in my case, my finals.

Although, in the event, Israel surprised the whole world by miraculously defeating the armies of several Arab nations in just six days, Israel still needed volunteers: many young Israelis remained at the front, and Israel needed hands to replace them on farms and kibbutzim. Most of the Ezra group ended up on Kibbutz Chafetz Chaim, close to the city of Ashdod. I, however, was still in London. Having no passport or travel document, I was basically stateless. I did not yet meet the criteria for naturalisation in the UK because an applicant had to have been a taxpayer for at least five years, and I was only going to start my working, tax-paying life that autumn.

I went to the Home Office and explained my dilemma. Could they help me get hold of some kind of travel document? They were sympathetic, but unable to help. They told me that I needed to obtain a letter from the Libyan embassy declaring that Libya was no longer responsible for me. I was so keen to join my friends on the kibbutz that I didn't consider how absurd and dangerous an undertaking this might be. Going to the Libyan embassy was certainly fraught with danger. When I discussed the venture with friends, one of them reminded me of a recent case of a Libyan expatriate who had been found at Rome airport, tied up in a box bound for Egypt. Even so, I was young, and perhaps the years I had spent in the UK enjoying democracy and freedom had made me a bit reckless. I paid little attention to the danger, and decided that I had to try and break this impasse.

12

Into the lion's den

I was not *completely* reckless; I knew that I had to take some precautions. I would be visiting the embassy without an appointment, and I asked an English friend from college, Nathan Scheiner, to accompany me. We agreed that, as a British citizen, he should be safe. I also asked Henry Shaw, the head of the Federation of University Jewish Students, whom I knew, to wait for a call from me. We arranged that if he didn't hear from me by two in the afternoon, he should phone the embassy and ask to speak to me. If his request was refused, he should use his judgement as to what to do next—perhaps organise a demonstration outside the embassy.

So, on a splendid day in early July, I presented myself at the Libyan embassy, with Nathan in tow. Stating my business to the polite young receptionist seated in the portrait-lined foyer, I anticipated a long wait. Surprisingly, I was quickly ushered into the inner sanctum, while Nathan remained in the foyer.

The official who greeted me was friendly enough as he asked me to repeat my name. 'Meghnagi, Meghnagi,' he mused, searching through files until he found one bearing my name. Suddenly his expression changed. 'Where have you been?' he demanded aggressively. 'The federal police in Libya have been looking for you for years!'

I started shaking, but managed to reply that I'd been in the UK the whole time, given that I couldn't go anywhere without a passport. That was the whole reason for my being there, I explained, to sort out my status.

'Hmm,' he muttered, 'we've searched everywhere for you, we've written to you....' Then, suddenly, he picked up his phone and told his secretary, 'Book me two first-class tickets on Libyan Arab Airlines for this afternoon.'

This sounded extremely ominous. I thought of that man who had been found tied up in a box at Rome Airport, ready to be smuggled out, and I had visions of being next. Trying not to appear worried, I surreptitiously started looking round for an escape route. I considered using a chair to break the window and jump out; I was young and strong, and the window was only about ten feet above ground level. While I was debating what to do, the official put down the phone, said, 'Excuse me, I just have to see to something urgently. Back in a minute,' and left the room.

Maybe I was being paranoid, but I suspected that he was leaving so that he could organise my abduction. It might all have been perfectly innocent, but I wasn't hanging around to find out! Having been left alone, I had a chance. I sidled out of the office and back into the foyer to join Nathan. I walked around slowly, pretending to admire the paintings while working my way towards the main entrance. At that point I shouted, 'Nathan, run!' and held the door open for him before throwing myself out. We flew down the road as if a thousand devils were after us, until we reached the post office where I had planned to use the telephone. Gasping, I managed to call Mr Shaw and report that we were safely out, and he need not send reinforcements. I also thought to take a passport photograph there, hoping it would be needed.

Having thanked Nathan warmly for his support I left him to make his way home, while I went straight to the Home Office in Holborn. It made such a change to go, not as a foreigner begging to be allowed to extend my stay, but to argue my case to be given a travel document. When eventually it was my turn to be seen, I explained what had happened and made it clear that I would not go back to the embassy unless someone from the Home Office came with me. Mercifully, I was assured that would not be necessary, and that a Home Office travel document would shortly be sent to my home. It was providential that I could hand over my photograph there and then.

Cleared to fly

The following week I received my British travel document, which made me feel both proud and ecstatic. I booked my flight to Israel and, through the head of the organisation Electronics for Israel, whom I had contacted, undertook to carry out a survey of the Israeli electronics industry. I thought with my knowledge of electronics and interest in journalism, I could be useful. I was given the name of an official in the Israeli Foreign Office who would be able to provide contacts.

I travelled to Israel in August, and found myself struck by the beauty and vibrancy of this promised land. I spent a week with my English friends on the kibbutz, picking potatoes. Then I spent time visiting family members I hadn't seen for years, who wined and dined me in their homes until I actually welcomed a fast day! Naturally I caught up with Mumu, then finally got round to visiting the official in the foreign office. We had a long conversation, and he gave me a list of companies to visit. I then spent a hectic week travelling round by public transport, visiting those companies and noting their details. On my return he called me to his office in Tel Aviv and offered me a position as his assistant. He explained that his job was to meet and greet foreign investors. He needed someone who was fluent in English and knowledgeable about technology to be the liaison between the investors and Israeli industry. It was a tempting idea, but I reminded myself I had a job with British Rail lined up for October, and my parents were still depending on me to find them more suitable accommodation. My mother still relied on me more than my other siblings. In any case, my fiancée was hardly likely to drop everything and move to Israel; she was about to start her Postgraduate Certificate in Education, and we had never even discussed the idea of living anywhere other than England, where all her immediate family lived. Politely, I turned down the offer. I was sure I would not change my mind during the year's grace I was given to decide.

The Six Day War ended positively for Israel, but not for the Jews who still remained in Libya. In the lead-up to the war, during, and afterwards, hatred towards Jews and Israel was incited by pro-Nasserite and anti-Western elements in Libya. Riots and violence broke out in Tripoli and Benghazi. There were many horrific attacks against the Jews, especially in Tripoli. The Jews tried to keep safe by locking themselves in their homes and relying on Arab friends for help, but some were nevertheless trapped by the mobs. At least seventeen Jews were killed, including whole families. Young Arab nationalists destroyed not only shuls, but over one hundred Jewish-owned shops and warehouses. King Idris intervened to organise the evacuation of the Jews of Tripoli and Benghazi to the safety of military camps outside the cities. With the country in a state of emergency, he agreed to arrange for the Jews to be evacuated to Italy until it was safe for them to return. Whether they would return or not, even if only to organise the liquidation of their assets and leave once more, would be a different question.

A long engagement

Once I was back in London I concentrated on preparations for my new job. I was given a pass for British Rail trains and the London Underground so that I could travel freely from my London home to Reading, where I would be training and working. I also needed to help my family before I started my new position; it was past time for them to leave their small, overcrowded apartment. I managed to find a large house for sale, close to transport and a short walk from my father's shul. Clement was already working as a salesman, so we pooled our fairly meagre savings for the down payment, obtained a local council mortgage, and were able to move the family into a roomy house.

Meanwhile, life had become quite difficult for Beryl. While she had been able to deepen her connection to Judaism during her last year in Birmingham, it was a different story once she graduated and returned to her parents' home in London. On the one hand, her PGCE studies were less demanding than her degree had been, and she had time to study once a week with a kind lady I found in the Lubavitch community. From her she learned to read Hebrew, and learned about the practicalities of Jewish observance, making copious notes on the laws of keeping kosher, observing Shabbat, etc. On the other hand, she felt very much the odd one out at home. Hers was a loving family, but she feared they felt her new-found observance was an implied criticism of them. Her elder sister was already married, and her mother and younger sister were quite tolerant, but her father was more than irritated when she refused to help in the family business on Saturdays, the busiest day of the week for the hardware and plastic laminate shop that fronted their home. It was hard for her parents to cope with the thriving business by themselves. Beryl tried to keep out of her father's way, and to just avoid breaking Shabbat. Because Orthodox Jews don't actively use electricity on the Sabbath, which begins on Friday evening, she would switch on the bathroom light before Shabbat began, but he would do things like switching the light off, and deliberately leaving down the cover of the toilet seat, a nasty shock to the system! She can laugh about it now, but it wasn't so funny at the time.

Added to that, as weeks and months went by and nothing was happening on the marriage front, my future father-in-law clearly had misgivings about my intentions (and from my present perspective, I can't say I blame him). I had always been honest with Beryl, who knew it would be a long engagement. Once I finished training, my salary would increase, but in the meantime I had taken on the responsibility of paying my parents' mortgage, since my qualifications put me in the position of ultimately becoming the highest earner in the family. Beryl was not earning yet, and I couldn't afford another mortgage for ourselves. I refused to start married life in rented accommodation as, rightly or wrongly, I was convinced that if we started out like that, we would finish up like that. Moreover, my mother's mental problems skewed her thinking and made her fear I would abandon my family if I got married. On the few occasions she met Beryl she wasn't exactly welcoming, and her limited English didn't help. I remember telling Beryl that I couldn't build our happiness on my parents' misery, and even said she'd be better off with someone with fewer problems, to which she replied, 'It took me long enough to find you; don't try to get rid of me now!'

Arrivederci Roma

My first year with BR took me all over the Western Region, learning different aspects of the job I would be doing. Beryl and I were finally both based in London, but since I was so often away, we rarely saw each other more than once a week, if that. In any case, London is a big city. We lived miles apart, and travel by public transport took a long time. The telephone bills mounted up!

In the summer of 1968 I had some holiday time, and given that my free travel perks with British Rail extended to rail travel in Europe, I thought I would use them to satisfy my craving to see friends and relatives in Rome. I would have loved to take Beryl with me, but we agreed that paying for her fare and accommodation would be too extravagant. After organising the visas for France and Italy I went to Martin's bank to get my travel document stamped, confirming that I was taking with me only £50, the maximum allowed by law at that time.

When the day came I decided to travel light. The journey from Waterloo to the cross-Channel ferry, then through to Termini in Rome, went smoothly, and I had a wonderful time catching up with people I hadn't seen since leaving Libya ten years earlier. Although they were fairly recent immigrants, many had already been saving money in Italian accounts before they were forced out of Libya. They were integrating well, forging new lives for themselves both socially and in business. I had no need to visit tourist sites, having done that years before, so we spent time reminiscing about the old days, and talking about people with whom we had lost touch.

On the way home I took the train from Rome to Modane, the French border town where passengers' papers were checked before they were allowed to continue all the way to London. By agreement between France and Italy, an Italian official checked all foreign passports on the train to save passengers having to get off.

I was enjoying a lively conversation with some fellow passengers when the Italian border official asked me for my passport. I handed him my British travel document, but he didn't seem satisfied. 'No, I want to see your Italian passport,' he said.

'I don't have an Italian passport,' I replied.

'Where is your Italian passport?' he insisted, becoming agitated.

'I've never had an Italian passport,' I said, beginning to regret having spoken to him in Italian. But then I realised he had heard me speaking to the other passengers, who were Italians; after two weeks in Rome I had regained my fluency, and it dawned on me that he must think I was a draft dodger or a deserter from the Italian army.

He got on his phone and called Rome, and I could hear him telling his opposite number, 'He looks Italian, he speaks Italian...he must *be* Italian. Do me a favour and check the military records.'

Clearly this was going to take some time, and what at first I had found amusing was no longer funny. I showed him the visa I had been given at the Italian embassy in London, whereupon he asked me to get off the train and go to the border control office, where the French border police were to hold me till they got instructions from Rome.

My heart sank. The next train to London was in twelve hours, and it was even possible that they would force me back to Rome till they sorted things out.

In the border control office, the French policeman asked what the problem was. I explained that the suspicions about me were unfounded, briefly outlining why I was travelling on a British travel document, complete with Italian visa.

'But excuse me,' the Frenchman interrupted, 'I have looked through your document, and you have no French visa.'

'Yes, I have!" I protested. 'I went to the French embassy myself and saw it being stamped.'

In reply he invited me to look for myself.

The travel document was made up of one long sheet folded into four sections. I took it, studied it, turned it over and over, and…he was right. There was a form from Martin's bank showing I had taken out £50, but no French visa. Then, suddenly, it hit me. The bank form was stuck on the document. I peeled it off and there, underneath, was a clearly stamped French visa. Seeing this, we both laughed, and he told me, 'Quick, quick, run to the train; it is about to leave. Good luck!'

I threw myself and my case onto the train just as it started moving. I found a seat, but only started to relax once we were well onto French soil. I resolved not to go to Italy again until I had a proper British passport.

Training travels

That trip had been a thoroughly enjoyable interlude (except for the hair-raising experience at Modane), but once home it was time to buckle down to some serious work. Beryl had gained her PGCE and started her first teaching job in September. As for me, in order to learn various aspects of railway work I was sent on more courses in different parts of the country. These training courses all over the Western Region had their fun aspects, but also their surprises. I often had to spend the nights away, and while the railways paid a fixed expense allowance to us, being strictly kosher did have its problems. I often had to eat in company with my colleagues, and while they would get their fish and chips, I would have to make do with stale two-day-old sandwiches. I didn't mind; I enjoyed their company, and our shared time helped form a bond between us.

During the last week of a four-week training period in Swindon, the centre of repair and maintenance for the Western Region, I was recalled to the office and told that my next training period was to start the following Tuesday, in Cardiff, and would last for a month. I was also told that the chief telecom engineer of the Western Region had asked the stationmaster at Cardiff to find me kosher accommodation there. I was very moved by his thoughtfulness. I knew that he was a religious Christian, but I hadn't realised that he was aware of the problems I was facing, as I never complained and was quite used to making do.

The following week I decided to arrive in Cardiff a day early so as to familiarise myself with the area. Since I knew that the kosher accommodation that had been found for me wasn't available till the following day, I went to a bed and breakfast I had seen advertised in the local paper. By the time I got there I had developed a really bad headache, so I went straight to bed even though it was only about 5 p.m. The landlady became worried, and offered me food, which I politely refused. Again she offered me tea, and again I had to decline. In order not to upset her I just thanked her and said I really didn't feel well, and in any case, I only ate kosher. She finally left me to try and cope with the headache.

A while later there was a knock on the door and in came a rabbi from the local community with enough hot, freshly cooked food to feed three people. That lovely Welsh lady had taken it upon herself to contact the shul and tell them about this Jewish guest who was unwell. The aptly named Reverend Fine couldn't do enough for me. Unfortunately, I felt really awful and couldn't eat the food he had brought, but I did take the chicken soup. Needless to say, he came back in the morning with a full breakfast. Feeling much better, I thanked him for his generosity and promised to see him at evening prayers.

After spending a full day at the office of the Cardiff engineer, I went to my new kosher accommodation, run by a Mr and Mrs Bernhard. They were a delightful old couple who had met and married after surviving Bergen-Belsen, where tragically they had each lost their first spouse and the rest of their families. It was truly lovely seeing their devotion to each other. They took an immediate liking to me, and we became very friendly. After two weeks there they refused to take any money from me. Despite my protests that British Rail was paying me a daily allowance, they were adamant. I stayed with them for four weeks, Monday to Thursday, going home for the weekends.

Some time later I needed to spend a few days in Cardiff and decided to stay in a local hotel rather than go to the Bernhards, because I was sure they wouldn't charge me. Somehow they found out that I was there, and were quite hurt that I hadn't gone to them. They actually made me feel I was doing them a favour in allowing them to be hospitable to me. From that day on, whenever I was sent to Cardiff I stayed with them and was treated like a son. We stayed in touch, and later we were delighted to welcome them as honoured guests at our wedding.

Encyclopaedic knowledge

In the months (and months, and months) of our very long engagement, finances were tight. Beryl was now in her first teaching job, saving all her salary and living at home, where her parents refused to take money for her board. As for me, as I said, I had taken on the main responsibility for paying the mortgage on my parents' house, and there was precious little left over. My pay as a trainee was not particularly high, but travelling round the Western Region for weeks at a time did leave me free to do some paid work in the evenings. Anything I could earn would be saved so that we could eventually use the money to buy and furnish our own home, and maybe also for a honeymoon (which, in the event, didn't happen until our fortieth anniversary!).

Beryl and I were discussing possibilities when I received a providential phone call from a friend, inviting us to a presentation of an 'amazing' encyclopaedia which was new in the UK. The presentation was taking place on a Sunday afternoon. We were free, a few friends would be there, and the person giving the presentation was a rabbi, meaning at least the snacks would be kosher. So we went.

It was in fact a well-presented recruitment pitch, and we were all very impressed with the quality of the *World Book Encyclopedia* and its junior version, *Childcraft–The How and Why Library*. The books were easy to read, beautifully illustrated, and likely to appeal, given that this was well before the days of Professor Google.

I don't usually rush into things, but this looked like an answer to our prayers. By the end of the meeting, we had both signed up as sales representatives. The rules were very simple: sell, sell, sell. The reward was a reasonable commission on each set sold, and the option of receiving our own set of *World Book* in lieu of commission after the fourth sale. The fact that I really believed in the product, and would have ample opportunity to drum up business, convinced me that this was a chance to be grabbed.

My first sales venture was in Swindon. I started by looking for Italian-sounding names in the local telephone directory, and discovered an area with a few that were promising. I didn't want to just turn up on doorsteps, so I picked a name and called to introduce myself. Having established that the family were recent immigrants with school-age children, I explained in Italian that I had books which would help with the children's education. Within the hour I was in their lounge, enjoying watching them pore over the sample books. To my delight, not to say amazement, they signed up for both the standard and junior sets. Better still, they recommended me to several other families who had come from the same Sicilian village, and by the end of the month I had sold to virtually every Italian family in the area. In each case I asked them to let me know when the books arrived, and went to spend a couple of hours helping the children get the most out of the books, of course at no extra charge.

All this involved numerous bus rides and was pretty tiring after a full day's work for BR, but I really believed in the product and found it very rewarding.

My next railway assignment meant spending a few weeks in Cardiff. As usual I stayed with my friends, the Bernhards. As usual, they were very helpful. They actually found a bike I could use, and gave me the addresses of some Jewish families who might be interested in the encyclopaedias. Excited and emboldened by my success in Swindon, I pedalled to a leafy residential area and went straight to the first house on my list. The man who answered my ring took one look at me and my books, muttered, 'Sorry, no books, bye,' and shut the door.

I felt like a balloon that had been fully inflated (to match my ego), then suddenly burst. I was about to give up when I noticed a similar house nearby, bearing the sign 'Lawyer' on the door. I rang the bell.

This time the man who answered spluttered, 'If it's books you're selling, you're wasting your time.' He tried to shut the door, but I put my foot in the way and said, 'Excuse me, but you're a lawyer, aren't you?'

'Yes,' he agreed suspiciously.

'Well,' I continued, 'when I need legal advice, I'll come to you; I'm a salesman, so please let me judge whether I'm wasting my time. May I come in?'

He was so taken aback that he just stood back and motioned me in. Once inside he let me do my demonstration for the family, and was so impressed by his children's reaction that he ordered both the *World Book* and *Childcraft*. He also asked if I had been anywhere else, and when I confessed my earlier failure, it turned out that he was a friend of the man who had turned me away. He promptly called him and asked him to give me a chance...which subsequently turned into a sale. On top of that, he knew the hotel magnate, Charles Forte, and set up an appointment with him for me.

I went back to the Bernhards and phoned Beryl to report my lucky break, then the next day I went to the Forte mansion, where I spoke with Mr Forte in Italian, our mutual mother tongue. He was very charming, but on seeing what I was selling, he led me to his beautiful library, which stood in its own grounds, and pointed out sets of all the best-known encyclopaedias and other reference books. 'Look,' he exclaimed, 'every book you can think of, and my children never touch them!'

'That's exactly why you need mine!' I replied.

Seeing his startled look, I asked him to call the children and let them decide. As I expected, they found the books totally absorbing, and I left with another order.

I seemed to have the knack, and I enjoyed doing the work. Then it occurred to me that I'd sold more than enough to entitle me to a set for our own future home, and it would be nice to have the books there waiting for us. I contacted head office in London with this request, only to be told that I should have made my intentions clear before making the latest sale. Since I hadn't yet received any commission I didn't see what the problem was, but they insisted that I would have to sell one more set before I could claim my own. Those were the rules, they said, and they could not be broken.

I was absolutely furious, and completely disenchanted. I had no doubt that the books themselves were an excellent product and good value for money, but I was not prepared to be taken in by sophistry. I needed to have complete faith in a company I was working for, and that faith had been broken.

'Just send me the commission on the sets I've sold,' I snapped. 'I quit!'

They tried several times to make me change my mind, but in fact I never sold another set of encyclopaedias. I concentrated all my efforts on my main job: railway engineering.

As for Beryl, she was as thrilled as I at my successes, but frankly relieved not to have to keep trying on her own behalf. Sales didn't suit her personality, and anyway her evenings were taken up with planning lessons and marking, so visions of her being a saleswoman had never really been feasible.

13

The wedding that wasn't, and the wedding that was

By 1969, Beryl and I were both working full time, respectively as an English teacher in London and a railway telecom engineer in Reading. We didn't smoke or drink, we didn't go on expensive holidays, we didn't own a car, and I had managed to earn some extra money by selling encyclopaedias. The prospect of our finally being able to get married was getting closer, but we weren't quite there yet. We resolved to put an idea to Beryl's parents. We asked if they would object to our having a civil wedding ceremony in a registry office, simply so that Beryl could benefit from reduced fares on public transport as my wife. This would be a big help financially, as she went to work and back by train, and in due course would need to travel to Reading to house hunt.

We stressed that since this would only be a civil wedding, not a religious one, it would simply be a formality which would not change our living arrangements. After a brief confab her father said they had no objection, provided my parents agreed. When I responded that my parents would never approve, and could not possibly be told, his answer was, 'Do what you like; just leave us out of it.'

We took him at his word, so having made (as we thought) all the necessary arrangements, a few months later, on 5 December 1969, we turned up at West Ham Registry Office. Goodness knows what the lady registrar thought of this couple who arrived with no fancy clothes, no flowers, no family or friends, no witnesses...no witnesses! Somehow it had escaped us that we would need two witnesses. I actually had to leave the building and waylay two random and somewhat bemused passers-by to come and oblige. And thus was the deed done. We left the office, gave each other a peck on the cheek, and went our separate ways.

Life went on just as before until one day Beryl's father, for some reason more frustrated than usual, rounded on her and exclaimed, 'If you ask me, he's never going to marry you!'

To which she sweetly replied, 'Well, as a matter of fact, he already has!'

At that time, Beryl and I lived about nine miles apart, and in telling me what had happened, she said she was surprised I hadn't heard the explosion. Her father went absolutely ballistic. He denied having had any conversation with us about a civil marriage, and was astonished and affronted that we could do such a thing without his knowledge. Her mother obviously did remember, but just looked the other way and kept out of it.

Despite the uproar, the ultimate upshot was that Beryl's father became convinced of my total commitment. From that point on, he was completely supportive, and even told us that he would give us a generous donation towards the deposit on our first home. (Mrs Epstein of the Jewish Refugees' Committee lent us some money towards the deposit, although Beryl reminds me that this was thanks to her being put on the spot and left alone in a room to write a letter justifying why we deserved the loan.) By 1970, we realised that we finally had enough money to put down a deposit on a house in Reading, the headquarters of British Rail, Western Region, where my job was based. Housing there was less expensive than in London, and Beryl had a teaching job lined up there for the coming academic year. At last it was time to look for a house so that we could fix the date of our wedding.

I put my protractor point on the address of the shul in Reading, drew a circle around it on the map with a one-mile circumference, and started looking. I found a promising property for sale: 37 Wensley Road. Beryl came to give it the once over and loved it. We paid the deposit, obtained a favourable mortgage through her teaching union, and hey presto, we were homeowners. I moved into the house immediately so that I could start cleaning and painting. And after a few problems trying to satisfy all the immediate relatives, especially my mother, the date for our wedding was finally fixed: 8 November 1970.

At long last, we were 'properly' married, at Lea Bridge Road Synagogue in Clapton, East London. It happened to be Remembrance Sunday, on which the fallen of the two World Wars are commemorated. Thank God we have a happier reason to remember the date. It was an incredibly joyful event for me, and for my new wife: the woman who had waited so patiently for so long, while putting up with being teased and showered with questions, could finally go public as Mrs Meghnagi—although she jokes that having waited so long to get the name, it's given her nothing but trouble ever since! (People are invariably flummoxed by the pronunciation, Meg-NAH-jee; she never had such problems with her maiden name, Freedman.) I am delighted and deeply grateful to say that after fifty-one years of marriage, five children and—at the time of writing—twenty-one

Married at last! My parents next to me, Beryl's next to her.

grandchildren, our feelings for each other are as strong as they were on that day.

Despite having had so long to prepare for our wedding, we still managed to make a gaffe: we had intended to return to our home in Reading for our wedding night (no expensive hotel for us) but hadn't anticipated the last guests leaving so late that we'd miss the last Underground train to Paddington, from which the train for Reading departed. We were saved by my new parents-in-law saying they were too excited to sleep, and would give us a lift all the way home in return for a cup of tea and a slice of wedding cake. Goodness knows what time they finally fell into their own bed!

We had a meagre one day 'honeymoon', which we spent travelling to and from London to see my Uncle David, who had been inconsolable when we left after the wedding. Although still single himself, he was a devoted family man. In Israel he had helped look after Frigia's children until Frigia came home from the hospital. Uncle David, whom we referred to as Dado, had arrived in London to stay in about 1965, and was very close to all of us.

Reading

Beryl and I settled down to married life. From the start we decided to continue our frugal living, and the order of the day became save, save, save. We agreed to live entirely on my salary, while hers went straight into a savings account.

We settled into our new routine: Beryl had to cope with the pupils in the aptly named Battle Secondary School, and I found myself travelling all over the Western Region from Paddington station as far as Carmarthen in Wales.

It is not widely known that British Rail had its own telephone system, but it did, and at this point my task was to test phones along the railway routes. This soon developed into assisting in the laying of underground telecom cables and testing the overhead ones. Many of my graduate colleagues just stood watching while the cable and telegraph gangs did the digging or climbing up telegraph poles, but I was keen to be hands on. I helped with the digging and did a lot of climbing. Indeed, I used to join the workers during the lunch break in their huts, or sometimes in the local pub, enjoying their company while eating my own sandwiches. They appreciated this and treated me as one of them, which certainly helped me learn the practical part of my work much more quickly. It was interesting and very healthy work, doing a lot of walking out in the fresh country air.

Soon I was put in charge of large projects, commissioning telephone exchanges dotted around the Western Region. Because some of them would take a few days, when possible Beryl would come with me so she could enjoy the sights, or mark school assignments whilst I carried out the work.

Then, one Monday morning, this idyll nearly came crashing down. Mr Cardani, the chief signal and telecom engineer for the Western Region, who had first taken me on, was promoted to the British Rail Board, and his replacement sent for me to discuss my future. Having congratulated me on my good work, he told me that he could no longer sanction my leaving early on winter Fridays. When I asked why, he explained since I had been carrying out 'on call' duties, he was worried that in an emergency on a Friday I would abandon the job and my colleagues, and just go home. He was much reassured when I told him that in Judaism we are not allowed to ignore an emergency which could put lives at risk, and of course railway signals are vital to passenger safety. I added that I had agreed a code with my office manager whereby he could call me on the Sabbath in a real emergency. This put his mind at rest, and my heart resumed its usual rate.

I can honestly say that my time working for British Rail was the happiest in my working life. I used to joke with my colleagues, saying that I was going to write a book called *Railway Sleepers* about the easygoing way work was carried out. There was a lovely, friendly atmosphere, especially with the Welsh contingent. They were funny and always smiling, and I was delighted when they had accepted the invitation to our wedding. (They had never been to a Jewish wedding, and enjoyed themselves in a bemused sort of way. They couldn't believe that the bar was free, and that nonetheless nobody drank much.)

One of my main tasks at work was to locate faults in buried cables, but the system in use was rather antiquated. Although based on old electrical theory, in fact it was mostly trial and error. I decided to find out what the electronic industry had to offer, and unearthed the solution hidden in a cupboard: an oscilloscope-based instrument called a Cossorscope, which was adapted for cable fault finding. It seemed nobody wanted to learn how to use it, preferring to use the old-fashioned system, which struck me as not only time consuming but not particularly accurate. I decided to acquaint myself with the instrument, and soon became very proficient with it.

Although my responsibilities were officially confined to the London area of the Western Region, I was frequently 'borrowed' by other areas and became the Western Region's unofficial cable fault finder, travelling from Paddington to Plymouth, from Cardiff to Carmarthen, carrying with me my trusty Cossorscope. Wherever I went, the local engineer's office provided me with a cable gang who would repair the damaged cable once I had found the fault.

On one never-to-be-forgotten occasion I was called to Paddington station to locate a cable fault. I had to be as sure as humanly possible, and after a number of tests I identified the fault as being too close to the live rail of the Underground. This was an area where British Rail and the Underground Authority shared the tunnel. I checked and checked again, as I would have looked a real idiot if the fault wasn't there, especially since they had to stop all the trains till the repairs were completed. I was relieved when we discovered I was right; the cable had been damaged by an overnight tamping (levelling the ballast) with a crowbar!

Much as I enjoyed my job, after a couple of years I was beginning to feel I was stuck in a rut. I was applying for vacancies in upper management but was constantly being passed over, while sometimes people with fewer qualifications were promoted over my head. This was clearly because I was too useful in cable fault finding, and the department was reluctant to lose me.

Close encounter of the worst kind

Life was good in Reading, where we quickly made friends both from work and the Jewish community, led by our minister, Rev Leo Sichel, and his charming wife, Gertrude. They were a warm and sincere couple, always ready with advice, support and hospitality, and we really valued their friendship. The highlight of our week was the Shabbat service at the Baker Street synagogue, after which many of the worshippers stopped off at the Sichels' home for *kiddush*. Over-generously provided with hot drinks and cake, we enjoyed socialising and listening to Rev Sichel as he spoke about topical Bible themes and moral issues.

However, as we were still newlyweds, we would spend the major festivals with our families in London. The plan for Passover 1972 was to be with my parents for the first and last days, and with Beryl's for the intermediate days. I had taken the week off as part of my annual leave, and Beryl was free as schools were closed for the Easter break.

Easter Monday was the first day on which we could have an outing, and we were on our way to London Zoo, with a detour en route to visit an elderly friend who was in University College Hospital. We had to change lines at Kings Cross station, which involved going down a long escalator. I was standing a couple of steps behind Beryl. We were about halfway down the escalator when I heard a loud clattering behind me. Glancing round, I saw a large metal-bound trunk tumbling down the steps. It had clearly slipped from the grasp of a young man, who was waving wildly to warn me. There was no time to think things through; I just knew that if I stepped aside, the trunk would hit Beryl, send her flying down the escalator, and land on top of her. Instinctively I put my left leg out to stop it...and put a stop to any and all plans for the next three months!

I won't attempt to describe the excruciating agony which shot through me like a lightning bolt. I just about managed to hop off at the bottom of the escalator before virtually passing out, which gave Beryl a terrible fright, as she hadn't been able to see what happened. I must take her word for what happened next, as I was pretty much out of it. The man whose trunk had, as it turned out, broken my leg, was one of a group of soldiers returning to barracks after weekend leave. Very upset on my behalf, they quickly called an ambulance, then gave Beryl their names and contact numbers.

I soon found myself being carried back up the same escalator, and we finished up at the hospital we'd been making for...but not in the way we'd intended (we never did manage to visit our elderly friend, as sadly she died before I was mobile again). By the end of the day my leg was in plaster from thigh to toes, and that's the way it stayed for the next three months.

After Passover, my in-laws drove us back to Reading, and I had an enforced rest from work. I was not allowed back into my office at the Western Tower as I worked on the eighth floor and would have been a liability in case of fire. I spent the time stomping about doing jobs around the house (including sanding and varnishing the kitchen floor while sitting on my behind), and always had a meal ready when Beryl got back from work. I remember making fresh pasta, leaving the strands to dry over a chair-back, and being the first in our family to bake challah for Shabbat.

After doing some research as to my rights, somewhat to my amazement I managed to get compensation for my injury from the British army. I had my qualms about suing the army, since it was thanks to them my leg had been saved when I was a child, but we needed the money! When the plaster finally came off, my leg was a sorry sight: a skinny stick with rhinoceros-like skin. However, with exercise and determination, thankfully I was soon more or less back to normal.

A new life

It was particularly important that I should progress once back at work, because to our delight we were expecting our first child. At that time a pregnant teacher had to leave her job at least eleven weeks before her due date. In our case that due date was in March, so Beryl was to carry on until the end of the autumn term.

While we were getting used to the idea of becoming parents, out of the blue one of our suppliers contacted me with an offer of a senior management position at his new factory, which produced radio communication systems. It took a lot of discussion and agonising before we decided I should accept the job. To their surprise, I gave British Rail a few months' notice (jobs on the railways were regarded as 'for life'). My boss, the head of the local signal and telecom department, became quite concerned about cable fault finding. I promised to train a number of engineers, which I did. I even wrote a handbook, which was still in use when I visited their office some years later.

This new company was situated in Biggleswade, and the nearest town with a shul was Welwyn Garden City, about twenty-five miles from my new job and fifteen miles from London. We took a day off and went there, looking for a house near the shul. We found one not far from Stanborough

Lakes, which boasted an open-air lido set in parkland. We really fell in love with the pretty town.

Crisis at Paddington

On the weekend of our second anniversary, we went to my parents for Shabbat, and then to my in-laws on Saturday night. With them we planned an outing to a popular beauty spot, High Beech in Epping Forest, for the Sunday, followed by a meal at a kosher restaurant. Having agreed on the details for the next day, Beryl and I went to the local cinema. That turned out to be a mistake. The film, an animated cartoon called *Felix the Cat*, had sounded innocent enough, but it turned out to be peppered with really offensive language. After half an hour of these expletives, we gave up in disgust and walked out.

It was just as well. As we walked back into the house I was greeted with, 'Elia, John Stratton phoned. Will you call him back? It sounded urgent.'

John Stratton was the Reading engineering office manager. It had taken him a while to track me down, and he sounded very relieved when I got through to him and asked what the problem was. He explained that there had been a major cable fault on Friday night and the signals were all out of action for about four miles, from Old Oak junction to Paddington station. All the trains had been stopped at Old Oak until early Saturday morning, and there were now only a few signals functioning, from a temporary cable. It was imperative, he said, that I should be at Old Oak early the next morning.

'Of course,' I said, 'just get me my Cossorscope and the box of instruments on top of it, and tell the cable gang to be there at nine.' Then a thought struck me. Since signalling problems could pose a threat to passengers' lives, we had an agreement that if there was an emergency on Shabbat, he would ring me three times in succession and I would answer the call. I asked, ' John, why didn't you call me this morning?'

'What,' he protested, 'and disturb your Sabbath?'

John was such a decent man. In the two years that I was put on standby duty, he did not disturb my Sabbath even once.

I told Beryl what had happened and that it was likely to take most of the day, so they would have to go without me. Even though we were supposed to be celebrating our anniversary, she didn't complain. That's her all over!

I arrived at Old Oak Common at about nine in the morning and was met by John Stratton, the Paddington stationmaster, the chief engineer and a host of other personalities, all looking to me to sort out Paddington station's problems. I hadn't been expecting this reception committee of bigwigs, and it was rather disconcerting. Three or four of them tried to 'assist' me by making all kinds of suggestions. I just did my usual: took my coat off, rolled up my sleeves and got down to business. I surveyed the route of the 900-metre-long cable and used my test equipment to carry out measurements first from one end, then the other.

The readings should have enabled me to calculate the distance to the cable fault. In those days it was not an exact science because a cable can have many faults, and when problems are found they are seldom caused by a clear break. However, I managed to achieve fairly good accuracy, and I knew if the readings from each end coincided, that would pinpoint the fault; if not, I would have to carry out further tests with half the top management breathing down my neck and waiting for results. Not a happy prospect.

What I saw made my jaw drop—the clearest result I had ever seen in all my work thus far. The cable was buried underground except for one spot, according to my reckoning 367 metres from its start, where it surfaced inside a small hut. When we all trudged down to the hut it was immediately obvious what had happened. It had been cold and rainy on Friday evening and someone, possibly a homeless person, had started a fire in there, and bang! Goodbye cable!

Once I had directed the cable gang to repair the cable my job was done, and it was not yet 10 a.m. I phoned Beryl with the good news and got back in time for us to have our outing together after all.

The next day in the office I was congratulated by John Stratton and my other colleagues and told to take the first train to Paddington, where the general manager wanted to see me. There the GM was very kind in his appreciation, and said he was puzzled to hear that I was leaving. When I explained my reasons he understood and said that he would rectify the situation, but it was too late. We had already started the process of moving. I assured him that before leaving I would run a course on cable fault finding, for which he thanked me, and told me that there would always be a job for me at British Rail.

14

Ice cold in Welwyn Garden City

I must admit I was quite sad to be leaving British Rail. I had thoroughly enjoyed my time there, and have sometimes wondered whether I would have done better to stick it out. However, the decision had been made, and we were looking forward to our new life in beautiful Welwyn Garden City, Hertfordshire, with its tree-lined avenues, attractive housing and sparkling fountain at its centre. By the time we moved in, there would be three of us, so we had decided not to waste time selling our Reading home, on which we had managed to pay off the mortgage. For the time being, we arranged to rent it to four police officers for twelve months, which would give us time to settle in to our new home.

In the meantime, there were some minor problems towards the end of the pregnancy. Worried that Beryl would be left alone if I was called away overnight, I persuaded her that, if they were agreeable, we should move in with her parents back in East London and arrange for her to give birth in the local maternity unit. This is in fact what happened. For me the move meant a two-hour journey each way to work, but it was worth it for the peace of mind. I well remember the generosity of one of my colleagues, who insisted on giving me the pram they no longer needed. It was a big, old-fashioned one with two large and two smaller wheels, and I got some very funny looks as I manhandled it from Reading to London, up and down flights of steps, on and off mainline and Underground trains, and finally pushed it for the twenty-minute walk from Upton Park station.

It was worth the effort, as very soon after, two days early on 13 March 1973, Beryl gave birth to our darling Deborah, clearly the most wonderful baby in the world. I was especially proud to welcome her as a fully-fledged British citizen myself, as I had received my naturalisation papers the previous year. After Beryl's then-obligatory ten days in hospital, we stayed in London for another couple of weeks until the baby had settled into some kind of feeding routine, benefiting from the help and advice of my mother-in-law. Then we returned to Reading to begin this new, and exhausting, stage in our lives. When we had decamped to London Beryl's bump had been hardly visible, and several neighbours asked us whose baby it was!

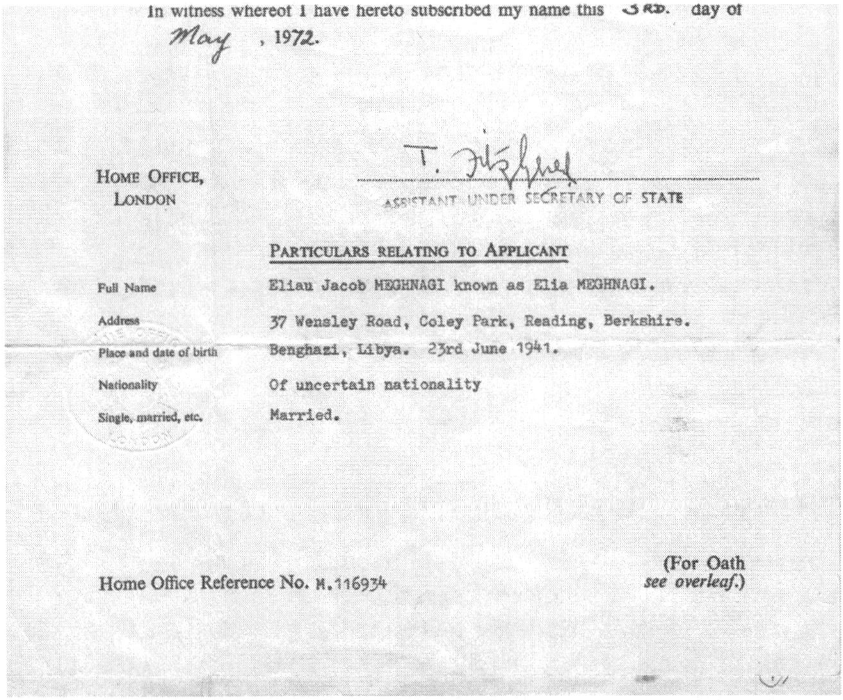

In witness whereof I have hereto subscribed my name this 3RD. day of May, 1972.

HOME OFFICE,
LONDON

ASSISTANT UNDER SECRETARY OF STATE

PARTICULARS RELATING TO APPLICANT

Full Name	Eliau Jacob MEGHNAGI known as Elia MEGHNAGI.
Address	37 Wensley Road, Coley Park, Reading, Berkshire.
Place and date of birth	Benghazi, Libya. 23rd June 1941.
Nationality	Of uncertain nationality
Single, married, etc.	Married.

Home Office Reference No. M.116934

(For Oath *see overleaf*.)

Part of my naturalisation document, stating that I was 'of uncertain nationality'. Beryl says, quite truthfully, that she married an alien.

Our moving date was 13 December, the day Deborah was nine months old. The journey from Reading to Welwyn Garden City was awkward by train, so Clem kindly gave us a lift, following behind the removal van. He left straight away to get back to work, so couldn't help when the first thing we discovered was that the previous owners had removed every single light bulb in the house. I quickly became friendly with our new neighbours and borrowed a few bulbs while it was still light enough to fit them.

The next problem was that the house was freezing cold. The central heating came from a gas back boiler in the lounge, but I simply could not see how to light the pilot. I had to bother the neighbours again to use their phone. I called the Gas Board but was told no one would be available until mid-January. If only we two adults had been affected we would probably have gritted our teeth, wrapped ourselves up, and waited, but the bitter cold was a health hazard to a baby. I had only one recourse: assuring Beryl that I would DO SOMETHING, I left the house and went to the nearby telephone box I had seen, to call the Gas Board again (I couldn't bring myself to disturb the neighbours yet again, and in any case I didn't want them to hear me embroidering the truth). This time, I reported that I thought I could smell gas coming from 56 Marsden Green. I was told that they would send an engineer to check as a matter of urgency. I rushed back to the house and shortly opened the door to a friendly young man who proceeded to prowl around searching for a gas leak…which of course he couldn't find.

Just as he was packing up his tools, I casually asked him if he knew how to light the boiler, and he was happy to show me and make sure I could do it myself. I did offer to pay whatever the charge might be, but he just waved me off with a 'Happy Christmas,' and left us to gradually warm up. I must say I'm not usually devious, but sometimes needs must!

Licences, provisional and otherwise

I had been given a week to sort myself out before starting my new job, and first on the list was finding a way to make the twenty-five-mile journey. I had taken driving lessons while at college, but had failed the test because my instructor had warned me the examiner would make a note of every mistake. Well, he was scribbling as soon as I got in the car, and well into the test, so I thought I had made a hash of it and simply gave up. Afterwards I was told that both bad and good points were noted, but by then it was too late. While I was with BR it hadn't seemed worth driving since I had free travel, though they had sent me and a few colleagues on a week's residential driving course, culminating in a test. The trouble was we were given very little actual driving time, and not one of us passed. However, I had been riding a bicycle for years and was used to being on the roads, so I obtained a motorbike licence, a motorbike and crash helmet. It wasn't a very pleasant way to travel in wintry conditions, and I would arrive home half frozen, in spite of the plastic suit Beryl made me, but I managed for a few months.

In the spring I applied to the Driver and Vehicle Licensing Centre (now DVLA, Licensing Agency) to add a provisional licence for a car to the provisional one I already had for a motorbike, intending to take driving lessons. When the envelope arrived, it contained my provisional bike licence, as expected, but incredibly there was also a full driving licence for a car! Unbelievable! I already had my eye on a little car, and this meant that ostensibly I could 'legally' drive to work and back unaccompanied.

Predictably, Beryl's sensible reaction was, 'I hope you don't think we're getting in a car with you until you've passed your test,' and of course I fully intended to do so, but this lucky break allowed me to get in plenty of practice beforehand.

In fact, taking the test was a bit of a gamble. Having no instructor with me, I would have a problem getting home if I failed. The nearest test centre was in the small town of Hitchin, notorious for its tight bends and blind corners, negotiable only by using the mirrors provided by the local council. Still, if I wanted to take my family for a spin, I had to chance it. By this time Beryl was again pregnant, and teaching English part time at a nearby college. When she mentioned to the students that her husband was taking his driving test that afternoon in Hitchin, they all chorused, 'He'll fail!' Mercifully, though, I managed to keep my head, and was mightily relieved to hear the words, 'I'm pleased to tell you…'. The examiner had looked somewhat askance at my full licence, but I just raised my eyebrows to indicate I was being honest, and thank goodness it paid off. We were now mobile. Freedom at last!

We took a drive to London to see our families. Our Fiat 500 was perfect for our needs, and I enjoyed the much easier drive to work. We certainly made good use of that little Fiat. We drove round the beauty spots in Welwyn, Hatfield and Hitchin, and even visited the home of George Bernard Shaw in the charming village of Ayot St. Lawrence.

Family expansion

On 14 April 1975 we welcomed another delightful daughter, Naomi. We were very happy for Deborah to have a little companion (though she was not too sure about it initially; the first time she saw Naomi being nursed, she yanked her off by her hair and exclaimed, 'Don't you dare do that to my Mummy!'). We felt that, even if we did not go on to have more children, our little family was complete.

We had become regular worshippers at Welwyn Garden's shul as soon as we moved into the area. We became friendly with the congregants, including the president, who realised we were an Orthodox couple and reasonably knowledgeable about Judaism. A little while after Naomi was born, he asked if I would set up Sunday morning Hebrew classes for the children, a challenge I was happy to take on. I appointed both Beryl and the president's teenage daughter, Jacqueline, as teachers alongside me. Somehow we managed to take our two children with us, with Beryl retiring to the kitchen in the early days to feed Naomi during the break, and Deborah happily occupied with colouring books. Jacqueline stayed with us until she left for university, after which we lost touch. (Some nine years and two more children later I joined my family at the kosher hotel in Bournemouth where they had been staying while I was working abroad. Among the crowd after the Shabbat service I was delighted to see Jacqueline, and also a young man called Alan Shaw, whom I had met at conferences for Hebrew teachers. It occurred to me that they would make a good match, and I was nudging Beryl to introduce them to each other when she pointed at the ring on Jacqueline's finger. They were there on their honeymoon. Well, I was right! Today I am pleased to say that Rev Dr Alan Shaw and Jacqueline live not far from us, and we have remained good friends.

Another move

A few weeks after joining the new company, I realised my timing had been bad. Britain had got itself mired in a major economic crisis, and it had not been the right time to have left one of the most secure jobs in the country. Shortage of coal owing to the miners going on a 'no overtime' strike caused power blackouts, and chaos to the industry. On the day we moved to Welwyn Garden City, the prime minister, Edward Heath, declared a three-day working week. This lasted for months, causing untold damage to the economy. Eventually this toppled Heath, resulting in the election of Margaret Thatcher as the country's first woman prime minister.

The 'lady not for turning' took on the miners head on: the irresistible force, Thatcher, against the immovable object, Arthur Scargill, head of the Miners' Union. The end result was a defeat for the miners that killed the mining industry, weakened the economy, and eventually brought 'Maggie' down.

The three-day week caused big problems for the company I had joined. Although they hung on for a while, after I had been there a year or so, they were forced to reduce staff. Since the work I had ended up doing was not something I had much experience with, I accepted redundancy.

I called an agency called Capital Appointments, specialising in engineering jobs. Its director, Maurice Wayne, agreed to take my details over the phone, and we went through the usual information. He then asked me if I was in good health, to which I replied, 'Thank God'. After a short pause, he said, 'May I ask if you're Jewish?' When I confirmed that I was, and wondered what made him ask, he said it was usually Jewish clients who answered in that way. Having completed the formalities, we started chatting on a more personal level, and discovered that he and Beryl came from the same part of London. His late father had been a warden in the shul she had attended every Shabbat before we were married, and had regularly invited anyone passing his house on their way home for *kiddush* and cake. Beryl had fond memories of these gatherings, where she had met Maurice and his future wife, Deirdra. The Jewish world is full of such coincidences.

Maurice found me a job with a London-based company called PPD, which dealt with pump systems. This was not my area of expertise, so I thought it would probably not be long term, but having it gave us the impetus to move to North West London, which we needed to do anyway in order to get our daughters and any future children into a Jewish school. The little nursery school Deborah had attended in Welwyn Garden was fine, but we felt she was ready for some religious input. We had already managed to find a suitable house, and had just moved in when I started my new job. She started attending the nursery attached to Mill Hill Synagogue, but would ultimately need to transfer to primary school.

Finding a school with the right Jewish values was important to us, so we attended an open evening at Rosh Pinah Primary, in Edgware. This would have been a long walk from our house in Mill Hill, (Beryl didn't drive at the time) but our kind neighbour Gitta Zarum already had children there, and offered to give Deborah a lift if she got in.

At the meeting, Rev Saul Amias, the school's founder and honorary principal, stressed that the school was oversubscribed. Once a child was accepted, he explained, any siblings would automatically be given a place, but acceptance would be on a 'names out of a hat' basis. Hating to be pushy, but feeling I had no choice, I later spoke to him quietly and explained that we had moved house specially for the sake of Jewish education and really couldn't rely on such a hit-and-miss system. At this he made a note of our name and told me not to worry. Sure enough, a while later we received a letter of acceptance, and I clearly remember Deborah jumping up and down and singing, 'Now I can go to Rosh Pinah, and Naomi, and the baby in Mummy's tummy!' Yes, another little Meghnagi was on the way.

A devastating loss

We were perfectly happy with our two lovely girls, but this time I was hoping for a boy, for a very sad reason. On Rosh Hashanah 1976 my beloved father had died, after a massive heart attack, and we thought we could give a boy his name, Yaakov. We had been worried about my father's health for some time, as there had already been two mild attacks a few months apart. His job was tiring, and his home life often stressful because of my mother's mental problems. Still, a routine check-up just days before we arrived for the two-day festival had shown no cause for concern, so we were looking forward to being with the family. Only Clem would not be there: he had married his American girlfriend, Miriam, the previous year, and they were with her parents in New York for the festival.

The first evening went well, but during the night we were woken by my mother's desperate cries. Rushing upstairs, we found my father suffering agonising chest pains, and immediately called an ambulance. Leaving a distraught Yvette to keep an eye on our sleeping children, Beryl and I went in the ambulance, and once at the hospital were left to pace anxiously while my father was wheeled away. Well over an hour later a young doctor came to say there was nothing to be done. In a daze we followed him, to see my father still lying unattended on the same trolley, in the corridor. I am still convinced that he could have been saved if they had got to him more quickly, but nothing we could do would bring him back. Shocked and disbelieving, we started the long walk home, dreading having to break the news. The reaction was every bit as bad as you would expect, and we still had to tell Clem that our beloved Pa had gone. He was just sixty-four.

It was all a nightmare. There can be no funerals on a festival, so by the time they can be held again there tends to be a backlog. To make a bad situation even worse, of all things there was a gravediggers' strike at the time. Desperate to show my father due reverence by giving him the quick burial required by Jewish law, I drove like a maniac to the office of the Spanish and Portuguese Synagogue (with Beryl trying to calm me down), only to be told it would take at least a week. Unheard of. Only thanks to the generous intervention of the Ashkenazi Kedassia organisation were we able to have the funeral as soon as Clem flew back.

Months later, anticipating our third child while still reeling from my father's death, I was glad that, boy or girl, there would be more than two of them to comfort each other when the sad time came for our children to mourn a parent.

It's a cliché to say that life goes on, but clichés have their basis in truth, and I still had to earn a living. Since I regarded my job at PPD as a stop gap, I even considered returning to the railways. I actually went to visit my old office, and was pleased to find the engineers were still using my book on cable fault finding. They would have been happy to have me back, but moving back to Reading would have meant no Jewish schools, so there was not much point.

Just like most other companies, PPD was going through hard times, and I heard that they were laying off some staff. One of my colleagues, a man in his late fifties, had been selected for redundancy, and it was obvious that his chances of getting another job at his age were extremely remote. I didn't see myself lasting long in a job I wasn't enjoying, so I offered to stand down in his place. At the same time, I entered my details into a government-sponsored jobseekers' site for engineers. I was still working out my notice when one evening I received a phone call that changed my life completely. The head of the signalling department of GEC-General Signals, a subsidiary of the major conglomerate GEC (General Electric Company) invited me to interview for a new position. It sounded just up my street, as the English say.

15

General Electric Company

Those who know me will confirm that I'm an easy-going person, but one thing I'm very particular about is being punctual. My meeting with the head of the signalling department of GEC-General Signals was so important to me that I actually arrived there an hour early. I wanted time to find out more about the company, with which I had had some dealings when I worked for the railways. I learned that the name was derived from the fact that the company was 50 per cent owned by GEC, and 50 per cent by the General Railway Signal Company (GRS) of America. That pleased me; I liked the idea of working for a multinational company. An added bonus would be that their very modern offices were in Borehamwood, just a fifteen-minute drive from our home.

Mr Waller, who had called me for the interview, explained that so far most of the work carried out by his department involved installing new signalling systems for British Rail, which was in the process of modernisation. Previously, contracts had been given either to GEC or to Westinghouse, but now these two major companies had to compete for orders with others. This meant that in order to stay relevant, the company wanted to expand into overseas projects, which would include tenders for telecom as well as signalling systems.

He sounded me out on my ability to form a small section with the task of preparing tenders for telecom. Since my work with BR had included dealing with suppliers, I confirmed that I would be delighted to undertake the suppliers' end of these projects. After a discussion of other roles I had taken with BR and elsewhere, and an agreement about my Sabbath observance, he offered me the job. Jubilation!

By this time I was free to start a new job, so the following Monday I arrived at the GEC offices. I was assigned a desk in the technical department, and was made a member of what was called the Officers' Club. This gave access to refreshment facilities for senior personnel and their business guests. My new colleague in personnel took my details and explained the work rules, including an entitlement to eighteen days paid sick leave per annum. That being the case, I promptly asked if I could take the next three days off as part of my sick leave. We all had a laugh, and that broke the ice with the personnel department. On my way out I nearly laughed again when I saw the accountant's name plate on his desk: A.S. WINDLE. No wonder he's the accountant, I thought.

I had been easing myself into the new job for a few weeks when there was another new beginning, this time in our personal life. On 1 August 1977 our third child was born, and was indeed the hoped-for boy. We would not normally have mentioned possible names to anyone before the circumcision, but it happened that my father-in-law's name was also Yaakov, so we asked how he would feel about our son having that name. To say he objected is putting it mildly! Sephardi Jews such as myself often name babies in honour of a living person, but he was an Ashkenazi Jew, and their custom is to name babies in memory of people who are no longer living. He felt that giving the baby his name was tantamount to wishing him dead, and no amount of reasoning on our part would budge him. We were still agonising over what to do literally ten minutes before the circumcision, when Beryl was giving the baby a quick feed to make him sleepy. We finally decided not to sour a celebration by making it into a family feud, but what to call this baby? Luckily, inspiration struck: after two daughters, I suggested the name Reuben, which means 'Look, a son.' So that's what we called him.

Life at my new job was pretty hectic because our office was getting lots of tenders from all over the world and we had to decide which ones to go for. We knew perfectly well that many tenders were not worth the paper they were written on; they were already earmarked for a particular manufacturer, but the clients were going through the motions in order to get a better price, or simply to prove to the relevant authorities that they had tried other manufacturers. We all understood the game, but it still gave us plenty of work.

After a couple of years working on small projects, my remit was expanded to include costings, researching cheaper alternatives, and working on major projects. At GEC the directors used to appoint a person in charge who would select a team of engineers to prepare the tender. At least once a month the managing director would call the team to a board meeting to discuss progress and any problems with the tenders. I thoroughly enjoyed these sessions where the directors gave all of us a thorough grilling in order to arrive at the best and most economical solution.

After about a year of this work, the managing director sent for me and invited me to join the sales team. He had noticed that at the board meetings I always took note of the cost of projects. I was happy to do this, but when

I asked, 'So who will be handling the engineering?' the answer was, 'You will.'

So I ended up doing two jobs. This meant that when an enquiry landed on my desk, I had to identify the best suppliers for every part that made up the system, both within GEC and other companies in the UK, and abroad. I had to get the best quality at the best price, while making sure it met or was closest to the specifications. Furthermore, I had to prepare my costing for parts, labour and installation, plus expenses covering travel, hotel, and even the cost of borrowing to finance the project, the company's overheads, the overseas agent's fees, and finally our company's profits. When all that was done, I had to prepare a schedule of manufacturing time, installation and, finally, testing and, if required, training. On top of all this I had to prepare myself for the monthly board meetings, where some dozen directors and engineers would dissect my presentation of work done so far and happily try to tear it to pieces.

All this was a tall order, but I did have plenty of assistance. This came partly from within our parent company, GEC, which was then a huge conglomerate employing some 250,000 people and manufacturing a large variety of products in the UK and overseas, and which owned such renowned subsidiaries as Marconi. In addition, I also received help from some of our suppliers. Despite the pressure I thoroughly enjoyed it all, especially since I had built an excellent relationship with the managing director himself, Tom Cunningham, better known as TPC. TPC really was a great managing director. He expected a lot from his staff, but he made sure we were well rewarded.

On overseas trips to meet with clients I sometimes had the support of directors and other engineers who came with me as a backup. On particularly important occasions TPC himself would come along, and then he would relax his usual aloofness and become very chummy. On these occasions he would be generous in the hotel bar, ordering food and drinks which were put on my bill (even though I could not actually partake, since it wasn't kosher). The logic behind this was simple: he was the one who approved my expenses, whereas his own expenses went to GEC head office for approval.

On one of these visits, when he had drunk a bit more than usual, he confided that he had been sent to a boarding school and had rarely seen his parents, who were usually abroad. He went on to say that the school had made him tough and successful, but when I asked him if he had been a happy child, the bleak expression on his face told me everything I needed to know. Soon after that, he left the bar.

I spent over ten years doing this work, and some of the more interesting overseas projects still stand out in my memory. I travelled all over the world, representing GEC and organising lectures and exhibitions. Flying and working alongside important and successful businessmen, it was hard to think of myself as being in their league: somehow I had made the transition from fugitive, to refugee, to British businessman.

On a short trip to Paris with just one colleague, I remarked that it would be nice if we could take our wives with us: they could see the sights during the day, and we could all meet up in the evenings. I thought he was joking when he replied, 'Who wants to eat sandwiches when they can go to a restaurant?' However, some time later it became apparent that he had been serious, and had treated his wife accordingly: returning from a longish trip abroad, he found a suitcase packed with his clothes on the doorstep of his home, and discovered he couldn't open the door as the lock had been changed.

Over the years I went on various trips abroad, on fact-finding missions, to organise and attend training and exhibitions, and for consultation with our partners in GRS of Rochester, USA. At a technical meeting in Rome, with Marconi Italiana, then a part of the GEC Group, I had the pleasure of awakening my dormant Italian. Although the discussions were conducted in English, during the coffee and lunch breaks I took full advantage of my knowledge of the hosts' language, to my pleasure and theirs. We soon built up a pleasant atmosphere of camaraderie and trust. I was fascinated how for so many technical expressions English was used, but with an Italian twist. For example, when one of them said, '*Il problema, non abbiamo il no-au*' I realised that he had said, 'the problem is, we don't have the know-how.' Ah, I thought, so that's how they say it!

On one occasion, my penchant for puns got me in trouble. TPC came into the Sales office and asked loudly if anyone could speak Portuguese. I jokingly replied, 'I can speak very poor-tuguese.' Whereupon he turned and said, 'You'll do. You're going to Lisbon. This actually turned out to be a fact-finding visit to learn more about a large railway contract in Recife, Brazil, but I did not have a chance to take part in that project, as I became involved in the Tel Aviv Metro, the Hong Kong Maglev, and the Seoul Metro project. I really relished the prospects of trips to Israel for the Tel Aviv Metro but unfortunately for me, GEC decided not to get involved for fear of losing the much larger Saudi Arabia railway contract. I did get involved in the Seoul Metro and help GEC win a share in the contract, for which I was presented with a commemorative plaque.

Caracas Metro

One day sometime in 1978, when I had been working at GEC for about three years, TPC dropped a large file on my desk. It contained the specifications for a new metro in Caracas, Venezuela. GEC had been asked to bid for the telecom system. The company with overall responsibility for implementation of the system was Bechtel of the United States, and they in turn had put out the tender internationally. It was a most interesting project, not the first one in South America for GEC; we had been working on a major railway signalling scheme in Recife, Brazil.

One of the elements in this Caracas specification called for a continuous telephonic link system between the cab (train) driver and the signal box. The request was for a wired system called a loop, despite the fact that the more modern wireless system (known as the leaky feeder) was more easily available and more economical. I had great difficulty in finding a manufacturer for the wired system until I finally discovered that the specification was written round the system used by the Paris Metro. Their engineering department put me in touch with their supplier, a company called Alberthal of Thionville, in the north east of France. I asked my assistant to call Alberthal and ask if they had heard of the Caracas Metro project, and Monsieur Alberthal confirmed that the specification was written round their system. He invited me to visit them so they could take me to see the Paris Metro system operating.

My assistant was on the phone sorting out arrangements for my visit when I caught the word 'lunch'. I didn't usually bother to mention my food restrictions, preferring to simply avoid eating at meetings altogether, but for some reason this time I said, 'Please tell him not to worry about lunch, as I only eat kosher.' Imagine my reaction when my assistant told me, 'Monsieur Alberthal says he also only eats kosher.' At this point I grabbed the phone myself and delightedly agreed on the arrangements for the following week.

Luxembourg being the closest airport to Thionville, Monsieur Alberthal picked me up from there and took me to my hotel. The next day he took me to the local shul, where I was warmly welcomed as the *minyan* man (he who completes the ten-man quorum needed for a full service). After the service we visited the factory and then drove to Paris to visit the Metro. We agreed that Monsieur Alberthal would follow up with a quotation for a complete system, including installation and training.

During a discussion over lunch in a kosher restaurant, I learned that his company had in fact been taken over by a Jewish charity which put all its profits towards Jewish education in France. He added that the head of the charity was intrigued that there was an engineer from GEC London who only ate kosher food, and asked if I would mind meeting him. Of course I was happy to oblige, so we stopped off on our way back to the airport. As we walked into the office, a bearded guy looked up, leapt to his feet and exclaimed, 'Elia!'

Of all people, the charity head had been a fellow student at Gateshead!

Nor did the coincidences end there. While swapping family histories with Monsieur Alberthal, he told me that his daughter had worked as secretary to Herbert Pagani, who was my mother's cousin! I dined out on stories of that trip for years to come.

Once we finished preparing our bid for the Caracas Metro, I sent it to Bechtel and waited. We didn't think we had much of a chance because the whole specification seemed to follow the French system, which was not commonly used. Even so, we felt we had to make a bid in order to signal our entry into the overseas Metro business.

A few months later we learned that, as expected, our French competitors had won the contract. I took a two-week seaside break with the family, and on my return a colleague pointed out an advert in the *Daily Telegraph*. Bechtel were seeking an engineer to manage the telecom part of the Caracas Metro project. I had spent so much time and effort on this that I felt I should have a go at it. If by some remote chance I got the job it would mean a major upheaval in our lives, involving leaving family and friends and relocating to Venezuela, but Beryl agreed I should at least try, and see what happened.

However, the deadline for applications was the following day. I called Bechtel and explained that I had been in charge of the GEC bid and would love to apply for the vacancy, but had only just seen the advert. I offered to take my application to them in person, unless they would be kind enough to take my details over the phone.

I actually thought this was pretty cheeky on my part, and was surprised and pleased when we went ahead with a question and answer session so that he could fill in the form then and there. That done, he invited me for an interview on the following Monday. Naturally I agreed, and spent most of Sunday reviewing the telecoms system specifications. At the interview I was fully genned up, and decided that the best tactic was to go on the offensive. I asked their technical director why they had decided to use an outdated system. I acknowledged that it had a good track record on the Paris Metro, but then held forth for some time, explaining the advantages of the more modern leaky feeder system. (For the technically minded, this is a special type of coaxial cable laid alongside the length of the track which is designed to 'leak' the speech signal at regular intervals so that there is continuous communication not only between the driver and the signalman, but also the train staff, inspectors and security personnel.)

Then, in response to his questions, I outlined the work I had been doing at GEC General Signals. After all this he got up, held out his hand, and calmly said, 'Congratulations, you have the job. Welcome to Bechtel.'

I couldn't find the words.

Salary, expenses, medical cover, etc., would shortly be explained, but in the meantime he offered me two business class air tickets to Caracas for a week's stay in a hotel at Bechtel's expense. This was so that Beryl and I could find an apartment and enrol our two older children in the American School (baby Reuben was six months old at the time). It also appeared that Beryl would be in great demand as an English teacher in Caracas, and domestic help would be easy to find.

He explained that the contract was initially for four years in Caracas, after which I would have the option to move to their headquarters in San Francisco. I was told that my generous salary would be paid into an investment bank, because the expenses they paid would be more than adequate to fund a decent standard of living.

It looked as if our financial future was secure. We had always saved the salary Beryl earned from the various teaching positions she took between babies, but childcare was not cheap. My own earnings were by now very respectable, but I still had to pay the mortgage on my mother's house, and school fees were quite high and likely to become higher.

By her own admission Beryl could hardly be called adventurous, but she surprised me by her enthusiasm; she was as excited as I. We felt it was a good time to make such a move, while the children were still very young and adaptable. They were likely to pick up Spanish fairly easily, and there was a strong Jewish community there with its own religion classes. With Italian as my first language, I was well placed to learn Spanish, and Beryl felt that her A-level French and Latin would be helpful. We had a few months before I had to take up my position, so we had time to prepare. We both started listening to Spanish tapes, and Beryl bought a few dresses suited to the hotter climate. All of us except the baby had jabs against various tropical diseases (he got his dose through his mother's milk), which was in fact quite traumatic. We were all vaccinated at the same time, which turned out to be rather unwise, as our reaction to the vaccinations was unpredictable. Beryl and the girls suffered very painful arms for some two weeks afterwards, to the extent that Beryl tied a ribbon round the girls' affected arms so they would remember not to touch each other there. I was actually very ill for a few days. I remember dragging myself into work feeling ghastly, but I couldn't tell them why because I hadn't yet said I would be leaving.

Nevertheless this soon passed, and we were getting ready to embark on our new adventure. However, they say that if something seems too good to be true, it probably is, and so it proved to be.

All this had happened quite quickly, and I hadn't said anything to my family until I was sure it was settled. When I did tell my siblings, they were happy for my sake. They were all working and self-sufficient, and were quite prepared to look after our mother, who was on medication, but her mental state was still precarious, especially since the sudden death of my father. I knew she would probably be upset, but I was not prepared for how upset she was when I did tell her. When she heard we were going, she completely went to pieces. She took an overdose, and had to be admitted to intensive care. I had had no idea she would react so drastically. Rightly or wrongly, I was the one she relied on and, feeling that she was losing me for good, she didn't want to go on.

I reported this very worrying development to Bechtel's personnel officer, who couldn't have been more sympathetic. He even said the company would pay for her to accompany us to Venezuela, but I couldn't see that uprooting my mother, whose move from Libya to England had precipitated her mental decline, would do anyone any good, least of all her.

I returned to the Bechtel office to tell them why I had to turn down the job, and also to return the airline tickets they had given us. The personnel officer was surprised that we hadn't taken advantage of the free trip, and was impressed when I said we wouldn't dream of doing so once we knew we had no intention of moving there. To me this was just the natural way to behave, but I suppose experience must have taught him otherwise. He was kind enough to say that they were sorry I wouldn't be joining them, adding that if my circumstances changed there would always be a job waiting for me.

Life went on in its usual routine, but we were feeling somewhat deflated as the exciting prospect of Caracas disappeared. We packed away the 'Learn Spanish' tapes and the new dresses that would probably be too flimsy for English summer weather. We consoled ourselves with the knowledge that we would still be within easy reach of family and friends…and at least we weren't likely to get cholera, typhoid, yellow fever or blackwater fever!

It was just as well that we made the decision we did, and stayed within reach of my mother. Over the ensuing years her mental health deteriorated further. She never actually became senile, but she was often confused and sometimes unreasonable. This could be very difficult, both for her and for us, but the situation did occasionally have its funny side. Once, she called me in the middle of the night. I managed to fumble the phone from my bedside table and, through my yawns, half-listened to her chatting away while I gave occasional monosyllabic replies.

Suddenly she paused and said, very sharply, 'You sound tired. Why do you sound tired?'

As gently as possible I reminded her what time it was. Beryl couldn't understand why I then burst out laughing, until I explained afterwards that Ma had protested, 'What are you doing up at half past three in the morning?'

I remained in my position at GEC and carried on as usual, working long hours and occasionally globetrotting. By the summer of 1979 Beryl and I were at rather a low ebb after a draining couple of years. The exciting prospect of a transatlantic move followed by the trauma of my mother's drastic reaction was not the only thing we had to cope with. We had been expecting another baby, but very sadly in November 1978 Beryl had miscarried at five months, when Deborah and Naomi were old enough to understand and Reuben was just toddling. After such a draining year, Beryl and I agreed that our batteries needed recharging, both physically and spiritually, and so we booked a holiday in Israel with the three children and, thankfully once again, 'one in Mummy's tummy'. We had been invited to stay with my father's brother, Moshe. He was very hospitable, but his small apartment was very humid, and we all had to sleep in one bed. Using the pregnancy as an excuse so as not to upset him, I contacted my dear friend Mumu, whom I hadn't seen in over a decade. He quickly found us an apartment to rent, in a block by the sea in Bat Yam. There was no air conditioning, but the wide spaces between blocks meant that we got a through breeze. We were dismayed to see there was no fridge, but without being asked Mumu brought us one. We had a wonderful holiday, if at times a queasy one in Beryl's case. We relaxed on the beach, saw some sights, and visited some of my relatives, who feted us like royalty.

Caracas was almost forgotten until one day when we were walking through the famous Machane Yehuda street market in Jerusalem. I noticed a man waving at us from a nearby bus stop. Recognising him as a friend from Gateshead, I hustled the family across the road to greet him. After embracing him warmly and making introductions, I asked what he was doing with himself. The answer was too ridiculous, but entirely true: 'I'm here on holiday,' he told us with a smile, 'but I'm actually the chief rabbi of Caracas.'

Medellin Metro

Once back at the office, tanned and refreshed, I found a large envelope on my desk marked MEDELLIN METRO. All I knew about Medellin, a city in Colombia, was that it was the capital of the illicit drug trade. In the envelope was a file containing a study for the plausibility of a metro system for this notorious city, which was making huge efforts to industrialise. It included plans for the metro and an invitation from the mayor for a presentation and a tour. I was in mid-read when TPC sent for me to tell me that I'd better go home early as the next day I'd be flying to Bogota. I'd be met by a Colombian associate, Carlos Moreno, and together we would fly on to Medellin.

I was usually given rather more notice than that, but Beryl and the children had (mostly) adapted to switching to 'Daddy's away' gear. I took the file home for bedtime reading. I had never realised what a beautiful city Medellin was: luscious, modern and classy. The city's mayor was inviting international companies involved in metro construction to visit the town to learn about the project and collect the tender documents. It was obvious to me that we needed to join a British consortium to include various GEC and Marconi companies as well as, possibly, GRS of the USA.

I arrived in Medellin on Wednesday, and was going to be there over Shabbat. The hotel receptionist warned me that it was dangerous to venture far from the central square after about 8 p.m. I asked if by any chance there was a synagogue nearby, and was delighted to see from their map that there was one within easy walking distance.

When I arrived there on Shabbat morning, I found it was part of an active social centre which was in the process of being rebuilt. Seeing a visitor, the president of the Jewish community welcomed me, handing me his card and urging me to call him if I needed anything. By a lucky chance my hotel was Jewish-owned and kosher, serving only fish meals, so I hadn't been going hungry, but I was hoping I might be able to find kosher meat for a change. He told me that this was difficult, as it had to be flown in from Bogota.

I went back to the shul for afternoon prayers, and asked him about the origins of the Jewish community of Medellin. He told me a fascinating story; the usual tale of Jews needing to escape persecution, in this case by the Catholic Church, which was trying to convert them. They had faced the choice of expulsion from Spain, or death.

Medellin = Modi'in?

What is the connection between Medellin (pronounced Medeyin) in Colombia, and Modi'in, in Israel? From the late fifteenth century onwards the Jewish communities of Spain and Portugal were subjected to the terrible persecution of the Spanish Inquisition, established by the monarchy and vigorously supported by the Church. The Jews, who had reached a very high standard of living and had become an essential element in the Iberian peninsula's economy, were given a heartbreaking choice: conversion or expulsion. Tens of thousands chose to leave, having had all their possessions confiscated. Those who remained to become ostensibly Christian were known by the degrading name 'Marranos' (possibly from the Arabic *muharram*, forbidden, referring to pigs), or *conversos*. Needless to say, the Church never trusted the sincerity of these forcibly-converted Jews, and the Inquisition continued to hound them, all too often condemning them to be burned at the stake.

Of those who left, the majority went to other parts of Europe, Turkey and North Africa, where they were welcomed, but a large number went to South America, including Bogota, the capital of Colombia. Although it was under direct Spanish rule, there the Jewish community thrived for a time, until the Inquisition started hunting them down even there. Tradition holds that, weary of living in constant fear, a number of families loaded everything they had onto wagons and set off with their cattle and horses, much in the style of American pioneers. They moved up the Andes Mountains until they eventually found a beautiful, sheltered valley, where they settled to build their homes and schools. They called this settlement Modi'in, in memory of the Maccabees, who came from the town of Modi'in in ancient Judea, and who had defeated the Syrian-Greek leader Antiochus when he tried to wipe out Judaism in the Holy Land. The surrounding wilderness they called Antiochia.

Today the name Modi'in has morphed into Medellin, and the province is Antioquia. I was told that many citizens of Medellin used to keep both a cross and a menorah, either at home or in their cars. I found this tale almost unbelievable, but when I took a taxi to the airport I noticed that the driver had a cross affixed to one side of his dashboard, and a menorah to the other. When I asked him what the menorah meant to him, he replied that he didn't know its significance, but it had been in his family for generations.

Mexico City

Every time I was away I missed my family, and spent as much time with them as possible when at home. The children were growing fast, and it was hard for me to miss stages in their development (though harder for Beryl, frequently having to cope alone). Wherever I went I brought back toys and clothes, some of which are still being worn by our grandchildren. I also brought back any exotic fruits I found, plus jewellery, including on one occasion a matching pendant and bracelet in smoked topaz for Beryl, without knowing it was her birthstone. On one occasion I presented Beryl with an elegant black chiffon evening gown. She held it up, smiled sweetly, then said, 'Thank you, but I'm afraid this really isn't my style; it's for the tall, willowy blonde you wish I were.' That still makes us laugh (and anyway, I don't wish that; apart from anything else, that would make her taller than me!).

Our very welcome number four, Judith, was born on 10 March 1980, a seventh birthday present for Deborah. In July 1980, Tom Cunningham called me to say that he had put my name forward to join a government-organised fact-finding trade delegation to Mexico City. Delegates from twenty of the top companies in the UK would be going, and he wanted me there to represent GEC-GS. The mission was for a week, Sunday to Sunday; I was expected to bring back information about the Mexican economy and any possible openings for GEC-GS. I was chosen because I understood some Spanish, and because I could represent both the sales and engineering departments of the company.

I remember that as I packed for the trip I was worried that our most recent addition, who was only four months old, wouldn't remember me when I got back (I needn't have worried, as it transpired, as the excited waving of her little arms and legs upon my return proved). Our group occupied most of Business Class on the Pan Am flight. After a pleasant journey with a five-hour stopover in Miami I arrived in Mexico City but, as it turned out, my luggage did not! After a long wait and much form filling it transpired that my luggage had been sent to New York. This was a problem, as I needed smart clothing for business meetings and had no idea when my case would arrive. The staff were very understanding, and I was able to buy what I needed at the airline's expense (the case arrived two days after we did, on Tuesday).

We spent the week travelling around visiting various manufacturers and industrial units, as well as the Aztec pyramids of Teotihuacán, just outside Mexico city, and other tourist attractions. Unfortunately for my colleagues, every morning a number of them had to forgo the day's programme as they were laid low by food poisoning. By the end of the week I was the only one not to have suffered the indignity of being on the receiving end of this Montezuma's Revenge. Thanks to my kosher, albeit boring, diet of fruit, hard-boiled eggs and tinned tuna, I was spared.

All the same, I was a bit anxious about getting a proper kosher meal for Shabbat, and when my daily phone calls to the only listed kosher restaurant in Mexico City came to nothing, by Wednesday I resorted to calling a local shul. I explained to the rabbi, David Masri, that I was having trouble ordering food, and he told me he would deal with it; I was to call him the next day. I had a very long day on Thursday and thought it was too late to call when I got back to my hotel, but he had left a message saying to phone, however late, so we spoke after eleven that night.

'Right,' he instructed, 'tomorrow you're going to my mother for lunch. In the evening you're coming to me for dinner. For Shabbat lunch, we're all going to my mother. And after Shabbat, I'll take you on a tour of the city.' My protestations about not wanting to cause all this bother fell on deaf ears, though Rabbi Masri reluctantly conceded that as I was going out of town the next day, I couldn't accept the generous offer for Friday lunch.

On Friday morning a group of us were meeting a representative of the British Embassy at a very big industrial centre well outside of Mexico City. It was an all-day programme, so I arranged to meet Rabbi Masri at the shul for the evening service.

By late afternoon I started to become concerned about the approach of Shabbat, since we were still on site miles from Mexico City. I explained the situation to our host, and instead of calling me a cab, as I had requested, he kindly put a car and driver at my disposal. I showed the driver the address of the shul, and off we went.

After about an hour's drive there were still two miles to go, and the darkening sky showed it was nearly Shabbat. I asked the driver to stop, and got out. I would have to walk the rest of the way. He insisted on driving very slowly alongside me (to the irritation of the other drivers on the road) to be sure I arrived safely. Mexico City was not quite yet a major centre for drug cartels, but there were some pretty unsavoury characters around. Only when the shul was in sight did he smile and wave goodbye.

As I entered the shul and was greeted by the rabbi, my first thought was 'So much for wondering if there was any Jewish life here!' The place was absolutely packed, particularly with women, which was something you didn't typically see on a Friday night in London.

I went on to spend a wonderful Shabbat with Rabbi Masri and his family, during which I was amused to be asked, 'Is there any Jewish life in London?' I reflected that it served me right for making assumptions. Having heard my reason for being in Mexico City, after Shabbat ended Rabbi Masri introduced me to a number of important business people who gave me plenty of business data and statistics for my report.

Just before I left, late on Saturday evening, the rabbi's mother invited me for Sunday lunch. She was almost offended when I said I'd be on my way home at that time.

'What,' she exclaimed, 'you call this a visit?!'

When I described my weekend to them on Sunday morning, my colleagues found it hard to understand how I had been so royally feted by complete strangers. How to explain that Jews regard ourselves as one family?

Back at GEC, I handed TPC my nearly fifty-page report full of facts and figures from the Mexican Ministry of Export. There was also a list of companies that were ready to become our agents. He was amazed that I had managed to gather so much information in such a short time; I knew that it was largely thanks to the contacts I had been given in the Jewish community.

16

Korean interludes

One day early in January 1981, the sales director told me he was sending me to South Korea, along with the factory manager, to meet a prospective new agent. My job was to report on our chances of winning part of the contract for lines three and four of the Seoul Metro.

Our flight brought home to me the meaning of long haul, and gave me time to reflect on how far I had come, not just in physical miles, but in terms of stages in my life. The young boy from Benghazi who had escaped to Cambridge had become a husband, a father, and an engineer for a respected British company, comfortably conversing in English and rubbing shoulders on equal terms with international businessmen. I had to give myself a mental shake to take it all in, with a sense of wonder and gratitude.

We were more than happy to be met by the aspiring agent, Mr Young Kim, who took us to the Lotte Hotel. After quite a promising discussion on our chances of success, he announced that he had booked a table for dinner at one of the hotel's dozen restaurants (the thirty-something-storey hotel made the London Hilton look like a garden shed). I was ready to panic. Anxious not to offend, I made excuses that I was very tired, I wasn't really hungry, and in any case, I was a vegetarian. Understanding my problem with non-kosher food, my colleague hissed, 'Elia, can't you get a dispensation from a rabbi or something? If you upset this guy, we've had it!'

I realised if I didn't do something he could report back that I was being difficult, so I took a risk: 'Mr Kim,' I said, 'the truth is I'm not tired and I'm not a vegetarian. I'm afraid I can't eat in the restaurant because I'm Jewish, and I only eat kosher food.'

I'm not sure what kind of reaction I was expecting, but I certainly didn't expect him to jump up and embrace me! 'You're Jewish?' he cried. 'My sister moved to Chicago and was alone and miserable, but then a lovely Jewish lady said hello and helped her. Now all her best friends are Jewish. Great people!'

Eager to assist, Young Kim went on to say we could go to the buffet restaurant on the top floor, where I could help myself to fruit, vegetables and boiled eggs. My colleague shot me a look which clearly conveyed, *I don't know how you got away with that.* From then on, my friendship with Young Kim was sealed.

Our schedule there was very busy, with multiple visits to the railways and the metro, and I tended to stagger back after a long day and want nothing more than to collapse in my room. Every time I went to collect my room key, whoever was on duty at Reception would invariably ask, 'Excuse me, you Dustin Hoffman?'

I was tempted to say, 'Shush please, don't tell anyone,' but refrained. Dustin Hoffman and I are both short and Jewish, but only Koreans ever saw a likeness. At least I got a less dramatic reaction than the Scottish fellow who turned up in a kilt, to gales of behind-the-hands giggles from the Koreans.

I travelled to South Korea many times. During my earliest visits, Seoul was under a midnight to dawn curfew. There was no native Jewish community in Seoul, but there was an American military base serving the United States Eighth Army four miles from the hotel, and there was a Jewish chaplain and Jewish soldiers and admin staff stationed there. On my first Friday, Young Kim kindly gave me a lift to the base before Shabbat so that I could attend the evening service at the Jewish chapel, where I met Rabbi Philip Silverstein and his charming Korean wife, Adina, who had enriched the Jewish people with her conversion. Of course, after the service and the subsequent Shabbat meal I had to walk back, accompanied by a soldier to show me the way. Returning to the hotel very tired I went straight to bed, only to be woken later by increasingly loud and persistent knocking. I got up and opened the door, only to be confronted by two young Korean girls trying to push their way in. It seemed that due to the curfew, sometimes call girls (or students of English, as they styled themselves) would find themselves stuck at the hotel, unable to get home.

'No, no, no,' I protested. 'Please, out, out!' It took quite some persuading on my part to convince them that they really weren't welcome. (When I told Beryl who had knocked on my door and she asked me what I'd done, I teased her, 'How could I have paid them? It was Shabbat!')

Once back home I had to write a report on our trip for the MD, but I left out the above details. In fact, we did win the contract for lines three and four of the Seoul Metro, but we shared it with the Americans, and I believe the French.

A couple of years later, my association with Korea was restarted. I had to deliver a catalogue to the office of an important South Korean company.

The catalogue described all the various London offices of GEC and its subsidiaries, together employing some 200,000 people all over the world. Whilst waiting I noticed a press release announcing that this Korean company (I'll call it the firm) had won the contract to build a major new railway line in Iraq.

I asked to see the director, and was allowed through. I wanted to find out if he was looking for subcontractors to design and install the signalling and telecom for this new railway project. I explained that my company, GEC-GS, was among the largest in the world, but had not been given a chance to bid for the project. I reminded him that we were in the process of building part of the Seoul Metro, and said we would be delighted to participate in this new project for Iraq.

Whatever the reason we had not been involved, I was informed that the tender deadline had passed, and the bids received would shortly be studied at company headquarters in Seoul. At this news I very politely pointed out that we were talking about millions of dollars; the firm had already won the contract for the whole project, and if we were allowed to bid, I was sure that—as had been the case with the Seoul Metro—our price would be more competitive than the others they had received, which would mean more money in the bank for his company.

He thought for a bit, then said he was prepared to give us a chance, but needed our prices within two weeks. Even though I knew that was impossible, I agreed, grabbed the tender documents and rushed back to report to my sales director and the MD.

The prospect of preparing a bid at such short notice made the MD's hair stand on end. I suggested he call the firm's London MD, blame me for being over keen, and stress that GEC-GS was seriously interested but would need a month to put together a really keen bid. He made the call, and after some haggling we were given one month to submit our bid. Luckily I was able to obtain a copy of the Bill of Quantities, a 500-page book listing all the parts needed, from point machines down to the nuts and bolts for the signalling and telecom system. Without going into technical details, I can say that by dint of many hours of overtime and extensive analysis of the components required, we managed to submit our price on time. We were confident that this would enable us to go ahead to the next level of tendering against a reduced number of competitors.

So began my longest project, involving over two years of work and some dozen trips to South Korea. The first of these trips was taken in order to explain our bid and reprice it, taking into account the many changes that we had been warned to expect. Knowing that my visits there were likely to be frequent and possibly prolonged, I renewed my acquaintance with Rabbi Philip Silverstein of the American military base. I was to become a frequent weekend visitor to the base, where Rabbi Silverstein and his wife Adina welcomed me into their home and the small shul he served. They were always there for me with kosher food and, equally importantly, friendship. They were also my gateway into meeting a number of fascinating people, the most *interesting* of whom was undoubtedly an unusually tall Korean called Yang Chung.

The DIY convert

On one of my early visits to Seoul, I was making my way to the American base on Shabbat morning on foot when I realised that I was lost. This could be a big problem in those days. I had been given a lift there before Shabbat, without noting the route, and accompanied back to the hotel in the dark. My notoriously bad sense of direction was no help. Moreover, while the hotel receptionist had written out the address for me, she'd written it in Korean. Luckily I spotted a traffic policeman who could help me, and he managed to say, 'Ah, you want American Buddha.' He pointed in the direction of a large arch with a big cross on it and the sign 'US Army Religious Retreat'. The Koreans clearly took the cross as the American equivalent of their Buddha. (One Korean friend told me that in Korea at that time 80 per cent of the population were Buddhist and 50 per cent Christian. When I pointed out that the maths didn't add up, he simply replied, 'Well, you know, Buddha, Jesus, just in case....')

When I arrived at the shul, Rabbi Silverstein greeted me particularly warmly. He told me that they were expecting a new congregant, a Korean who wanted to meet me.

'Why me?'

'Because,' he said, 'we told him that you are very strict about keeping Shabbat, eating kosher, and so on.' He then briefed me on this remarkable man's story. Yang Chung had grown up in a village a few miles from Seoul, and was brought up as a Christian. As an adult he had begun to question some of the tenets of his religion; he read the Bible, and he didn't understand why Christians didn't keep the laws he read of—why they did not keep the Sabbath laws, or practise circumcision.

He decided to give up Christianity. Instead, he decided he wanted to be like the Bible's forefathers, Abraham, Isaac, and Jacob, and vowed to live like them. His doctor supervised while he circumcised himself and his boys.

He kept the laws of the Old Testament as he understood them. He rested on Shabbat, refrained from eating animals forbidden in the Torah, and grew his hair long.

He became a real oddity in his village.

He had not realised that Israelites still existed. He thought they had disappeared and were just a relic of history. Then, by chance, he read in his local paper an article about the 'Israelite' community in Seoul. Excited, he contacted the editor of the newspaper, who gave him a number for the American base. He called and had a lengthy conversation with Adina, Rabbi Silverstein's wife. This led to his walking several miles every Shabbat morning to the shul. Unable as of yet to follow the service, he sat with the Jewish children learning Hebrew before lunch. He had been doing this for several weeks, but he was growing disillusioned, having realised that none of the American Jewish army personnel observed their religion in the 'proper' way. He was discouraged and almost ready to give up. But then the rabbi had told him about the visitor from London, yours truly, who did observe the laws in the traditional way. And that is why the rabbi was so keen for me to meet him.

Shortly, a tall, imposing figure came striding towards us. With his long hair, floor-length robe and sandaled feet he really did look like one of the patriarchs. We were introduced, and when he saw the black *kippah* on my head his face lit up.

After the short Shabbat service the rabbi went off to teach the children, leaving me and my new companion together. As his English was very limited, I took him to find a book we could look at in the library. I spotted a large, illustrated volume called *Faces of Israel,* and we started leafing through it. He was fascinated by the rich mixture of people he saw, and became very excited when we came to a page with pictures of Yemenite Jews in their full regalia: white ankle-length robes, large caps, long beards. They obviously looked just like his idea of Abraham.

Jabbing the photograph, he turned to me and asked, 'This here…live… now?'

'Yes,' I confirmed.

'Where?' he demanded.

'In Jerusalem.'

He got up, called Adina and they spoke for about five minutes.

I asked her what he said.

'He wants to go to Jerusalem. He wants to live with these people.'

For all I know, he may even now be enjoying a cup of Yemenite tea in Jerusalem. I do hope so.

This small army synagogue, built and financed by Uncle Sam, was certainly frequented by a motley assortment of congregants. One couple I met, attached to the US forces, were Michael and Maeve. When I was first introduced to Michael, I thought he must be Rabbi Silverstein's assistant; he looked like a stereotypical Orthodox Jew, beard and all. He and his vivacious wife invited me to their home, where I had an eye-opening evening.

Maeve told me she had grown up in Toronto, the daughter of Irish immigrants. One Friday evening, bored with watching TV, she had gone for a walk around the neighbourhood until she heard voices singing. She followed the sound of the unfamiliar but haunting music to a building which turned out to be a shul. She went in, and was directed to the ladies' gallery. Intrigued and enchanted, she started going every week, and this ultimately set her on the long path of studying to become Jewish. She was already a vegetarian, so the dietary changes were not onerous for her. She told me about the final test she had taken in Jerusalem, before conversion. A friend had accompanied her to give her support. When one of the rabbis asked her to name the three pilgrim festivals, she confidently stated the names of the first two, Pesach and Sukkot, before becoming stuck on the third. Her friend hissed 'Shh…', and that jogged her memory. With great relief, she blurted out 'Shavuot.' By the time I was their guest she had been Jewish for some years. She was actually indignant that so many Jewish people paid so little heed to their religion, when she herself had worked so hard to be able to follow it.

I was interested to hear how she and Michael had met; they seemed like an ideal Jewish couple. I learned that they had actually met at a vegetarian society, and was taken aback to hear that in fact Michael was still in the process of studying to convert. They had married in a civil ceremony, and were waiting for Michael's conversion so they could marry in shul. The son of Italian immigrants, he had grown up in a mixed Jewish and Italian district of New York, where many people simply assumed from his appearance that he was Jewish. He had spent so much time in a Jewish milieu that he became interested in the religion; laughing, he told me that he had decided to convert in the spirit of 'If you can't beat them, join them.'

Talks, talks and more talks

After two weeks of discussions and technical amendments I returned to the UK to work further on the now greatly expanded project. Over the following months we hosted a delegation of railway personalities from KNR (Korea National Railway) in the UK. They were trying to decide on the best high-speed system to use. Then we in turn led a delegation of heads of British industry in Korea, where I had to organise a presentation to KNR by the various delegates, including GEC, Marconi, Rolls Royce and many others. Thanks to GEC, we had assembled the heads of a dozen of the top companies of the UK, and I had to quickly find a hall to accommodate them and the assembled top engineers and managers of KNR.

I decided to ask the commercial attaché at the British embassy in Seoul to help me find a spacious hall and an overhead projector.

His offhand reply was, 'Sorry, not my job.'

I was incensed. What was he there for then? I'm afraid I raised my voice and told him to just get on with it. Somewhat taken aback, he did help me find a hall which hosted over two hundred Korean railway engineers, and this contributed to the success of the visit. The presentations went well although, as a non-native English speaker myself, I did sympathise with the Koreans. Their repeated lack of response to jokes told in the course of the presentations showed that their generally excellent command of English didn't extend to idioms. This verged on embarrassing. Luckily, the plentiful food and drink laid on afterwards was understood by everyone.

Once back in London we began working hard on the new specifications for the Iraqi railway job. In the meantime our agent, Young Kim, was keeping in constant touch with his contacts in Korea. One day he phoned me from his hotel in London, where he had stopped off on his way back from a trip to Paris. He wanted to update me on the latest news on the Iraqi project and others. Given that he had only ever seen me eating boiled eggs, peanuts and lettuce leaves, I thought I'd treat him to a slap-up meal at Reubens, the well-known kosher restaurant near Baker Street (now on Baker Street) renowned for its salt beef.

He absolutely loved it, and boy did it show! He was slurping and chomping so loudly that the other diners began staring at him. I tactfully pointed out that, as he had always so helpfully told me about Korean customs, now I had to tell him about English customs, and that the English considered it bad manners to eat noisily. He was very surprised, explaining that that was how Koreans show their appreciation of good food, but thereafter became the model of English decorum. He welcomed my suggestion to send his compliments to the chef.

The next day he was able to get his own back. We were waiting for a train at Marble Arch station, and he was pacing up and down the platform as the ash from his cigarette became longer and longer, threatening to fall. He looked so agitated that I asked what was worrying him.

He blurted out, 'Elia, I'm going to burn my finger! Where is the ash tray?'

He was scandalised when I explained that it was fine to just drop the stub over the platform edge. Such behaviour was unheard of in Korea: so rude!

He travelled back to Korea on Saturday, and that night he called me from his stopover in Anchorage, Alaska: I was needed for an urgent meeting in Seoul on Monday morning.

Of course this was before the days of online booking. It could have been a problem, but I knew where to find a travel agent who, unusually, was open on Sunday. I bought a first-class ticket to Seoul, went to Gatwick, and boarded my Cathay Pacific plane. I was browsing through a magazine while waiting for take-off when two police officers approached me and asked me to please leave the plane with them for a few minutes.

Bewildered, I obliged, and was asked to show some ID. My passport wasn't good enough for them, but luckily, I also had my GEC club membership card with me. Satisfied with that, they asked me how I had managed to buy a ticket on a Sunday morning.

My next-door neighbour happened to be a travel agent, I explained.

So how had I paid for the ticket, they wanted to know.

I just about managed to suppress my sarcasm when I said, as politely as I could, 'Have you heard of a credit card?'

They finally agreed that I was bona fide, apologised and let me back on board, where suspicious glances from the other passengers made me rather uncomfortable. Strange how you can feel guilty when you know quite well you've done nothing wrong. And this was just the beginning of a twenty-two-hour journey!

I normally travelled business class, and here I was travelling first class with Cathay Pacific, yet all I was able to eat was smoked salmon and fresh fruit. I counted myself lucky to get that; at such short notice, there had been no time to order kosher food.

I spent only two days in Korea, where I was required to be present at a Monday morning meeting between our agent and KNR.

I flew back home to continue working on the big Iraqi tender. After all the trips back and forth, with competition from other companies, we were on the home strait, but not there yet. Now we had only four weeks to submit our final bid. Of course, they never really mean it; 'final' is a very flexible term in international bidding, but nevertheless we worked to meet their requirements.

I contacted our sister companies and various UK and overseas suppliers to make sure we got the best prices and guaranteed delivery dates. By the end of November 1982, we were ready with our bid. Then, a week before Christmas, we received a telex from our clients requesting all bidders to telex their prices by 5 p.m. Seoul time on Monday, 2 January 1983.

I showed the telex to our MD, pointing out that they wanted the information by 8 a.m. our time on that date, which would be straight after the Christmas and New Year shut down.

So we'll have to send it before the Christmas shutdown,' the MD replied.

I countered that in that case our prices would be available for all our competitors to see (via the inside men we knew they had).

We mulled over the problem, and I managed to come up with a plan: I would send a deliberately garbled telex from an outside agency to arrive in Korea ten minutes before the deadline. I asked my brother Ever to open his office early in the morning at 7 a.m. which is exactly 5 p.m. in Korea. Of course, it would be incomprehensible; and I instructed our agent, Young Kim, to explain that since our company was still closed for the holidays, we must have used a telex agency. He would then promise that as soon as GEC reopened, we would send a new telex, with our apologies and a promise not to use that agency again. That is exactly what happened, and with the information obtained by Young Kim (who had his own inside man), our bid offer was third from the bottom.

A week after we sent in our offer we were invited back to Seoul to explain it, and to prepare a new offer after some changes. Two other competitors were also invited, one British and one Dutch. Five firms were turned down.

Enter Mr Moon

At this point, an unexpected telex arrived for me from a Mr Moon in South Korea. He was offering us his services as the agent for the Iraqi project in exchange for a 4 per cent commission. He gave us names of companies in the UK for which he had obtained significant orders, and claimed that he could practically guarantee us the contract. He wanted me to fly out and see his capabilities for myself. It did occur to me that there was a difference between practically guaranteeing a contract and actually winning it, and it could be that he thought we already had it in the bag.

Nevertheless, I couldn't ignore the telex so I phoned the companies he had mentioned, who confirmed that he had indeed helped them as he claimed. They also all told me that he was a force to be reckoned with. Armed with this information, I went to see TPC.

TPC asked if there was enough margin in our proposed bid to pay an extra 4 per cent to this Mr Moon on top of the 4 per cent we would be paying our own agent, Young Kim (a good chunk of which he would spend on entertaining relevant Korean and Iraqi personalities). The answer was 'just about', but it would be a very tight squeeze.

The sales and technical directors joined the discussion, and we all agreed that it was very strange to contact us so late in the day. Moreover, Mr Moon was already the agent of the only non-British company still in the running for the contract, and we wondered why he was giving up on them.

The upshot was yet another trip to Korea for me.

By the time I arrived, Young Kim had already been put in the picture, and I asked him to put his contacts to work. I needed to know who Mr Moon's 'inside man' was, and any other relevant information he could gather.

The next day Mr Moon picked me up from my hotel and took me to a high-class restaurant where he had booked a private room. A long, low table laden with all kinds of food stretched the length of the room, flanked by two attractive young ladies kneeling on the floor. We two men sat alongside them on plump cushions, and I had to point out what I wanted and 'submit' to being fed! It was rather surreal. I was extremely relieved to see plenty of fruit and vegetables, so at least there was no problem in that direction.

Between mouthfuls, Mr Moon, who was feeding himself, filled me in on his background. He had retired from the army as a highly decorated officer, and now had many useful contacts through the army's old boys' network. For various reasons he felt the European company he had been representing had little chance of winning the contract, and now he wanted to pitch for us.

I let him do most of the talking, and I was certainly impressed. When we finished our meal he took me back to the hotel. I thanked him for an enjoyable (if somewhat strange) afternoon, and told him he would hear from us soon.

Young Kim and I then compared notes. He had found out that Mr Moon's inside man was very high up in the Korean company to which we were tendering but was due to retire and would thereafter have no further input.

Back in London, with the MD's approval, I faxed Mr Moon to say that, regrettably, our margins would not allow for an extra 4 per cent outlay. Essentially, we were convinced that he had contacted us because he was virtually sure we would win, and wanted to profit from that with little effort on his part. I couldn't really blame him: that's business.

The thief of Baghdad

The following weeks saw incredible activity, whereby the remaining competitors fought hard to win the contract. Some of the tactics we witnessed were quite Machiavellian, sometimes including bribery and downright lies. Take the following story as an example. During one stay in Korea, after a long late-night telephone discussion with my London office (3 p.m. in London was midnight in Korea) I went down to the hotel bar to listen to some music before going to bed. I sat down next to a sad-looking American and asked why he was looking so miserable. What he told me was rather worrying.

The previous evening he had sent a telex from the hotel to his firm in the States. It had included some uncomplimentary things about the Korean director he was dealing with. At that morning's meeting, the director had asked him to explain the derogatory things he had written about him, showing him a copy of the telex he had sent to the States. Trying to cover his embarrassment, the American had said that the fact that he had a copy of the telex proved that what he had written was accurate.

It was clear that some companies paid hotel telex operators for a copy of every telex sent from their premises. After hearing this story, I arranged with my office to communicate mainly by phone, and to use a previously agreed code when sending a telex.

After many more visits and endless discussions we beat the other two companies and were invited to Korea to negotiate the contract conditions and sign a Letter of Intent, prior to signing the final contract. Still, the business of international trade can be cutthroat. Beyond illegally obtained telexes, bribery was common too. Before we were at long last able to sign the contract we had to overcome yet another intervention by one of our competitors; they offered the Korean company an incredible last-minute bribe to snatch the project from us. This occurred during the month-long negotiation of the contract document with our Korean counterpart. I received a phone call at 2 a.m. from my managing director. He told me that this competitor had offered the Iraqi minister of transport over a million dollars if he would use his influence to transfer the currently underway railway contract from GEC to them.

Apparently, the information my MD had received was 100 per cent reliable. GEC's agent in Iraq had therefore offered this minister half a million dollars, with more to come in the future, but had been turned down. My MD was actually prepared to go to two million dollars if we had enough slack to cover it, and asked me my opinion.

'Mr C,' I said, 'it's two o' clock in the morning here, and I'm too tired to think straight. I'll talk to Young Kim in the morning and get back to you tomorrow, but please don't give that Iraqi thief a penny till I call you back.'

After said discussion with Young Kim, he contacted the mayor of Seoul, who was against this kind of extortion. It was agreed that the mayor of Baghdad would be invited to Seoul for a ceremonial public signing of the contract, and GEC would cover most of the reception costs. This would make it public knowledge that our winning the contract was a fait accompli, and obviate the need for bribery of any sort.

Before joining GEC this kind of international intrigue, bribery and counter-bribery had been quite foreign to me, an ex–British Rail engineer used to giving my best for my employer and only expecting my regular salary in return. TPC appreciated the work I had done securing the contract and decided to give me an ex gratia bonus after the contract signing, despite the fact it was against new company rules. That may explain why he was suddenly moved to a smaller GEC subsidiary in a remote part of the UK. Luckily for me his successor, Mr Sidebotham, honoured the arrangement, but I did feel bad for TPC.

The final stage was back in Korea, this time with a contracts manager who had to check that everything was correct according to company and British law, while I made sure the technical aspects were in order.

Faux pas

After over a year of hard work, international travel and intrigue, it was finally time to go through the 'Letter of Intent', designed to iron out any differences or misconceptions prior to the grand signing of the contract itself.

So there we were, seated at a long table in Seoul, with the British contingent on one side and the Koreans on the other. Each of us was given

TO: E Meghnagi

FROM: E Sidebotham

12th December 1983

LETTER OF INTENT - PROVISIONAL CONTRACT OBTAINED
IN KOREA FROM HYUNDAI FOR KIRKUT/HADITHA RAILWAY

In view of the hard work which many people in the organisation have put into tenders and subsequent work to reach the above position, I propose that those closely involved with work in Korea should receive some recognition for this fact.

I would like you to know that your efforts under difficult circumstances negotiating with Far Eastern clients have been recognised and as a gesture an ex-gratia payment of £1500 is being put forward on your behalf and you will be receiving it in January. Unfortunately, we are unable, at this late date, to pass it through in time for Christmas.

I am pleased, in this instance, to be able to put forward a payment such as this on your behalf but, of course, you will recognise that it can only be operated in cases where genuine effort over and above that normally expected has been made and success achieved.

E Sidebotham.

The letter from my new MD, confirming the ex gratia payment in recognition of my efforts.

a copy of this document, which was in fact a three-centimetre-thick book. I was impressed that my legal assistant, DB, had obtained an advance copy, to which he had added his comments and objections. He gave one copy of this to the Koreans' chief negotiator, and one to me. Once I saw the corrections he had made, I was less impressed.

The first line of the document produced by the Koreans began with: 'This is letter of intent' which DB had corrected to 'This is *a* letter of intent...'

This change immediately made the Koreans' chief negotiator suspicious. He demanded that DB explain the presence of this additional 'a'.

This was impossible to do, as the Korean language has no 'a' or 'the'. DB made an already embarrassing situation worse by saying, 'It just makes more beautiful English.'

The response from the Koreans was, 'If you added something, it must be to your advantage. We shall study all your comments and corrections and we'll meet again next week.'

I was furious. DB had had no business correcting the English. He had inadvertently insulted the Korean author of the document by criticising his English, and it would cost us a wasted week.

For me this was potentially a huge problem. It was the middle of March. Monday 16 April, just over a month away, was the beginning of Passover, for which I simply had to be home. It was bad enough being away for weeks on end; I simply couldn't contemplate being stuck in Korea for that major festival, and missing the *seder* with my family—a ceremony on the first and second nights of Passover that involves the retelling of the story of the Exodus, complete with symbolic foods and a festive meal. But the delay caused by DB's faux pas had made that eventuality a distinct possibility. Who knew how long this final review would take?

I phoned my office in London, advising them that DB (who was actually senior to me in the company) had made an enemy of the Korean English-language expert, and that he should either stay in the hotel, from where we could keep in touch, or preferably be recalled. In the age of the telephone and telex, I could keep in touch with him each day as we progressed.

He was recalled.

The following Monday we returned to the negotiating table, and to make things more friendly I got up and asked the Korean chief engineer to please move along a little and make room for me, as I wanted to sit next to him. 'Now we're on the same side,' I said, 'so let's get on with it.'

Everyone laughed, appreciating my rather theatrical gesture, and we carried on reviewing the Letter of Intent.

By Thursday 12 April all the *t*'s were crossed and the *i*'s dotted. We celebrated by hosting a reception attended by the British ambassador and other British and Korean dignitaries. One area in which those Koreans beat us Brits soundly was in the consumption of whisky.

The next morning I booked my ticket for London, to leave Seoul on Saturday night. I was ecstatic that I would be back in time for the *seder* on Monday night, one of the most important family rituals in the Jewish calendar. I called Beryl to tell her that all being well I should be arriving around midday on Sunday. I also apologised for having left all the considerable preparations for the eight-day festival to her. It wasn't just that she had had to do all the cleaning and changing over the house to rid it of leaven, and then do all the cooking for the festival. As had been our tradition for some time, my mother, my sister, and my younger brother Ever—with his wife and three children—would be coming to stay for the whole week, making a total of thirteen people in the house. Beryl was wont to observe that with the crowding, noise, and mess, it must have been pretty much like the exodus from Egypt commemorated by the festival.

Now Christians have many saints, but they are all dead. Jews also have saints, but they are very much alive. They are called wives. That is why on Friday nights in observant Jewish homes the world over, the beautiful poem by King Solomon, '*Eshet Chayil*', is sung to the woman of the house, opening with the line: 'A woman of valour who can find? Her worth is far beyond rubies'. Although this passage from Proverbs that has become a hymn has had some deep esoteric meanings ascribed to it, I love its simple, plain message: It is an ode, a thank you to my wife and the mother of my children, for the many roles she fulfils. And as I have already mentioned, in my wife's case this included doing all the Passover preparations, plus coping with a large percentage of my family living in her home for eight days—and all without complaint. At least she *usually* had me there to help in the lead up to the festival—but not this year.

I started packing. I'd been away from home for over four weeks, and by this point I was counting the hours; Friday night to Saturday night seemed more like a hundred hours than a mere twenty-four!

The next morning, Shabbat, I was sitting in the hotel lobby listening to soft music while dreaming of the flight that would take me home that evening, when Young Kim's secretary hurried in to tell me I was needed very urgently in the office. It was a short walk away, so we went together. And that's when Young Kim dropped his bombshell.

'You can't go tonight.'

I felt as if a tractor had driven over me. After the initial shock, I said firmly, 'Young Kim, I *am* going tonight.'

For the first time in our long and cordial relationship, Young Kim and I clashed. I insisted I had to leave, and he started shouting that I had to stay. He actually kicked a chair viciously, and spat on the floor.

That pulled me up short. Young Kim had *never* behaved like this before. I could just picture that whatever was behind this, my insistence on leaving would mean something going wrong at the last minute, and everyone saying I had torpedoed the project for the sake of my religion. 'OK, Kim, I'll stay,' I placated him. 'Now, what's so important?'

'The president wants to see you on Monday morning,' he announced, suddenly all smiles. He meant the president of the firm, not of Korea (possibly more important). He promised to pick me up on Monday morning.

The rest of that Shabbat was thoroughly miserable, and when it ended I called Rabbi Silverstein of the American base and glumly told him about my predicament. Being a true gentleman, he picked me up and took me to a local bar frequented by American forces, where we had a drink and a chat. He wasn't in the least surprised at my situation. 'I just knew you'd be stuck here for the *seder*,' he said. 'I know the Koreans. Things move more slowly here.' He went on to say that he was expecting some five hundred people for the *seder* on the base and as soon as he had received my call, he had arranged to make me his assistant. The two of us would conduct the proceedings, and I would stay in the US Army Religious Retreat. All the cleaning and koshering for the festival had been done with the help of Uncle Sam, and food had been provided by Lubavitch, New York.

I made my way back to my hotel feeling very downcast. True, I would have a proper *seder*, but being away from home and leaving my family in the lurch was a depressing prospect. Unable to sleep, I got up in the small hours to call Beryl at 7:30 p.m. London time—with some trepidation.

As soon as she heard my voice, she calmly said, 'Hmm, if you're talking to me on the phone you're obviously not on a plane. And if you're not on a plane, that means you won't be here for the *seder*.'

I couldn't believe she was taking it so well. My mother, along with Yvette, plus Ever with his wife and children, were already there, and I knew that my mother in particular would react badly to my absence. Stupidly, I asked Beryl how she was going to manage, and she laughingly replied that she had hardly been waiting for me to do all the cleaning and shopping at the last minute. Obviously trying to make me feel better, she said they'd miss me terribly, but they'd cope. I even remember her saying, 'One day we'll laugh about this.'

All I could do was apologise profusely, wish her luck, and promise that I'd fly home on the third day of the festival, when travel is permitted according to Jewish law.

As I hung up the phone an almost palpable wave of depression swept over me. Never since our wedding had I been away from her or the children for this most important family festival. For those unfamiliar with Passover, imagine combining the celebrations of Thanksgiving, Christmas Day, birthdays and wedding anniversaries into one. That's how important it is.

Imagine leaving all the preparation and cooking to your wife while she also deals with four pining children, *and* accommodates your sister, your brother and his whole family, as well as your mother who, thanks to her wartime experiences, is prone to attacks of hysteria…and then not even turning up yourself. It takes a very special woman to put up with that without complaint.

Later that morning, Young Kim collected me to meet the president. Having just signed the Letter of Intent for this enormous project on behalf of GEC, I was thinking about the hours, days and months it had taken to reach this point. I had agreed to meet the president for the sake of my employer, my colleagues (some of whom were under threat of redundancy) and of course for the UK, to which I owed so much.

I was still wondering what on earth he wanted with me when we reached the imposing building and took the lift to the top floor. I didn't have long to wait. Walking towards me came a tall, clearly senior figure with his hand outstretched. As I shook it, he exclaimed, 'Mr Meghnagi, job well done!' Then, with a 'Thank you for all your efforts,' he presented me with a parcel before withdrawing to his inner sanctum. And that was it!

Back at the hotel, I unwrapped the parcel to reveal a glass case containing a jade and gold-plated replica of the crown of the last king of Korea (either it was a miniature version, or the king had a very small head): another treasured souvenir for our display cabinet. It was a nice gesture of recognition and was really appreciated. He couldn't know, after all, that it cost me and my family a great deal of heartache and inconvenience.

Later still, when I visited Rabbi Silverstein at home before Passover began, he presented me with a plaque, adorned with the insignia of the United States Eighth Army and the logo of the chaplains of the United States Army, which read: ASSISTANT COMMAND CHAPLAIN KOREA 5743.

Being the senior chaplain at this enormous base, he had the authority to organise this. I felt truly humbled to be shown such consideration by him and his lovely wife. I still cherish that plaque, and am often asked to tell its story. What was amazing was that the plaque was already prepared. Either he had anticipated that I was going to be stuck in Korea, or that was just how fast they worked at the American base.

So there I was, stuck in Seoul for the two *seder* nights. The US Army Religious Retreat was a haven of peace for members of the US forces needing a quiet place to rest or recover, surrounded as it was by beautiful gardens and wonderful views, so I had very comfortable accommodation. At that time Rabbi Silverstein was the senior chaplain to the forces in Korea, in charge of chaplains of all faiths, and the pass he had given me meant I was welcomed and treated with great respect. In my allocated room I found a note from him with details of the services and the *seder*.

At the appointed time we made our way to the enormous dining hall. A *seder* at home might well accommodate thirty-plus people, but here were ten times that number seated at some thirty tables...not just military personnel, but many admin staff, and visiting businessmen who had booked a place.

Most of the tables were marked with a letter of the alphabet, including one with a G.

'That table is reserved for guest Christian chaplains and senior officers,' the rabbi explained. 'They think it's G for generals, but you and I know it's G for gentiles.'

I was deeply grateful to join the rabbi and his wife at their table, and to have the honour of helping him run both of the *seders*. It was comforting to see on each table the same symbolic foods I was used to, arranged on their special dish, although I decided it was impractical to carry out my personal custom of walking round with the *seder* plate and rotating it above the heads of all the participants during the singing of *Ma Nishtana*. After a unique and special Passover experience, two days later I was extremely grateful to finally be home, having been away for over a month. I had a gift for everyone and an especially warm hug and kiss for Beryl. They all admired the plaque and the crown, and teased me with the title 'King Elia'.

The Hebrew at the top means 'Memento', and at the bottom is the Jewish year, 5743, in Hebrew letters. I value this plaque as my only connection to the military, however tenuous.

Replica of the Korean crown: This is the gift that made me miss my family *seder*.

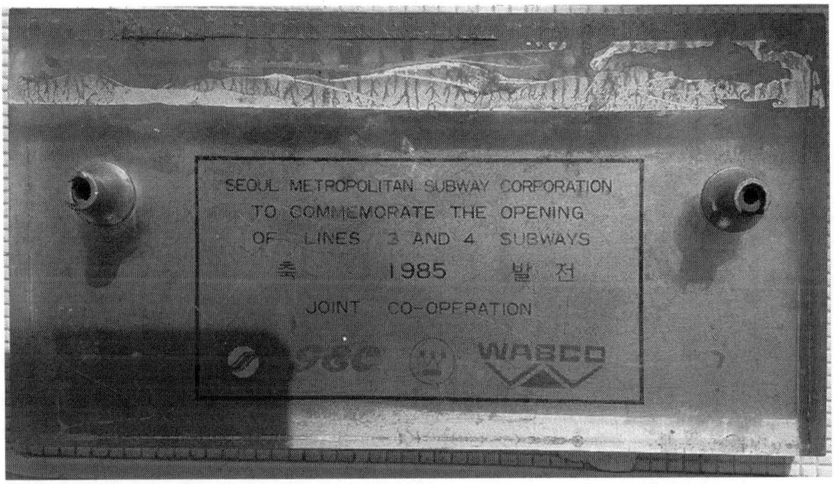

GEC Seoul Metro: The plaque I received for my part in winning this project.

Jetlagged as I was, overwhelmed by the hubbub of immediate and visiting family, I couldn't have been happier.

Recently, while preparing this book, I tried to locate Rabbi Silverstein and found that, following his service in South Korea, he returned to the USA and served as rabbi to the Beth Shalom Synagogue in Columbia, South Carolina, loved and respected by the whole community which he served with great gusto and devotion. I was saddened to learn that he passed away in 2015.

17

I scream, you scream

When I returned to GEC I was greeted as a hero, which was quite embarrassing! The new MD presented me with the ex gratia payment for all my hard work and its successful conclusion. However, there was one person with whom I most certainly was not popular: our new vice chairman, Steven Levi (name changed to protect the guilty). Because of his surname everyone assumed he was Jewish, but he vehemently denied it.

We knew each other. We had been together briefly in Korea, and on more than one occasion had been joined at business meals with the Koreans by an American colleague, Rudi. Rudi was used to my dietary habits, and was always more than happy to let me sneak my food onto his plate while I just pushed around a few lettuce leaves. However, he was not the most tactful of men. He would tease Steven for not doing the same, saying things like, 'Hey, Stevie boy, why are you eating all this non-kosher food? Why can't you be like Elia?'

While I'm sure he meant it in good part, he was doing me no favours, because I could see that 'Stevie boy' would absolutely seethe when this happened. He would also glower visibly whenever Young Kim, who had become my personal friend, insisted that I travel with him in his car, while more senior management followed in another.

On the one hand, I could sympathise with Steven's position, but on the other, he went out of his way to make life difficult for me. At one point, he tried to overturn the agreement I had made with TPC about leaving the office early on Fridays in the winter months. Since he was not then the head of my department, I just ignored this; I knew I had nothing to worry about, especially since I was putting in a huge amount of unpaid overtime because of the Korean and other projects.

However, now he was the new vice chairman, he had more power. Just after I returned from Korea he announced that he had arranged for me to attend a meeting in Rome on Yom Kippur, even though he knew perfectly well that even non-observant Jews don't work on that most important day in the Jewish calendar.

When I pointed out that he could have checked for an alternative date, his comeback to me was, 'Do you think the whole world has to stop because of your Yom Kippur?'

Since he refused to consider changing the date of the meeting, which was with Marconi Italiana, Rome, I contacted them myself and found that the date was only provisional and could easily be changed.

An hour later a telex arrived for Steven Levi saying that the meeting had been postponed until a few weeks later 'at the request of GEC London'.

I should have used more foresight in my attempt to go round him, because he came storming in, screaming, 'How dare you change the date? You think the whole world has to revolve around your religion!'

Most of my colleagues had already gone home for the day. Realising there was no point arguing with him, I just calmly walked out (which probably annoyed him even more).

A few weeks later, when I had taken a week's holiday to coincide with the festival of Sukkot, there was a knock on the door. Steven Levi had sent an assistant to my house to say there was an emergency and I was needed in the office. I was still in shul, but Beryl answered the door, and promised the guy that she'd give me the message.

When I got home, instead of waiting until after our family lunch, I immediately walked the four miles to the office. When I asked about the emergency, I was told that it was nothing urgent; it just concerned something on a Critical Path Analysis chart I had produced for a tender in South America, which listed all the dates when equipment, installation and testing had to be done.

I gave Steven Levi the answer, pointing out that it wasn't my project and I had only been helping out. Many other engineers in the company would have been just as capable of answering. Despite the fact that I had taken official leave for a week, I was happy to help.

Then, in early 1985, came an absolute bolt from the blue: I received a letter stating that, owing to the economic situation, I was being made redundant. Signed: Steven Levi.

My knees actually buckled. I could not believe it. After all my hard work, after the major part I had played in bringing home a huge contract in Korea, not to mention saving GEC millions in inducement money, aka bribery payment, I was being made redundant? And I was the *only* employee to be facing this? It was clear that there was no coincidence that I was the only Orthodox Jew at GEC. I had to go to the office to collect any personal belongings, then suffer the humiliation of being escorted from the building, watched by sympathetic but powerless colleagues. Knowing I would receive a reasonable severance package was little comfort. I didn't have a very high opinion of Steven Levi, but I had never thought he would sink so low.

When the shock had subsided slightly I contacted a lawyer, and when I described the circumstances surrounding my dismissal, he said I had an excellent case for discrimination. He was sure I would be entitled to significant compensation, but also warned me that I would probably never have a job in the engineering industry again: I would acquire a reputation as a troublemaker, and no one would want to touch me.

Taking his advice (which may have been a mistake), instead of seeking legal redress I wrote to the GEC Group Chairman, Lord Weinstock. I explained how I had been instrumental in winning a multi-million-pound contract and had saved GEC half a million pounds in bribe money, and enclosed a copy of the letter of appreciation sent to me by the previous MD.

In due course my GEC office invited me to a meeting 'to discuss my future'. When I asked about Steven Levi, I was told that he had been transferred to another branch of GEC. I was stunned, and felt vindicated. It was obvious that Lord Weinstock must have had a quiet word with them.

I said I appreciated being given the chance to talk, and thanked them, but… 'Once bitten, twice shy'.

In the interim, I had already started my own company called Intertex (International Technical Exchange), with an office in London and a branch in Seoul.

The idea had come to me one day when I was sitting with Young Kim at the hotel bar listening to the piano. A man had come up to me and introduced himself as the manager of the hotel. He explained that the hotel kitchens were due for a complete refit, and they needed new industrial ovens, fridges and freezers for the forty-storey hotel. The British embassy had helped by sending him catalogues and a list of suppliers, but he had no time to contact all the companies himself and decide what to order. He needed one person to look at what was available and advise on the most suitable equipment, taking into consideration the size of the hotel and the number of units needed.

I had realised at that time that there was a need for an intermediary in cases such as this, and after my redundancy I had the chance to put an abstract idea into practice. Over the following months I built up a reasonable list of clients, with myself serving them in this capacity, with help from my contacts abroad.

In addition to this, I also called a telecom company in Dorset, whose director I knew because I had brought him business with BR and in Korea.

When he heard about my redundancy, he invited me to be his part-time commercial manager. We agreed that I could do this by working one day a week in Dorset, and another day from home. I was paid a good basic salary, plus commission on sales I made. I was glad to land him some big contracts, so it was lucrative for both of us. The director was a real gentleman, the best of British, and I only wish I could remember his name.

To our relief, despite the shock redundancy we were doing quite well financially, with our combined incomes from my work and Beryl's earnings from the part-time teaching positions she somehow managed to juggle with taking care of home and family.

Snowcrest

My two brothers had been in the kosher food business for some years, working for the Israeli company, Osem, in their London branch. Ever was the office manager, virtually running the company, while Clem was a very successful salesman. As an Italian speaker he was able to sell Israeli spaghetti to Italian restaurants! It probably helped that in his ever-present hat he looked like a refugee from the Mafia (even though he's the kindest, most honest person you could meet). They were contacted by the three owners of Snowcrest, a long-established British kosher food manufacturer. The owners wanted to retire and offered Clem and Ever the opportunity to buy the business.

My brothers were definitely interested but realised they would need a third partner; someone who had practical experience and could also help with a share of the financing. They needed someone who understood machinery and electrical installations to run the production side; in other words, me. Mind you, Ever had his doubts about my qualifications. 'What do you know about food?' he demanded, to which I replied, 'I eat, don't I?'

I felt I couldn't let down my brothers, and thought it was a great opportunity to go into a family business respected by the community. It would be a way of combining my engineering and religious knowledge. We agreed that I would be production director, a position which, in my innocence, I thought would be straightforward, leaving me time to carry on with my other work.

How wrong can you be?

We took over the company in late 1987, a new beginning in more ways than one, as Beryl and I were looking forward to the arrival of our 'bonus'. Our second son and fifth child, David, was born on 12 January 1988, to our delight and that of his siblings. They were all very helpful in looking after him, which was just as well: I was frequently putting in over fourteen hours a day fixing machinery and electrical equipment, and supervising production staff. Within a year, Intertex and my work for the Dorset company had to be shelved for good.

When David was born I was forty-six and Beryl forty-two, considered quite elderly for new parents at the time. It was a tiring time, though I found it quite easy to make the transition from the world of international business to that of the more parochial kosher food industry. Dealing with the queries and requirements of various rabbis and customers was not so very different in principle from negotiating contracts, while maintaining and repairing machinery kept my hand in on the engineering side.

One of my hardest and all-too-frequent tasks was acting as a stand-in for various kosher supervisors, including the regular milk production supervisor, when he couldn't be there for one reason or another. This meant being at the farm at 4 a.m. to supervise the whole process—milking, pasteurising, and bottling—so that our supervised milk could get to the kosher shops and our factory, and onto the doorsteps of many Jewish homes, first thing in the morning. I still managed to get back to the office for a full day's work. In my time, I have supervised the production of soft cheeses, cottage cheese and, in our own factory, yoghurts. Nowadays we no longer deal with farms, but our range includes non-dairy ice cream, crisps, soya mince and blintzes, jams, packs of frozen pastry, and we are the only major kosher company in the UK to bake cakes and biscuits for Passover.

In the factory, if there was any problem with the machinery it was up to me to sort it out. To call in electrical engineers would normally have meant a break in production, and in any case experience told me that outside experts might exaggerate the problem and tell us we needed new parts—which would then take days to arrive. An excellent example of this was when our large electric oven with a rotating platform stopped working. We were using it to bake cakes and biscuits for Passover, which was just a few weeks away. A delay in repairing it would have been disastrous, so I asked the office to call in the firm that specialised in repairing bakery equipment.

Their engineer came, and within ten minutes he gave his verdict, and left. According to him the oven needed a new motor and other bits and pieces. The price would be £1,500 for labour, plus the cost of the parts, but those parts would take two weeks to arrive. Two weeks! That would make it much too late to have our cakes in the shops in time for Passover; a scenario not to be contemplated. I left the office, went down to the bakery, and after a thorough examination I found the problem. It was nothing to do with the motor, and within the hour I'd fixed it. Many years later it is still working perfectly.

This does not mean that I'm such a brilliant engineer. It's just that all too often the people you call in want a quick fix. Simply replacing parts is quicker, and they make more money.

A few months later we had another breakdown that cost us some £2,000, but had an inadvertently stress-relieving outcome. We had just appointed a new, highly-skilled factory manager, Antonio dos Santos, a Portuguese man who proved to be a devoted and loyal employee and remains—many years later—a personal friend. We explained to him all the rules that a kosher food factory had to abide by, adding that we would be closed the following Wednesday, it being Yom Kippur.

When we got back to the factory on the Thursday I went to check that things were running smoothly on the floor, and was surprised to see Antonio looking really upset. He was embarrassed and reluctant to tell me the problem, but I finally winkled it out of him: he had wanted to do something nice for us, so the previous day he had come to the factory and prepared a whole 400-litre batch of vanilla ice cream, ready for freezing after the holiday. However, he had forgotten to close the tap fully, and overnight the whole 400 litres had dripped down the drain.

He was practically cowering, obviously waiting for me to sack him, or at least insist on his paying for the lost ingredients. Instead, I simply burst out laughing.

He couldn't understand why I wasn't even angry with him, so I explained: since Snowcrest is a strictly Orthodox Jewish concern, it was forbidden for anyone at all to work there on Yom Kippur, the holiest day in the Jewish calendar. By inadvertently wasting the ice cream mix, he had saved me from the dilemma of having to decide whether to save it somehow, or throw it away. I told him I was just grateful that God had acted so promptly!

After that he was scrupulous in sticking to Jewish law. He even kept on his locker door a translation of the *Shema*, our basic declaration of faith, which he read every morning before starting work. Not being Jewish himself, he nevertheless was and still is a great admirer of our moral code. He was with us for many years, and we were very sorry to see him go when advancing Parkinson's disease made it impossible for him to continue. He returned to Portugal, and still phones every year to wish us a happy Passover. He has put his holiday home in Braganza, Portugal, at our disposal any time. It's very rewarding when treating your staff as friends is appreciated.

During the course of our association, Antonio found out that he did have some Jewish ancestry himself. Quite recently he phoned me from Portugal to tell me of the sad loss of his father-in-law, who had been descended from Jewish *conversos*. He had left a note asking for some Hebrew words to be put on his grave, and Antonio was calling to ask my advice as to something suitable. After some thought I sent him the words from Genesis, where Noah is described as '*Tzaddik haya bedorotav*' (a righteous man in his generation). If you happen to be visiting this particular Catholic cemetery in Portugal, among the crosses and Christian symbols you'll see one headstone engraved with Hebrew letters, with the translation in Portuguese.

A kosher food factory has to have a rabbinical supervisor on the premises, and in our case, we needed a supervisor appointed by the religious authority Kedassia, but equally approved by the KLBD (the Kosher London Beth Din). Ours was a pint-sized Dane named Mr Levy, with a beard practically down to his knees. He looked like a cast member from *Fiddler on the Roof.* The fact that he was a friendly, helpful person never interfered with his duties as supervisor, which sometimes led to confrontations with the factory staff, but nothing ever became personal, and no disagreement lasted beyond the day. However, Antonio was a bit of a joker, and delighted in teasing this Mr Levy. He knew that in a factory such as ours, the oven had to be lit by an Orthodox Jew. One day, he called out 'Mr Levy, please go to the office and find me someone Jewish to light the oven.'

Mr Levy promptly turned and started trotting up the stairs. He was near the top when he stopped, whirled around and exclaimed, 'Just a minute, I'm Jewish! I can light the oven!'

He wasn't too pleased to see Antonio doubled up with laughter.

The truth is, they really liked and respected each other. Antonio loved mischief, and Mr Levy loved wagging an admonitory finger at Antonio's midriff, which was about as high as he could reach. They were both good, honest people who certainly livened up proceedings.

Beware the wives of March

Preparation for the festival of Passover, as I've already mentioned, is a mammoth task. These days men do tend to contribute more, but the organisation is still regarded as mainly the woman's task. At home the house must be cleaned from top to bottom to remove any trace of anything containing leaven. The usual crockery, cutlery and pots and pans in the

In the yard at Snowcrest. Left to right: myself, Rabbi Dunner (grandson of senior), Ever, Rabbi Dunner senior, Clem, Mr Levy.

kitchen are swapped for sets kept specially for that week. It makes spring cleaning a piece of cake in comparison.

In a kosher food factory the task of Passover cleaning is on a huge scale. All the machinery has to be dismantled, sterilised and reassembled in readiness for the Passover run. I had always helped at home whenever possible, but if Beryl counted on my being on call because I wasn't in Korea, she was disappointed. At Snowcrest, the three months leading up to Passover spell work for all of us almost round the clock. People often ask us why we wait so long to start production, but the truth is that many Passover ingredients are not available till shortly before the festival, which falls in March or April.

One of the main ingredients we need, used in products like sorbets, jams and soft drinks, is citric acid. We typically order it months before it is needed because it is often produced only in Europe or the Far East. One year, just before we were about to start our Passover runs, we were told that the citric acid from our usual supplier could not be used, as they had introduced a new ingredient which was not permitted for Passover. This meant the money we had spent on the sixty twenty-five-kilogram bags we had already received would be wasted. Even worse, I knew it would be impossible to find alternative suppliers, obtain rabbinical approval for an alternative product, *and* get delivery in time. I was desperately concerned that a major part of our production was going to have to be cancelled that year, greatly affecting our profits and, just as worryingly, letting down our loyal customers. That night, I couldn't sleep. I twisted and turned, trying to think of a solution.

Then, suddenly, it came to me.

I could hardly wait for the morning, when I phoned the manufacturer concerned and asked when they had introduced the problem ingredient. To my everlasting relief, I heard the magic words that the consignment we had received predated the change.

Once the rabbinical authorities received confirmation of this from our suppliers, we got the go ahead. I had never been so happy to start production. We were saved.

Over the next few days we were inundated by calls from other kosher companies in the UK, and even one in Gibraltar, pleading with us to sell them some citric acid. We tried to help as many as possible, even our competitors.

Another Passover incident concerned our strawberry and raspberry squash. Unlike our orange and lemon squash, which are made with pure juice concentrate, these are made with artificial flavouring. One year I decided that it was wrong for children to be drinking something with no food value, so I added some lemon juice concentrate to the strawberry squash in order to improve the vitamin content.

The first batch went to a local supermarket. The following day we got a request from the supermarket to send a driver to collect all the bottles we had delivered, because they were substandard. The lemon juice had neutralised the red colouring, so that what had left the factory a pretty pink colour now looked like plain water. I was reminded of the saying 'If it ain't broke, don't fix it!'

Interestingly, today it is recognised that less colouring is healthier, and in any case citric acid contains vitamin C. Clearly, I was ahead of my time!

Normally we order our orange and lemon concentrate from Brazil, but on one occasion there was a problem with their production, so we ordered about ten 200-kilogram drums from Sicily. We sent a rabbi from London and one from Milan to the orange and lemon groves to supervise the process, and soon the drums were on their way to us.

Then, of course in the middle of the night, I got a call to tell me that our drums were stuck in Messina because the ferry from Sicily to the Italian mainland was on strike. Eventually, after talking to all kinds of people, we got our juice concentrate. The quality and freshness were first rate, but by the time it arrived we had just four weeks until Passover. We worked round the clock, with lots of extra temporary staff, and managed to get maybe 60 per cent of our normal production run to the shops, just in time.

We had to take all these setbacks philosophically, as part and parcel of the food business, or suffer heart attacks.

Luckily, there have been many happier occasions to help us maintain our sanity. One such occurred one year in mid-December, when I noticed an unusual request in the weekly order. When I saw the words 'Hilton Hotel' I shuddered, remembering the awful time so many decades earlier when I had gone there to be told I could expect no more help from my parents. This, however, was much more positive: an order for 200 croissants and 2,000 mince pies! We did not usually make these products, but such a prestigious order made it worth our while. When I accompanied the driver to deliver them, I asked the manager why they needed so many kosher goodies. The answer was that a conference was to be held there with a large American contingent, many of whom had requested kosher food for breakfast and tea. To avoid any mix up between kosher and non-kosher, he had decided that all the delegates would enjoy our Snowcrest goods.

Another cause for pride was when we received a call from 10 Downing Street, requesting ice cream, croissants and doughnuts. An Israeli minister was due in the UK for talks at Downing Street, and was known for eating only kosher food. We were honoured to oblige, but I was very disappointed when the previous owner of Snowcrest, Joe Steinhart, begged us to let him make the delivery to Number 10. Oh well, you can't win them all!

My Muslim brother

One of the biggest dreads in a food factory is a visit by the Health Inspector. It seemed no coincidence to us at Snowcrest that a procession of inspectors would invariably turn up just at our busiest time, in the weeks leading up to Passover: Health, Health and Safety, Weights and Measures; one by one they would appear, ready to pick us to pieces. Replacing tiles, repainting, replacing scales, etc, would cost us a small fortune and interrupt production.

One year we had a visit from the Health Inspectors' department. During his thorough inspection he found that one of our electric hand dryers was not working. He noted it down and insisted it must be fixed or replaced within two weeks, even though there were four others in working order.

The next day, an inspector turned up from the Health and Safety Department. He demanded that we take down the electric hand dryers and replace them with paper towels. I politely told him what the previous day's inspector had said, but he would not hear of it. 'Put paper towels,' he demanded. 'People don't have the patience to dry their hands properly with the electric ones.'

We ended up installing both.

Once we were contacted by a Jewish doctor in Reading. He complained that the bottle of orange squash he had bought for Passover had gone fizzy. He conceded that the half-used bottle had been left in his car for weeks in warm weather, but was still demanding a new bottle. Even though this was six months after Passover, and seemed unreasonable, 'The customer is always right', and we fully intended to replace it. The trouble was we lost his contact details (inefficient, I know), so we had to wait for him to contact us again.

He didn't. Instead, a month later we received a call from our local authority's Health and Safety department saying that this doctor had called them with his complaint. Our protests about the age of the bottle and its being kept in unhygienic conditions fell on deaf ears. We were to expect a visit from two inspectors.

I quickly informed the factory. The workers always wear aprons, gloves and caps, but I told Antonio to make doubly sure. On full alert, we waited...and waited...and waited. Nearly two weeks went by, and we were just beginning to think they had bigger fish to fry when two burly gents turned up at my office.

I welcomed them, and offered them a drink, trying to put things on a friendly footing. The senior of the two looked as if he might be originally Turkish, and since my grandmother had had Turkish connections I asked if this was so, thinking it would give us something in common.

Instead of answering, he asked me where I was from, and when I replied, 'I'm from Libya', he declared, 'So am I!'

That's it, I thought. *Goodbye, Snowcrest!*

'Which town?' he asked.

'Benghazi,' I replied.

'So am I!'

Then he added, 'Which school did you go to?'

This was where I thought the coincidences must end, since the student body of the school I had attended comprised mainly Europeans and just a few wealthy Arabs. But when I said 'Istituto De La Salle,' he jumped up, embraced me, and exclaimed, 'So did I! We are like brothers!

All my best friends are Jews from that school, and I often visit them in Rome!'

My brother Ever had been watching these goings on from his office, and came rushing in, looking worried. He needn't have been. This charming man, whose name was Younes, explained that he was a Bedouin who had escaped from Gaddafi and his killers, who had been on the lookout for him, and immigrated to the UK. He was quite indignant that a fellow Jew had tried to make trouble for us simply because we had failed to make contact with him. He had a look round the factory, and had a chat with Mr Levy, our supervisor, making suggestions for a few minor changes. He also told his somewhat bemused companion to look after us, as we were 'his brothers' and Snowcrest was a reputable kosher company.

Before he left, he said, 'I'll speak to this doctor tomorrow morning, after I've done my interview with John Humphrys on Radio four. Then I'll get back to you.'

That's how I found out that Inspector Younes was the most senior inspector in Haringey. He had just completed a BBC TV series called *Restaurants from Hell*, in which he exposed some terribly unhygienic commercial kitchens, and many shops and restaurants falsely claiming that their food was halal.

True to his word, next morning he called me to say he had sorted out the doctor, and we should just send him a parcel of our goodies and an apology to close the chapter. I thought to myself, how ironic: a Bedouin making peace between Jews. There's an example for the world.

Shortly afterwards, Mr Younes called me again to ask if I would speak to the elders at his mosque about the process of setting up a board to check the credentials of halal traders, something similar to our kosher authorities. It was an interesting idea, but he must have become involved in other matters because he never followed up on it.

Mr Hasham, the Hashemite

One evening I was just going to bed when the night foreman at the factory phoned to report a strong smell of ammonia. Since it was February, we had people packing various products for Passover, so I told him to send everyone home and go outside to wait for me. This was in the days of the original factory in the East End (we moved to more modern premises about three years after taking over the company). I made the journey from outer London in twenty-five minutes, half the usual time, as the roads were deserted. Access to the ammonia cylinder was awkward, but wearing a special mask I managed to get to it and seal the leak.

The next day Ever and I agreed that we could not continue working with ammonia, and had to find an ice cream machine that used safer gas as soon as possible. We tracked down an auction for industrial machinery, and Ever went and paid a deposit for two machines. He gave a cheque for 25 per cent of the cost, on the understanding that we would pay the balance within two weeks, and then collect the machines.

The only problem was that we didn't have that much money, and our bank refused to help. We were at risk of losing the machines and our deposit, but then we found out that our local authority was running a scheme to give short term loans to deserving businesses. I must admit I was dubious we would qualify, but I called anyway and was put through to a Mr Hasham, the man in charge of the loans department.

I explained our situation and tried to make it sound really critical, which wasn't far from the truth. I certainly didn't want to have to go through another ammonia leak emergency. Mr Hasham listened patiently to my story. Our ammonia machine was one of the top in the business, but a recently-introduced law now required a full-time ammonia engineer to watch over it and to make sure that emergency leakage arrangements were clearly identified all over the factory. Employing such a specialist was simply not practicable for a small company like ours. This made matters even more urgent. After asking a few questions our prospective saviour arranged to come the following Monday.

Upon his arrival, two things were immediately obvious: he was very distinguished, and he was a Muslim. Seeing me, he asked if ours was a Jewish company, which was a bit worrying. When I warily confirmed his assumption, he smiled and said, 'That means I must help you.' Intrigued and delighted, I asked him to explain, and he told me his moving story.

As his name suggested, he came from a very distinguished Hashemite family that traced its roots back to Mohammed, and they expected great things of him. Some thirty years before, at the age of eighteen, he had left his home in Pakistan to study in Chicago. Finding it hard to make friends in an alien culture, he had become very lonely, depressed, and eventually suicidal. One day, standing on the shore of Lake Michigan, he had become overwhelmed by his feelings and waded into the lake, intending to end it all. At this point a young man came rushing into the water after him, put an arm round his shoulder and led him to a nearby building, which was actually the shul of which he was the rabbi. Having helped him dry off, wrapped him in a robe and given him a hot drink, the rabbi spent time talking to him, and offered to be there for him whenever he felt down.

What impressed Mr Hasham so much was that it made no difference to this rabbi whether the person in need was Muslim, Jewish or whatever; he was a human being who needed help.

The result of this pivotal moment was that Mr Hasham was able to finish his studies, qualify, and come to work in the UK. He promised himself that if he ever came across a Jew in trouble, he would do his best to help. He now had two daughters who were studying medicine, and he had asked them to begin their careers as doctors volunteering in Israel.

It was quite a story, and one from which we were fortunate to benefit. This fine man arranged a loan for us at a very low rate of interest, to be repaid over ten years. Full of gratitude, we were able to pay for the two new, safer ice cream machines, and carry on the business.

I find it truly heartening that each time our Jewish company was in trouble, it was a Muslim who came to our aid. It reinforces my lifelong belief that irrespective of religion, race or colour, people can rise to the occasion and help a needy fellow human being.

PART THREE

Extra-curricular

18

This and that

Throughout my childhood, my mother pushed me constantly to work harder at school, fully convinced that I was destined for great things. Her reason, as she often reminded me, was that I was *'Nato con la camicia,'* meaning born with a shirt, that is, still inside the amniotic sac. According to Italian folklore, this means the baby will be lucky in love, though my mother conveniently left out the 'love' part. I can understand how this belief has come about, since apparently only one in eighty thousand babies is born in this way (I looked it up).

Being a sceptic, I took this with a grain of salt, but hearing it so often did make me push harder in whatever I did, as if I had to prove my mother right.

That is probably why I have always looked to participate in extra-curricular activities in the Jewish world, such as teaching, organising lectures, and giving talks myself. With Beryl's help and encouragement (for I certainly have been lucky in love) I have written for Jewish newspapers, met some very interesting personalities, and travelled all over the UK visiting small communities.

Frogs' legs

Over thirty years ago my dear friend Yossi Zaltzman (sadly no longer with us) who was then secretary of the Jewish Memorial Council, asked me if I would take on the role of the Chief Rabbi's roving education adviser to small communities. This involved travelling to Jewish Sunday schools in small communities, as well as Sunday sessions teaching the Jewish pupils in boarding schools within a 100-mile radius of London. Although the job was not salaried, expenses were fairly generous, and I took it on because I felt it was very important work.

Of course it was tiring spending the best part of Sundays driving and teaching, but I really enjoyed it. On Sundays when our own children were not in their own classes I would take the older ones with me, which was enjoyable bonding time. We would eat our sandwiches together and demonstrate the grace after meals for my pupils (somewhat to my own children's embarrassment, I must say). I would have classes of about fifteen students, teaching Jewish law and history, the meaning of the festivals, maybe some Hebrew reading, plus some Hebrew songs to liven things up.

I served many important schools, like Eton (where my car looked pretty miserable parked alongside the flashy one belonging to the TV personality David Frost) and Rugby School, famous for inventing the game of rugby. There the school chaplain was an enlightened man who believed that Jewish pupils, and those of other faiths, should learn about their own religion. He even provided a room in his own home for my sessions. One Sunday when I was showing slides to illustrate the beauty of God's creation, as praised in Psalm 104, he attended with some of his own Christian pupils. His attitude accorded perfectly with my deeply held belief that what unites the three major faiths is much greater than what divides them.

One Sunday, the headmaster of Rugby asked me if I could find a speaker on Judaism for him, as part of a series of talks on world religions to be given to the whole school and staff a few weeks later. This was to be an hour-long talk, followed by questions and lunch. I agreed to find a suitable speaker, pointing out, however, that he would not be able to stay for lunch. Back home, I enlisted Reverend Saul Amias, a very experienced public speaker, who was happy to give the talk. However, in shul on Shabbat the day before the talk, he apologised and told me that he would be unable to make it. With no time to find an alternative, I had no choice but to tackle it myself.

During my usual lesson, given prior to the talk, I was told that the previous week's speaker, a Buddhist monk, would be a hard act to follow. Very encouraging! We adjourned to a large hall where I was confronted by over three hundred pupils, staff and visiting parents, all waiting eagerly for words of wisdom from yours truly. I had prepared the talk in my head while driving there, and took as my starting point the then topical controversy receiving large coverage in the newspapers regarding the practice of cutting legs from live frogs in India, to be sent to France. I explained that this practice had been forbidden in Jewish law for five thousand years, and that in fact the opposite of kosher is the word '*treif*', meaning 'torn from a living animal'.

I went on to list names of famous Jewish figures in all walks of life, from science to entertainment, explaining that the link between them all was a common history and a unique book, the Bible, whose ethics and morals had been adopted and adapted by most nations and some major faiths of the world.

After that it somehow flowed smoothly, and stimulated a barrage of questions and some friendly, if sometimes lively, discussion. During the Q&A a young girl asked what I would have done if I had come face to face with Hitler. I replied that I would not have hesitated to kill him. We are taught to preserve all human life, I explained, and if we know we are under threat, we defend ourselves.

My weekly trips on behalf of the JMC went on for a few years, until the organisation decided to discontinue that facet of their work. I must admit that I sometimes wondered if I was actually doing any good, a lone voice in the wilderness talking to youngsters who otherwise had very little connection to their Jewishness. Then, years later, I was at a charity dinner when a very obviously Orthodox young man came up and greeted me by name. Seeing my blank expression, he said he had been in my class at Rugby. My lessons had given him the impetus to join the Jewish Study group at university, and he had gone on to study Judaism and become completely observant. When I called Yossi to tell him this thrilling news, he replied that the JMC had received several letters with similar stories. *Well,* I thought, *I just wish you'd told me at the time!*

Chaplain Weisman's Libyan adventure

During my time working with the JMC I often had the pleasure of working alongside a man who was, and still is, a legend in his own time. Rev Malcolm Weisman was the chief rabbi's minister to small communities and senior chaplain to Her Majesty's Armed Forces. As such, he travelled throughout the UK and indeed the world, dedicated to keeping even the most remote British subjects in touch with their Jewishness. A warm and uplifting speaker, he attracted enthusiastic audiences to his talks in shuls and meeting halls, and more than earned the Queen's honour of OBE for his indefatigable service.

One Sunday I was addressing a sweet twelve-year-old girl in her seaside town of Eastbourne. The shul, usually almost empty because of the tiny community living there, was this time filled to capacity. I had taught this lovely, intelligent girl for several weeks, preparing her for her bat mitzvah, and couldn't resist commenting that while God could not usually manage to fill that lovely shul, she had done it. Rev Weisman, who had organised the ceremony, concluded the ceremony with an upbeat and rousing address.

Malcolm had his own tale to tell about Libya and Libyan Jewry. In 1960 he was posted to Benghazi as Jewish chaplain to the British Armed Forces, who had a base there. Shortly after arriving he was taking a break on the beach and asked a local for the address of the nearest shul. That evening a sergeant agreed to escort him there for evening prayers, but on the way they realised they were being followed by a man in uniform.

They made it in time for Malcolm to be greeted and join in the prayers, then hurried back to the base…where he was told he had been taken for an Israeli spy, and must leave in a hurry before he was arrested!

Back in London he learned some very upsetting news: the police in Benghazi had gone to the shul to take him in for questioning, and when they found that he had returned to the base they had rounded up all the men who were still in the synagogue and taken them to the police station to be interrogated.

They were forced to spend a couple of nights in the local prison, and only released when the police finally conceded they were telling the truth. After all, it was easy enough to check the chaplain's credentials with the base.

Reverend Weisman returned to Libya three months later but avoided making contact with the Jewish community for fear of bringing them under suspicion and putting them in danger. This incident is a good example of the precarious conditions the Jewish community were subjected to.

As for Malcolm, I'm delighted to say that after more than sixty years of service, he is still going strong. May he be blessed with many years in good health. They don't make them like that anymore!

One project I was almost involved in never actually ended up getting off the ground, which I've always regretted. In the 1980s, a community in Majorca contacted Alexander Rosenzweig, a director of the JMC. They were descended from so called Marranos, Jews who had been forcibly converted, and wanted help setting up evening classes in Jewish education. We discussed the possibility of going there to investigate practicalities, but before this could happen Alexander suddenly passed away. Subsequently the JMC decided to end their involvement in Jewish education, and the Majorca project was abandoned. That was a real pity, because there was a large group of lost Jews there seeking to find their way back. I have often wondered about them, and I did read that in 2011, a leading rabbi of the Beit Din of Bnei Brak recognised the Chuetas of Majorca, a group descended from *conversos* who married only amongst themselves for many centuries, as halachically Jewish.

One project I was able to participate in came about more recently. Out of the blue, I was contacted by two young women from Milan (I later learned that my dear friend Rabbi Mino Labi, also originally from Libya, had suggested me). As part of their PhD project they were recording testimonies of people who had lived in now-defunct Jewish communities, to be kept in an archive in Milan. They came to my home and recorded a four-hour interview, obviously in Italian (much to the chagrin of our children, who do not speak the language). I find it comforting that I was able to play a small part in preserving the memory of my childhood home.

CDEC

CENTRO DI DOCUMENTAZIONE EBRAICA CONTEMPORANEA

Mapping Living Memories: the Jewish Diaspora from Libya across Europe and the Mediterranean

Testimonianza di:

Meghnagi Elia

Londra, 18 Dicembre 2013

Intervista a cura di:

Barbara Spadaro
Piera Rossetto

Title page of my testimony, now held at the Contemporary Jewish Documentation Centre in Milan.

The Simon Wiesenthal Centre (SWC) UK

One day in the late 1990s I saw an advert about a series of lectures on anti-Semitism to be held on university campuses, organised by the Simon Wiesenthal Centre. They were to be given by lecturers from the UK and Europe, and were open to the public as well as university students.

Simon Wiesenthal was one of my greatest heroes; the man most feared by the thousands of Nazis in hiding after the war. Having survived the Holocaust himself, he spent the rest of his life devoted to their capture and punishment, wherever they were hiding. The suffering that my parents' generation, and earlier, had endured during the Holocaust has never been far from my thoughts. How devastating it was to know that the world had still not learned the lessons of the Holocaust, fifty years later, and still allowed this horrible disease to flourish, even thrive, in places you would least expect: universities, so called centres of education and enlightenment.

I felt compelled to play some part in fighting this scourge, so I contacted the SWC and ended up helping organise the events. I was then invited to join the organisation, and accepted immediately. Over the following years I helped set up events in London and abroad. These included weekend lectures in Berlin and Venice, designed to educate undergraduates about anti-Semitism and give them guidance on how to fight it.

The Berlin conference took place in 2000. The German authorities went into overdrive to make it a success. The irony of holding a conference on anti-Semitism in the Reichstag building, the seat of Hitler's Third Reich, was not lost on us. While there I was very impressed by a young German cleric, Christian Weber, who came to all our lectures and told us about the work he was doing with German neo-Nazis. He would befriend them, dress like them, and ride his motorbike with them. He had so far earned the trust of many, who ultimately agreed to visit Israel. He wanted them to have a taste of the vibrant Jewish culture which Germany had lost. His work included raising money for these trips. His mission was to make them understand the evils of anti-Semitism, and it was a dangerous one.

He actually told me he was unmarried because it wouldn't be fair to put a wife through the worry of what might happen to him at the hands of these violent gangs. At the time he himself had not yet visited Israel because, he said, he felt unworthy to be there. I deeply admired this Lutheran priest, and told him he would be very welcome to come for a meal if he was ever in London.

A few months later our phone rang. It was Christian, saying that he was on a special mission in London for a few days and would love to see me. It was a Friday, so of course I invited him for supper that evening, and said he could join us for the Shabbat evening service beforehand.

I remember exactly when it was because our daughter Judith was getting married that Sunday. She was rather crestfallen, thinking that having a stranger at the table for her final Shabbat in our home might cramp our style, but she really had nothing to worry about. He was a charming guest, and had us laughing when he described his visit to our shul. Out of respect he had covered his head, and was greeted by a member who made a point of welcoming visitors. When asked his name he said 'Weber', which is actually quite a common Jewish surname, but then threw the guy off balance by adding his first name—Christian. He told us he was impressed by the way children were encouraged to take part in the service. At the end, the rabbi made *kiddush* and the children in shul went up to the *bimah* to sip some grape juice from the cup. 'If I did that in my church,' Christian declared, 'I'd be crucified!'

At a Venice conference a few years later, we delegates had to wear a badge showing our name and home country. As we entered the hall I saw someone coming towards me who looked somehow familiar, and when he was near enough for me to read his tag I was amazed to see that it said: 'David Meghnagi, Italy'.

He did look rather like my brother Ever, without the broken nose, and was in fact my cousin, whom I had not seen since visiting Tripoli as a youngster. Of course, neither of us had known the other would be there (my cousin was a guest at the conference, not one of the organisers, as I was). We greeted each other enthusiastically, and it caused quite a stir when we walked in arm in arm, displaying our badges: 'David Meghnagi, Italy' and 'Elia Meghnagi, England'. I was to go on to discover that this cousin of mine was not only head of the psychology department at Rome University, and an accomplished author of academic texts on psychology and history, but was also engaged in Holocaust studies, and involved in overseeing a project cataloguing music that was composed in concentration camps.

In 2014, I was part of the committee working on the logistics of an exhibition staged by the Simon Wiesenthal Centre in cooperation with UNESCO. It was called 'People, Book, Land: the 3,500 Year Relationship of the Jewish People to the Holy Land,' and was displayed in the Houses of Parliament, schools and university campuses throughout the UK, Europe and America.

A few years ago, I was unable to attend a SWC committee meeting, and discovered after the fact that the board had voted in my absence to appoint me as a director of the UK branch of SWC Europe. I was delighted to accept this honour. I am still very involved with the Simon Wiesenthal Centre, and even during the coronavirus pandemic we managed to organise lectures, exhibitions and internet-based Zoom meetings.

I like to think that my father, of blessed memory, who had to fight and suffer humiliation and the loss of his livelihood thanks to fascist persecution, would be proud of me for my work fighting fascists and neo-Nazis through this excellent organisation.

19

Nostalgia and communal life

When I was about eleven years old, my classmates and I were given a lovely surprise: our class teacher, Fratello Roberto, introduced us to a new teacher. Unusually for a school exclusively run by friars, the new teacher was actually a young woman just arrived from Italy. She was going to be our music teacher. We had never had one before, and whilst half the class did not seem to care very much, I was ecstatic.

I come from a music-loving family. My father was our shul's favourite *chazan*, and even organised a choir, which was unusual in our type of congregation. In London he acted as *chazan* for the nearby Persian shul, and was so loved that an admirer even flew in from Rome to record his most famous piece, the *kedushah* of the Yom Kippur *mussaf* service. If only I had taken a copy of that recording!

When I say I come from a music-loving family, I do not mean only my nuclear family. I have relatives in my extended family in America, Italy, Israel and the UK who are very active in cantorial music. The Israeli opera singer Claire Meghnagi represented Israel in 2009 in the prestigious BBC Cardiff Singer of the World competition. Miriam Meghnagi is a singer, composer and ethnomusicologist in Italy, as is Evelina Meghnagi. Both are involved in cultivating and disseminating Sephardi music.

As for my immediate family, I married a music-loving girl whose voice is pure magic. Our eldest daughter, Deborah, sings in a Jerusalem-based women's a capella group; our elder son, Reuben, travels the world serving as the main *chazan* for the High Holy Days; our younger son, David, sings and plays at weddings and other celebrations, while our youngest daughter, Judith, is a singer-songwriter who performs to female-only audiences in the USA and Israel, and has released two albums. I mustn't forget our second daughter, Naomi, who also has a lovely voice, but focuses her talents on painting, sculpture and ceramics.

So you can see why—to return to my story—when this young woman came to teach us music, she touched something deep in me…in my soul, you could say. She put it differently; she taught us that *'musica e' l'arte del mezzo,'* meaning 'music is the central art'. When I was with this teacher, I felt I was in my element. Her lesson was always at the end of the day, and two like-minded friends and I would walk home with her afterwards, singing the songs we had learned that day.

Then, towards the end of term, we were waiting for her lesson to begin, but she didn't appear. We never saw her again. It transpired that for some reason the authorities had revoked her permit, and she had to return to Italy. That was the end of our music lessons; the school never replaced her. Even after all these years, I still remember the sadness I felt at losing that teacher. I have never forgotten the story she told us to help teach us the tonic sol-fa, but it does not translate well into English.

I was thinking of those musical days when considering which shul to join when we moved to Edgware in late 1979. For me a combination of spirituality and music is ideal, and in Edgware United Synagogue I found both. While living in Mill Hill I had often attended services at a Sephardi shul, particularly on the High Holy Days. However, when we moved about a mile down the road to Edgware, to be within walking distance of the children's school (we could hardly expect our kind neighbour to continue taking them when her own children had left), this brought us much closer to Edgware United; it was a three-minute walk from our new home. I grew up with the idea that you should not walk past one shul to go to another, so this was literally a godsend. I was soon welcomed into the choir, which was in need of a baritone, and became a member of a closely-knit group of friends.

When they were small, one or other of our five children would often join me in the choir box. During our earliest years in Edgware I would occasionally visit the Sephardi minyan for Rosh Hashanah and Yom Kippur, as I did love the tunes of my childhood, but after a while I stopped, not wanting to let the choir down during the most important services of the year.

The responsibility of office

One Saturday evening in 2004 my friend and fellow chorister, Peter Hartman, turned up with a most unexpected proposal: he told me he was intending to stand for the position of synagogue warden, of which there are two, and asked me to stand alongside him.

I was absolutely bowled over. By that time I had belonged to the shul for decades, but it had never entered my head to stand for any kind of office. I really felt he should ask someone else, but tall, elegant, eloquent Peter is very persuasive, and I finally capitulated.

Edgware United Synagogue, my second home for over forty years.

In due course we were elected joint wardens, and it proved to be the beginning of a rewarding partnership in which we complemented each other well. Although it could be demanding and time-consuming I thoroughly enjoyed it, and served for four years before standing down. I also shared that highly rewarding and exacting position with great friends like Mike Potashnick, Simon Gavzey, and Stephen Goldman, who still continue to do a superb job. I just felt it was time to give someone else a chance.

I consider myself fortunate to have served for those four years alongside the indefatigable Rabbi Benny Rabinowitz, who was described by the eminent Dayan Michael Fisher as one of the most knowledgeable and hard-working rabbis in London. With his enthusiastic help and encouragement we started the Shabbat afternoon summer lectures, which became one of the most successful series in Edgware, especially when the Edgware *Kollel* became involved in supplying many of the speakers. I was particularly happy that these lectures were open to men and women, seated separately, so that couples could come together.

In 2014, I was surprised and humbled to be presented with a certificate marking the tenth anniversary of these lectures and my part in their success. In light of the recent devastating loss of Rabbi Lord Jonathan Sacks, from

YOM HASHOAH
Holocaust Remembrance Day 2019
Jude
Remembering the past, changing the future
EDGWARE UNITED SYNAGOGUE
Wednesday 1st May 2019

Programme

Rabbi David Lister

Rabbi Ben Kurzer
Reflections from Poland

Service
led by **Chazan Yossi Schwarz**

Candle-lighting Ceremony
Monica Burman
Juliette Cohen
Seth Goldman
Ruby Posner
Daniel Singer
Yehudo De Wolff

Kaddish

Elia Meghnagi
Out of Africa - the forgotten victims

The Rt. Hon. The Lord Pickles

Hatikvah
National Anthem

Flyer for a shul event at which I spoke about how the Libyan Jewish community suffered in the Holocaust…a fact of which most of those present were unaware.

Flyer for an event I organised at Edgware United Synagogue in 2011.

Introducing guest speaker Ishmael Khaldi, an Israeli Bedouin, at the event.

which we are still reeling, I am all the more gratified that ten trees have been planted in my name in the Lord Sacks Forest in Jerusalem. I received the certificate from our present incumbent, Rabbi David Lister. Rabbi Rabinowitz was a hard act to follow, but Rabbi Lister has proved to be a worthy successor, always there with a smile whenever and wherever he is needed and giving his all to the Edgware 'family'. I remember when he had been through an in-depth interview with our selection committee and was waiting in the library for our verdict. Our feelings were summed up by our shul elder, the late Joe Perlmutter, who exclaimed, 'Lock the door and don't let him out till he's signed!' Knowing that I was a member of the committee which appointed him gives me tremendous satisfaction.

When Rabbi Rabinowitz retired after twenty-six years of devoted service, I was honoured to pay tribute to him at his farewell reception, in the presence of the then chief rabbi, Lord Sacks, and other dignitaries. In my tribute to his round-the-clock availability to help any member of the community, I recall comparing him to a church vicar of whom a member of his congregation complained that six days a week he was invisible, and one day a week he was incomprehensible. Unlike that vicar, I said, our rabbi was available eight days a week, day and night.

Rabbi Rabinowitz finally realised his great dream, and he and his wife Dalia now have a lovely apartment in Jerusalem. This happens to be quite

At the farewell reception for Rabbi Rabinowitz. Left to right: Rabbi Rabinowitz, Andrew Dismore MP, Dayan Menachem Gelley, myself.

Myself and the ever-smiling Rabbi David Lister.

close to our daughter Deborah's apartment in Arnona, an elegant neighbourhood in South Jerusalem with a large English-speaking community. Whenever Beryl and I are lucky enough to spend the weekend with our eldest and her delightful family, I usually go to the local shul, where I join Rabbi Rabinowitz's 'Edgware corner'. Needless to say we take advantage of any break in the prayers to reminisce about the good old days in Edgware.

I am pleased to say that I am still quite active in communal life, helping in various activities. These include organising short talks in shul on winter Friday evenings, continuing my involvement in the aforementioned Shabbat afternoon summer lectures, and the fortnightly Siddur Travelogue sessions, which are normally held in our home.

Moving from the communal to the personal, I must share that this memoir isn't actually my first literary endeavour. Chicco is a character I created when our eldest daughter, Deborah, insisted at the age of three that I tell her my own stories, rather than read her one from a book. Chicco stories became a family tradition, and all my children enjoyed them. Whenever possible, I continue the family tradition by telling Chicco stories to the next generation—twenty-one grandchildren (so far) and various of their friends have enjoyed them over the years. My next project, God willing, will be to write them down. Deborah is now a successful editor of many books, including this one. Hopefully the daughter who prompted Chicco's creation will help me get him onto the printed page, too.

Child of survivors

In these pages I have recorded the details of what happened to the Libyan Jews during the Holocaust. My father's luxury home goods store was destroyed, and for all of us it was a terrible struggle to try and survive and keep out of the clutches of the fascists and Nazis. My mother's mental health was permanently affected. As far as I know, my parents never considered the possibility of claiming reparations, though they probably knew that family members in Israel were in fact receiving money from Germany.

If I thought about it at all I probably assumed that only Israelis whose relatives had died in the camps were eligible. It therefore came as a great surprise when, a few years ago, Clem told me that he had met the secretary of a local social centre for Holocaust survivors, who had pointed out to him that our parents had missed out by not claiming compensation. Even more surprisingly, he said there was still time for me and Clem to claim for ourselves (Ever and Yvette were born after the allies liberated Libya; they were definitely not eligible). We were highly doubtful, but thought we might as well follow his advice and apply.

It took months of letters going back and forth between the UK, Israel and Germany before our claim was recognised as valid. At last a letter arrived from the Conference on Jewish Material Claims against Germany, which referred to me as a 'child of survivors'. Clem received a similar letter, and we had a good laugh at the idea of being children again after so many decades. Of course, I appreciate the regular payments into my bank account, but my gratitude is tinged with sadness that my parents missed out on this compensation, which they needed so much more than I.

Coming up to date

My branch of the Meghnagi family came to the UK as poor immigrants, and found a welcome home here. I have told my story, and will round it off now by giving an update on those who found their home in the UK with me. As I have already described, my father died in 1976, but my mother lived until 1997. Eventually wheelchair-bound, she spent her final years in a care home. What we at first took to be a stubborn refusal to eat was eventually diagnosed, to our horror, as cancer of the oesophagus, and she passed away on the same day as Princess Diana. What a sad end to a lady who just a few years earlier looked so young that she had been mistaken for my sister.

Clem and Miriam live in Golders Green, and have three sons, one in America, one in Israel, and one in the UK, and a goodly number of grandchildren. Ever lives in Stamford Hill. He and his wife Helen divorced, but remained on good terms till her death. He has a son and daughter in Israel and a daughter in the UK, and enjoys being with his grandchildren and great-grandchildren. Both Clem and Ever have needed treatment for heart problems, but thank God have made good recoveries. All three of us are still involved with Snowcrest, to a greater or lesser extent. As for Yvette, life hasn't always been easy for her. Despite her incomplete education, she mastered shorthand and typing (in English!) and went on to secure responsible positions, first in a publishing house, and later as a bilingual secretary for Alitalia. Always one to make lasting friendships, she has been less lucky in love. Now divorced, she is fulfilling her long-held dream of living in Jerusalem.

As for us, Beryl and I are both still happily living in Edgware. Beryl retired from classroom teaching some six years ago, but keeps herself in the game giving private lessons. I still work at Snowcrest, although I go in to the factory for fewer hours these days. Our youngest son, David, now works with me at Snowcrest, and lives near us in Edgware with his wife Esther and their two children. Our four older children all made their homes in Israel: Deborah, as mentioned previously, is a book editor and writer living with her husband Jonathan and their two children in Jerusalem; Naomi has four children and lives in Modi'in, where she is engaged in selling the beautiful functional ceramic art she makes; Reuben also lives in Modi'in, with his wife Rachel and their seven children, and, after following in my footsteps as an electrical engineer, now runs his own business as a building contractor; while Judith lives in Ramat Bet Shemesh with her husband Yehoshua and their six children, where she runs her own business, teaches music and continues to build her singing and song-writing career.

20

Reflections

Today there are no Jews in Libya. In 1969, Muammar Gaddafi took over the country and expelled the few Jews still living there, allowing them to take only a single suitcase and a mere $20 each. He also forbade all those who had fled in previous years to return, cancelled all debts to Jews and confiscated *all* Jewish assets, estimated by the Association of Libyan Jews in Rome to be worth between 350 and 400 million dollars. A number of families were never heard of again, presumed murdered by the mobs before they could flee. Indeed a friend of mine, Rafael Luzon, who now lives in London, told me that he had tried desperately to ascertain the fate of his uncle and family, who had disappeared. Years later an Arab friend reported that he had discovered their fate: they had locked themselves in their homes, hiding from the mob in Tripoli, but then a so-called friend of the family knocked on their door, shouting that he had come to take them to safety. Instead of doing so, however, he led them straight to the waiting mob, where they were all stabbed to death…father, mother and children. Only their eldest daughter survived, because she was out of town. To this day, despite extensive enquiries by their relatives in Rome, no one knows the whereabouts of the family's remains.

There may still be some beautiful synagogues standing in Libya, turned into schools or mosques, but many have become ruins, purposely destroyed by Gaddafi or simply left to crumble now that their faithful are gone. I understand my own, the Grand Synagogue, has been turned into a Coptic Church. Cemeteries have been turned into roads and airport runways. Repeated attacks on the Jews of Libya that began with the fascists, continued with Arab nationalists and culminated in Gaddafi's barbarism, put an end to a 2,000-year-old community that had been filled with love for and attachment to the land and its people, especially the Berbers, who make up the majority of the population and with whom the Jews share a history of friendship that goes back to Roman times. Many thousands of displaced Libyan Jews settled in Israel, some in the USA and the UK, and a large number in Italy. They and their descendants, numbering over 200,000, are to be found today in all walks of life, as professors, doctors, chefs, engineers, rabbis, singers and artists, and of course highly successful businesspeople.

Their ranks include the founder of an Israeli political party, the mayor of a London borough, and a British member of parliament.

Who knows where Libya would be now, if it had not expelled its Jews? It is no coincidence, after all, that Islam's conquest of medieval Spain ushered in a golden age for the Jews of the region. The Arabs' categorisation of Jews as *dhimmi*, second-class citizens, may have been derogatory, but it actually raised their status from that under which they had previously suffered within Christian Spain, where they had no legal status and no rights whatsoever. Indeed, in medieval Europe they were always at the mercy of the whims and fancies of the current local strongman, whether prince or cardinal. Under the Muslims they were somewhat protected; second-class citizenship is at least a form of citizenship. The was an extraordinary period when both cultures thrived enormously and fed off each other. The similarities in language, religious beliefs and literary culture were a great source of inter-communal respect and friendship. Even after Spain became Christian again and expelled both Jews and Moors, the exodus of Sephardi Jews meant that Jewish communities all over the Muslim world were enriched, including that of Libya.

The Muslims enriched the world with their mathematics and algebra, much of which was transmitted to the West by those Jews in Muslim lands who shared their learning with their brethren in Christendom. Many Jews even became ambassadors to the West, intermediaries between Arab and Christian. Would that that relationship had continued.

I had a cousin named Herbert Pagani. Even as a child he showed signs of the talents which would later bring him fame as an artist, filmmaker, musician and singer-songwriter. During his childhood and adolescence, he moved between Italy, Germany, France, and his birthplace, Libya. The day after the coup which brought Gaddafi to power, Libyan police broke into the Pagani home in Tripoli and destroyed hundreds of his canvases and drawings. My cousin spoke evocatively and passionately of what it is to be a Jew. He also wrote a public letter to Gaddafi, who had destroyed the last vestiges of the Libyan Jewish community; the letter was published on the occasion of the Second World Convention of Libyan Jewry, in 2005. With the kind permission of *Jewish Renaissance* magazine, I include an extract here of his open "Letter to the Colonel" because I think it encapsulates the feelings of many Libyan Jewish exiles. The translation from Italian is by Annalena Limentani.

> '...so, what are you complaining about?' the Colonel would say in his tent. 'You wanted to leave, and we let you leave.'

Yes, of course, you even encouraged us to go, stripping the few crazy ones who were still attached to the land of their rights and property. Don't worry, though, I'm not writing to you out of homesickness. I'm not one of those poor, unhappy persons who trip off to Tunis for their holidays to re-live the childhood they spent in Italy. Because if there's one thing I refuse to accept it's that catastrophic illusion of resemblance, that so small yet so great distance—base, yet head-spinning—that separates the tear from the drop of rain. Just as, when you're lost in a souk, you look for your mother, see her, shout her name, she turns round, and it's not her. When I shout she turns, and it's always her: Jerusalem. And when I want to go there, I go.

Why I am bothering to write to you is to tell you that this community of ours is very much alive. It's growing, and prospering. It's made a new life for itself, *'hamdullah'*, because after it lost everything, it had no choice but to press forward.

We're like bees, Colonel. If the lord of the farm steals our honey in September, we make haste to make more, before winter sets in, and if we go on stinging you with our claims for damages, it's more out of dignity than out of interest, to remind you of your debt, but above all, of your loss: we are producers of goods, materials and morals, and we always have been, you know that, because we're not afraid of work, because, for us, work has never been punishment, but expression. No, a blessing, rather.

The proof: just a month in refugee camps in Latina and Capua, and our people left the hovels and set off in search of work, and Italy, who gave us shelter, and citizenship, thought she was giving us charity, but soon realised that she's made an investment.

But you, like all the governors of the new Arab world, wanted to wash the Jews out of your social fabric. So doing, you've ruined the fibres: trade, craft, farming, the professions, everything's come loose and been swept away, like sand in the Ghibli, and all the experience you purchase in the West will never replace the ancient experience that you had of us, we whose vocation has always been communication: among beings, groups, races, disciplines, principles, states, civilisations.

That same vocation was indispensable for the grandeur of Islam, of the Russian Empire, the Ottoman Empire, pre-Nazi Germany, and you could have made it yours, if you had wanted to.

Just think, dear cousin. A troubadour was born on that slice of hell you govern. With the inexplicable, almost perverse love that Jews have for the stepmother land that adopts them, he could have made wings for your kings, for your heroes, for your saints and martyrs, and then sent them off to tell the world that your country exists. He could have sung the praises of that desert of yours, with words that would have made that rose of sand you have instead of a heart fall in petals.

But Allah, who is great, and sees far, desired to have us depart, by your hand, so that I could go off and sing my songs below other skies, and so that your nation could go on, as in the past, with its exciting task: to fulfil its role as the flyleaf of the Great Book of Islam.

Shalom v salaam

Herbert Avraham Haggiag Pagani

Looking back at my childhood and adolescence in Benghazi, I can honestly say that despite the dangers, the beatings, the frequent provocations and even killings, there was also a good side to life in Libya: a largely friendly, helpful, multi-cultural populace coexisting in relative harmony. To me this proves that no religion or race, whether Jewish, Muslim, Christian or other, has a monopoly on compassion, decency and bravery. I may have had to rescue my brother from a beating; my family may have had to hide from angry mobs—but those who hid us were also Arab, also Muslim. For every fellow Libyan filled with hatred for us, there were always some who were genuine friends.

A relative of mine who opened a shop in Rome created a sign in Arabic and placed it over his door specially to welcome Libyan tourists. When they do visit, drawn by his sign, he tells me that they will reminisce with him about the 'good old days' when they did business with their Jewish friends and neighbours.

Personal experience has shown me that we are remembered kindly and with nostalgia by many, especially the older generation, less affected by Gaddafi's poisonous diatribes. In 2004 there was a reunion in Rome for past pupils of Benghazi's Istituto De La Salle, from Friday to Sunday. Beryl persuaded me that I simply had to go and meet some of the *fratelli* of whom I had spoken so often. Both she and David were on their half-term break (she from teaching, he from studying) and they came with me, along with my two brothers. Having spent an enjoyable Shabbat together, early on Sunday morning we boarded the coach which took us to the main event: an all-day conference during which each past pupil had to mount a stage and recount his memories of the school. We Jewish alumni sat at our own tables—not to discriminate, but to make it easier to serve the kosher meal

Fratello Amedeo with his arm around my shoulder at a school reunion in Rome, 2004. Clem is on his left.

which was provided. We were also given Hebrew prayer books so we could sing the grace after meals together, and also pray the afternoon service. During both of these the others, mostly Christian but some Muslim, listened respectfully and with keen interest. Chatting afterwards, the goodwill shown towards us was palpable, and of course fully reciprocated. So it seems that some in Libya miss us as much as we miss them.

This is not to say that we are universally appreciated. David Gerbi, a psychotherapist originally from Tripoli and a resident of Rome since 1967, is the head of the World Organisation of Libyan Jews. He obtained permission to visit Libya in 2002, when Gaddafi was still in power, and has been back several times since then, in efforts towards reconciliation. He was allowed to visit again in 2007 because he supported the normalisation of relations between Libya and the United States, but when he started trying to restore Tripoli's ancient Dar Bishi Synagogue, he was detained, interrogated, and summarily dispossessed of his belongings and deported.

On a further trip in early 2011, he volunteered at the Benghazi Psychiatric Hospital. Later that year, after the liberation of Tripoli, he was given permission to resume work on the synagogue, but seeing him there, a mob gathered, shouting 'There is no place for Jews in Libya.' Again, he was forced to leave.

Nevertheless, there have been positive signs of hope. I believe that my parents would be jumping for joy if they could see the gradually changing political landscape of the Middle East today, specifically the steps towards rapprochement between Arabs and Jews. Israel has long benefitted from peace with neighbouring Jordan and Egypt, but with the recent signing of the Abraham Accords, a cold peace has become decidedly warmer. The UAE, Bahrain, Morocco and Sudan have established relations with Israel which seem genuine and warm. These countries are welcoming Jews and acknowledging the historical closeness that once existed between Jews and Arabs. Some of their hotels and airlines are even setting up kosher facilities, while Israel is reaching out to them with help in technology, medicine and agriculture.

Ahmed Shebani, president of the Democratic Party of Libya, has written several articles, including a recent one published in the *Jewish News*, London, asserting that the expulsion of the Libyan Jews was not only a big mistake, but a crime against humanity. He declared that the Jews had always been a peaceful element in the country, played a crucial role in its economy, and that it was historical fact that Jews predated Arabs in Libya by over a thousand years. Indeed, in his article in the *Jewish News* he wrote that the original population of Libya was mainly Berbers and Jews. Of course, as I have mentioned elsewhere, there was also a large Greek population.

In his reply to an email I sent him, he referred to me as 'brother', and promised that he would be working hard to get us welcomed back; he said he would fight for us to receive compensation and have our property returned to us. Brave people like him are becoming increasingly vocal. He is looking forward to translating this book into Arabic. The effect of this on all of us is incalculable. Who knows, I may one day be able to travel to the land of my birth and visit my shul, and the graves of my relatives. I ended the foreword of this book with the word *inshallah*. I conclude with the Hebrew equivalent:

Be'ezrat Hashem: with God's help.

Acknowledgements

Putting this book together has been pretty much a family affair. My first thanks go to my wife, Beryl. When the first Covid-19 lockdown came into force in March 2020, her immediate reaction was, 'This is your chance to get on with your book.' She has spent countless hours as my eagle-eyed proofreader, and has even thanked me for giving her a sense of purpose during what felt like interminable lockdowns and restrictions. Then our daughter, Deborah Meghnagi Bailey, opened our eyes to the work entailed in being a professional editor. Her eye for detail, breadth of vision, and insistence on accuracy kept me on my toes, and turned my efforts into a proper book. Thanks also go to our son, David, who has frequently come to my rescue in my battle against a seemingly malevolent computer, and also to our Naomi, Reuben and Judith, whose excited enthusiasm spurred me on. To round out the family effort, Reuben's wife Rachel, another publishing professional in the family, did an excellent job proofreading the final galleys before printing.

I very much appreciate the Vallentine Mitchell team, Stewart Cass, Sue Garfield, Toby Harris, Lisa Hyde, Deborah Mulqueen and Jenni Tinson, for their friendly and patient help in navigating me through uncharted waters.

Finally, I must thank the many relatives and friends whose oft-repeated, 'You should write a book,' finally convinced me that this was a project worth undertaking.

Portrait Gallery

Spot the difference: 8 November 1970; 8 November 2020.

Left to right: Myself, Clem and Ever at the small outdoor gathering (thanks to Covid restrictions) for my 80th birthday in June 2021.

Back in Cambridge shul on my 80th birthday. All but one of my children managed to be with me (Naomi was unwell).

My sister, Yvette, in about 2012.

Our children standing behind us at Judith's son's bar mitzvah in 2018.
Left to right: Reuben, Deborah, Judith, Naomi and David.

Deborah and family at her elder son's bar mitzvah at Bustan Abu Ghosh, Israel, in September 2021. Left to right: Deborah, Adiel, Matanel, Rav Jonathan Bailey.

Naomi (Tate Maghen) and children (Tajtelbaum) at her youngest son's bar mitzvah in Modi'in, Israel, in February 2019. Left to right: Josh, Esti, Yitzhak, Naomi, Betzalel.

Reuben and family in September 2021. Back row, left to right: Aviel, Dalia, Shira, Rachel (née Hanstater), Reuben holding Hila. Front row: Meital, Elad, Ma'ayan.

Judith and family in September 2021. Back row, left to right: Bracha, Judith, Rav Yehoshua Gerzi, Leah, Yaakov. Front row, left to right: Gavriel, Shlomo, Chaya.

David and family at his son's brit, London, February 2022. Left to right: David holding Libby, Esther (née Stonefield) holding baby Noah.

This was the online card for my 79th birthday from my grandchildren, who call me Nonno, Italian for Grandpa.